PROPHET OF THE PARKS:

THE STORY OF WILLIAM PENN MOTT, JR.

[handwritten inscription:] To Shan, Thank you for your tremendous contributions to CALIF. State Parks. Enjoy! *[signature]* 10/26/99

BY

MARY ELLEN BUTLER

[handwritten inscription:] To Shan; Thanks for your support. Think big as WPM jr. always did! Sincerely, Mary Ellen Butler Oct. 26, 1999

Published by

The National Recreation and Park Association
22377 Belmont Ridge Road
Ashburn, Virginia 20148

A Publication of the
National Recreation and Park Association

ISBN #0-929581-78-4

DEDICATION

This book is dedicated to four beautiful children, Anthony, Shane, Jacqueline and Noah, and any brothers or sisters they may have in the future. I fervently hope they will have an opportunity to learn to love and respect the world of Nature.

TABLE OF CONTENTS

ACKNOWLEDGMENTS

I wish to thank the many persons who helped make this book possible and to ask forgiveness from those I inadvertently fail to mention. The list starts with members of the Mott Memorial Fund, including five persons in particular. Jo Hemphill worked prodigiously to organize voluminous files, tape hours of priceless interviews with William Penn Mott, Jr., and collect comments on Mott's legacy from national leaders. Richard "Dick" Trudeau offered overall leadership and invaluable guidance to the project every step of the way. William Penn Mott III and John Mott contributed important family materials, relevant suggestions and continued inspiration on the need to tell their father's story. The Mott brothers and L.W. "Bill" Lane, Jr., wrote checks to get planning for the book underway.

Daphne Muse and G. Gary Manross critiqued the initial outline. Those who read, corrected and improved parts or all of the manuscript included Trudeau, the Mott brothers, Burton Weber, Martha Bauman, Joel Parrott, Jan Pynch, Howard Bell, Jo Mele, Hulet Hornbeck, Brian Thompson, Dennis Anspach, Les McCargo, Kenneth Mitchell and Denis Galvin. Editing services were graciously and expertly provided by Harlan Kessel. Donald Butler, my patient and understanding husband, gave me moral support as well as technical assistance with tempermental computer equipment.

Librarians, the unsung protectors of historic information, were of immense assistance. They include the staffs of the

Oakland History Room of the Oakland Public Library; the Bancroft Library of the University of California at Berkeley, the California State Railroad Museum Library in Sacramento, and the J. Porter Shaw Library of the San Francisco Maritime National Historical Park. Staff members of the Oakland Department of Parks and Recreation, the East Bay Regional Park District, the California State Parks Foundation, the California Department of Parks and Recreation, the National Recreation and Park Association and the National Park Service opened their files and welcomed me with a friendliness and hospitality for which I am most grateful.

Lastly and significantly, a very special thanks to Laurance Rockefeller, who personally endorsed the project with a generous gift to cover research and travel expenses.

FOREWORD

I am greatly honored to write the foreword to *Prophet of the Parks*, a lively and entertainingly written book that will both inspire readers and offer practical insights into the lifetime park career of William Penn Mott, Jr. Bill was a legend in the park movement at all levels: local, regional, state, national, and international. He was a modern-day John Muir in his environmental concerns and constant attention to conservation of our natural resources as well as their appropriate uses for recreation.

Bill had great vision. And, he had the rare ability to spur the teamwork needed to get the vision implemented. His impatience was discomforting to some, but his strong feelings on many controversial issues have often proven right with time. In the more than thirty years that I knew and worked closely with him, he was always anxious to get people together to solve problems with bold solutions, even when they were unconventional and — according to some doubters — impossible to achieve. He was sure that any difficult job could be done one way or another and then went out and found, or, if necessary, created, the tools to do it!

Bill vigorously contended that parks offered a unique opportunity to serve as educational vehicles for students of all ages. How he set about turning that hunch into reality at each level of his career offers proof that when you believe in something strongly enough you find a way to make it happen.

By any measure, Bill was a special, beloved individual. His lifelong commitment to parks, and to the public that deserves them, is of transcending importance. The leadership path he cut through institutional redtape and sluggish bureaucracy is illustrated step-by-step in the pages that follow. I commend this book to your study and enjoyment. In every aspect of his life, Bill Mott's achievements left all of us a much better world.

L.W. "Bill" Lane, Jr.
Former Publisher, Sunset Magazine
Former U.S. Ambassador to Australia
Recipient, National Park & Conservation Association's
William Penn Mott, Jr., Award (1994)
Chairman, Presidential Commission on the
Centennial of National Parks (1972)

INTRODUCTION

Though I had long known of his wonderful work, I didn't meet Bill Mott until the final years of his life. He was still fully engaged in imaging our future and in helping shape it. The years hadn't diminished his enthusiasms or clouded his visions. He possessed the wisdom of age and the passion of youth. He greeted me with his natural kindness and curiosity and invited me to feel comfortable in his presence.

When we met I was reporting on environmental issues for CBS and the CBS affliate in San Francisco, KPIX Television. I first interviewed him about his dreams for the San Francisco Presidio National Park. I was immediately taken by his ingenuity and by his belief that we human beings and nature can have better days ahead, and by his determination to help us achieve them.

In this age of cynicism and low expectations for our society, he spoke of possibilities and maintained high standards. He was realistic but not jaded, and for me, he was utterly inspiring. He helped me crystallize my own feelings and beliefs, and in the spring of the year he passed away, he gave me one very fine day I'll never forget.

Under a gloriously crisp and sunny sky, my photographer and I took a hike with Bill in Briones Park, an East Bay Regional Park District preserve in Contra Costa County, CA. I wanted him to reflect on what he had accomplished thus far, and to talk about his goals for the coming years. Our final objective that day was to climb Mott Peak (named after him by the regional park district's board of directors). But along the way we took our time admiring the green hills, the flowers of the season, the long vistas undisturbed by roads and dwellings, and the hawks and vultures soaring overhead. He trod easily over ground he knew well and had labored to protect. We passed groups of other walkers on the trail. Invariably, as soon as they recognized the man they called "Mr. Mott," they thanked him for all he had done to make places like Briones possible. Lively conversations ensued, and he never failed to encourage those he greeted to become activists on behalf of parks, public lands, and open space.

Finally, we trekked up the gentle slope of the hill that bore his name, and slowly savored the view. I remember the sweet breeze, the clean air, and the feeling that I was very fortunate to have had this time with him. Before heading down and back to our vehicles, and with the camera rolling, I asked Bill what his principal concern was for the future of our parks. Without missing a beat, he said that public apathy disturbed him most. He said that tens of millions of us visit and appreciate our parks every year, but only a handful of us advocate for them in the arenas of politics and public opinion. We take parks for granted, rarely recognizing what it costs to create and maintain them. He argued that parks need a strong constituency to flourish, one that mirrors the true size and diversity of the population that uses them. As the world becomes more crowded, he said, that constituency will become more important. His passion was infectious. He urged me to get involved. Ever since then, I have.

It's comforting to know that in many ways Bill Mott will always be with us. He lives vividly in the memories of those of us who had the pleasure to meet him. His ideas will be as germane and important in the future as they have ever been. And all around us, his legacy remains in the projects he pursued and the land he protected. His wisdom is written there for us to read, on the slopes of gentle hills and in the comings and goings of the seasons.

— Doug McConnell
Host and Senior Editor
Bay Area Backroads
KRON-TV
San Francisco, CA

PROPHET OF THE PARKS

WHAT THEY SAY ABOUT WILLIAM PENN MOTT, JR.

President Bill Clinton

"Bill Mott [was] one of the most vibrant and dedicated people I have ever met. When he visited Hot Springs National Park in 1985, he was interested in every detail about the Park, its history, and its people. Though my time with him was brief, I was deeply impressed by his commitment to preserving our national parks. He [was] one of a kind."

Dianne Feinstein
U.S. Senator from California

"California, with its majestic coastline, mountains, lakes and inland valleys, provides some of the most scenic vistas in the world. But nature's bountiful endowment to the state could well have been jeopardized if it hadn't been for a courageous and bold fighter for open space and parks. William Penn Mott [was] a relentless and visionary crusader for the preservation of what is most beautiful and precious in our magnificent state. He served his state and, as director of the National Park Service, our nation, with distinction and dedication, and his legacy shall endure always in the great beauty that is ours to behold and at which future generations will marvel."

Edgar Wayburn, M.D.
Past President, Sierra Club

Bill Mott "was a warm and vital man who instilled energy, enthusiasm, and inspiration wherever he went. His vision was both deep and broad. Early on, before many others, he realized the importance of a global outlook. When he died he was working on a long-range plan for the Presidio, to turn it into a Pacific Rim Environmental Center, a project he had first envisioned many years before. His ideas went beyond his very considerable accomplishments."

California Governor Pete Wilson

Bill Mott "was an extraordinary Californian...whose most fitting memorials are a legacy of protected natural treasures and a heightened awareness of their contribution to the quality of our lives."

Bruce F. Vento
Congressman from Minnesota

"Bill was a dedicated career professional who always displayed enthusiasm and love for our National Park System." He "was always willing to give the counsel needed and work as hard as he could to get the job done."

Former Tennessee Governor Lamar Alexander

"Bill Mott always understood that people preserve those places and things that they love and understand. He also recognized long ago that the keys to understanding are education and communication, two endeavors in which he always excelled. Without his keen ability to communicate the necessity for preserving parks and open space, our natural estate would be infinitely reduced."

Laurance S. Rockefeller
Longtime Park Supporter

"Bill Mott's concept for the Horace Albright Development Fund was embraced by our Trustees at Jackson Hole Preserve Inc., and by myself, as a way to properly honor and memorialize Horace Albright and to assist the employees of Horace's beloved National Park Service in their professional development. Funds were raised from other sources by the National Park Foundation to match our gifts and over a period of six years, an endowment was raised that now exceeds $2 million. More than 150 employees have benefited through grants from the Fund, and have successfully increased and improved their abilities as professional National Park employees. This is another example of public and private interests working together, and we were delighted and honored to participate."

Bob Baker
Former National Park Service Regional Superintendent

"So often in government, heads of agencies are very short sighted and are very uncomfortable with the long view. Fortunately, Bill Mott did not suffer from this critical leadership quality. He not only was committed to the strategic view but inspired others to do the same."

Bob Barbee
Former Superintendent, Yellowstone National Park

"Bill Mott had a 100 percent commitment to the necessity of parks, preserved space and proper land use as a social concept and its essentialness to the fabric of American life."

PROPHET OF THE PARKS

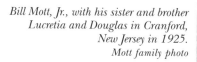

Bill Mott, Jr., with his sister and brother Lucretia and Douglas in Cranford, New Jersey in 1925.
Mott family photo

1921 - William Penn Mott, Sr., Matilda Young Mott, William Penn Mott Jr., Douglas Mott, Lucretia Mott
Mott family photo

1931 - William Mott at University of Michigan
Mott family photo

Chapter 1

Visionary by Nature

I love to think of nature as an unlimited broadcasting system through which God speaks to us every hour, if we will only tune in.

GEORGE WASHINGTON CARVER

If Hell ever visits Earth, it did so during the summer of 1988. From July through early September, eight huge forest fires burned in and around Yellowstone National Park. They sent billowing black clouds of smoke high into the sky and pillars of red-hot flames shooting up tall trees. They chased tourists and employees out of the park, consumed twenty-four small buildings and threatened but, thanks to stalwart firefighters, did not destroy historic landmarks like Old Faithful Inn.

The fires ultimately consumed 1.4 million acres, of which nearly one million acres were within the park. Nature, in the combined form of lightning strikes, extremely low humidity and freakishly high winds, caused some of the fires. Man, leaving spark-laden spores of unextinguished cigarettes and campfires, caused others.

Fire is a natural phenomenon. But in the world of politics, responsibility for even the most natural disaster must somehow be assigned to human frailty. Taking heat from their constituents and embarrassed by extensive media coverage of the inferno, elected officials looked for someone to hold ultimately at fault for the destruction.

Into this natural and political firestorm stepped William Penn Mott, Jr., the feisty, highly-respected, and 78-year-old director of the United States National Park Service. Mott had weathered many controversies during a long and successful career.

In the San Francisco Bay Area, he had started his long climb toward eminence in the parks movement as superintendent of parks for the City of Oakland. After seventeen years, he accepted the post of general manager of the East Bay Regional Park District. Five years later, he ascended to the post of director of parks and recreation for the State of California. After eight years in Sacramento, he returned to Oakland to run the California State Parks Foundation, which he founded in 1969. He reached the pinnacle of success as director of the National Park Service, from 1985 to 1989.

During that time span, Mott's colleagues panted to keep up with him. They called him the man with "an idea a minute." He created Children's Fairyland, the first three-dimensional children's theme park in the world and a precursor to Disneyland. He doubled the size of the East Bay Regional Park District and greatly enlarged the California State Park system. Upon his appointment as director of the National Parks, he became the only person, as far as is known, to progressively lead park systems at the city, regional, state, and national levels.

But now, a horrified world watched on television as the Yellowstone fires ate through acres of old growth wilderness. Most Americans did not understand why they continued to burn — or were allowed to spread so rapidly in the first place. If ever Mott's extraordinary record of leadership were tested, it was during the summer of 1988.

Yet there he was on August 29, 1988, flying into the park from National Park Service headquarters in Washington, D.C., a trim, square-shouldered, white-haired man with an infectious smile and crinkly blue eyes behind wire-rimmed glasses, telling the world not to worry.

During an inspection of a section of the burning landscape, Mott acknowledged to the gathered newspaper reporters, magazine writers, and TV crews that this event seemed like an unexpected catastrophe. But what he said next set them to scribbling furiously in their notebooks.

Unexpected, yes, he agreed. Catastrophe, no.

"These fires are really a predictable part of Nature's grand land-management plan," he explained to the astounded media representatives. "In fact, they happen once every several hundred years for a purpose."

Mott pointed to a nearby stand of lodgepole pines, Yellowstone's dominant tree. He explained that the heat generated by forest fires causes the lodgepoles' pinecones to pop open, allowing their seeds to fall to the ground. There, they germinate and begin to grow into new trees. When fire strikes every few hundred years, it gets rid of accumulated deadwood and makes way for new generations of growth. The massive burns, then, while not a good thing from the human perspective, are not a bad thing from nature's point of view.

Backing his staff, who were also trying to place the frightening conflagration in its historical context, Mott assured the public its beloved Yellowstone, the oldest national park in the world, would quickly recover from this natural disaster. Not so much in terms of human time, he said, but in terms of geologic time. And it was geologic time that mattered in the interconnected and interdependent natural universe of which mankind was — or should be — a servant, not a master.

Ranchers, who had a traditionally uneasy relationship with the national parks; merchants who depended on the tourist trade; and Wyoming congressmen, whose constituents were the first two groups, were outraged. Some called for Mott to resign. Wyoming Senator Malcolm Wallop, in the middle of a re-election campaign, went further, calling for Mott's removal on grounds he had shown insufficient aggressiveness in fighting the fires. But Mott stood by his principles, which mirrored those of the park rangers and park scientists he supervised. "Fire is a terrible thing and people get emotionally upset about it," he told the *New York Times* several weeks later. By then, the winds had died down, rain had fallen, and the flames had slowly subsided. "They have to blame somebody so they blame the Park Service. But next summer most of Yellowstone will look no different than before and there will be more visitors to the park than ever."

As for stepping down in disgrace, Mott refused to consider it. "I don't understand the personal attacks on me — this business about asking me to resign," he said. "I haven't done anything wrong, and I am not going to resign." President Ronald Reagan, Mott's ultimate boss and the man who had approved his appointment as National Park Service director, agreed. Mott remained in office for the rest of Reagan's second term. He resigned on April 15, 1989 only after incoming President George Bush appointed his own Park Service officials.

Soon thereafter, Mott returned from Washington to his home in Orinda, California, in the East Bay hills near Oakland and across the Bay from San Francisco. Just over a year later, on May 30, 1989, Memorial Day traffic into Yellowstone National Park topped out at twenty-five percent heavier than it had been on Memorial Day, 1988, shortly before the fires erupted. In fact, for all of May 1989, while Mott puttered in his garden, some 200,000 visitors entered the park, well over the 175,000 who had done so twelve months earlier. On Thursday, July 6, 1989, the *San Francisco Examiner* announced, "Worries That Fire Would Cut Tourism Prove Unfounded." By 1996, the forests were growing again and wildlife was booming. Mott's prediction had proved correct.

William Penn Mott Jr.'s unswerving faith in the ability of Nature to heal and sustain itself was just one of many strong beliefs he lived by. His response to the Yellowstone fires was just one of many times he carried out those beliefs. Not all of us can stay the course as firmly, paint our achievements on as large a canvas, or influence the thinking of as many people as Mott did. But we can learn from his life how to get more out of our own. Sharing Mott's sense of spirituality and vision, his work ethic and deep trust in his fellow humans, his amazing accomplishments and the legacy he leaves us today are what this book seeks to do.

DIFFERENT FROM THE BEGINNING

William Penn Mott was born on October 19, 1909 in New York City, the first of three children born to William Penn Mott Sr. and Mathilda Young Mott. His birth was followed by those of his sister, Lucretia, in 1911, and brother, Douglas, in 1912.

William Penn Mott, Sr. was a traveling salesman who loved to go camping when he had time. Mathilda Mott had been trained in nursing but spent most of her time taking care of her fast-growing family.

On their father's side, the Motts traced their family history back to the LaMotts, three brothers of French ancestry who belonged to the Religious Society of Friends (popularly known as Quakers) and who emigrated from England to America during Colonial times. After dropping the prefix from their names, the brothers went on to establish themselves in different parts of their adopted nation. The descendants of one brother evolved into the upstate New York apple growers who eventually founded the Mott Applesauce Company. The descendants of a second brother migrated to Michigan and became known as "the General Motors Motts." The descendants of the third brother settled in the Rhode Island area. Although available records are lacking, it is the third group that apparently gave rise to William Penn Mott's antecedents. "My branch of the family were the poor ones in agriculture," he once told an interviewer.

As for the William Penn part of his name, Mott Jr. thought he might be related on his mother's side to the famed English Quaker who founded the state of Pennsylvania, but, if so, neither he nor other members of his generation knew the details.

Nonetheless, several Motts came into national prominence during the 19th and early 20th centuries, achieving historic notice in their pursuit of the social and humanitarian goals important to their faith. James Mott was a 20th century Philadelphia businessman and social reformer who supported his wife, Lucretia Coffin Mott, in her fight for women's rights and against slavery. John Raleigh Mott was an early twentieth-century evangelist who founded the World's Student Christian Federation, received the Distinguished Service Medal for his religious work in World War I and shared the 1946 Nobel Peace Prize for work with the YMCA and with displaced persons. Charles S. Mott became a director of the General Motors Corporation and founded the Charles Stewart Mott Foundation in 1926. Today, the Mott Foundation, located in Flint, Michigan, pumps millions of dollars into educational and community-development programs.

William Penn Mott, Jr. never spontaneously mentioned his connection to this distinguished heritage. It did not come up in his speeches or writings. "The thing most significant to me," he did say — when pressed about his heritage — "is that as a Quaker you appreciate nature and the simpler things of life and you're taught to listen and not butt in on other people's conversations."

A remark in Mott's typical down-to-earth manner, it was evidence that he appeared reluctant to talk about his patrician bloodlines. Yet, when the values he expressed throughout his career are taken into consideration, even the most cursory glance at his Quaker background lends inescapable credence to the idea that this visionary, contemplative man's approach to life was infused with a spirituality carried down from his ancestors.

THE QUAKER CONNECTION

From their beginnings, the Quakers (so nicknamed after founder George Fox said he "trembled" at the word of God) stressed inward spiritual experiences rather than specific outward religious practices. Along with this individualized style of worship, Quakers are also known for their humanitarian activities. In the United States, they have been pioneers in removing barriers to racial and gender equity. They have worked steadily to reform prisons and mental institutions and to offer equal educational opportunity for all.

These egalitarian practices seem close to the heart of the principles that motivated Mott throughout his life. As a leader in the parks movement, he placed top priority on educating the general public about the need to protect nature. He called this goal "interpretation" and espoused the need for it wherever he went. He also believed in educating himself, as his lifelong devotion to reading, writing, thinking, and studying evidenced.

In addition, Mott broke down racial and gender discrimination by hiring women and members of minority groups previously shut out of parks work and by urging members of those same groups to take on leadership responsibilities. He relished the challenge of getting poor, inner city kids outdoors where they could learn good work habits and become contributing members of society. And one of the first things he did upon ascending to his first parks management position was to get rid of "Do Not Walk on the Grass" signs by planting grasses hardy enough to survive the feet of the common people whom, he strongly believed, the parks were meant to serve.

It seems clear that Mott carried a strain of populism within him that came out time and again in his desire to make parks accessible to everyday people. He used the word "intrinsic" rather than "God-given" to express his belief in the sacredness of the land, reflecting his privately held faith in universal and nonsectarian terms.

One thing seems certain, as we will see in looking at Mott's life and work. The boy grew up to be the man who saw the natural world through a deeply devout prism. While never publicly proselytizing, he became in private life a lifelong and dedicated lay leader of the Presbyterian Church.

THE CALL OF THE OUTDOORS

As William, Lucretia, and Douglas grew into childhood, Mott Sr.'s company transferred him frequently. The family moved from New York City to Windsor, Connecticut, Buffalo, New York, and Cranford, New Jersey. In Cranford, after school and during the summer, the Mott children had plenty of time to read and to create their own fun in their semi-rural neighborhood of wood-frame houses and grassy lots. In keeping with an inborn and elfin sense of humor, little Bill Mott was not above getting into mischief now and then. One time he and his buddies held hands while the boy in front touched an iron railing and the boy at the back a live socket. Everybody in line got a shock. On Halloween they put a pushcart on the streetcar tracks and sent it careening down a hill.

But Bill's love of outdoor activities went beyond boyish games and pranks. No matter where the family lived, he found himself noticing the natural state of things. In quiet moments, he often made some kind of garden. In Cranford, he remembered, he created "a funny little rock garden." It was no more than a collection of stones artfully arranged and rearranged over and over on a small patch of ground, but the pastime somehow resonated deep within him.

Bill realized early on that he liked plants, rocks, animals and other things associated with the Earth. In school, Lucretia excelled at math and Doug favored science. Bill was a good student, too, but was more attuned to the overall sweep of the outdoors and the aesthetics of nature than in the details of machines.

As a young boy he began to sense the presence of a benign spirituality, some kind of reckoning behind the natural world he was drawn to. One Independence Day when he was nine years old something took place that strengthened this still-forming belief in a universal power that was fundamentally good. As often happens with children, a simple experience left a life-long impression.

"It was the 4th of July following the end of the First World War," he recalled, "and for some reason everyone had fireworks but Toots [Lucretia], Doug and me. It seemed like everybody else was going to celebrate and we had nothing." Bill felt sad and helpless, but there was no money for pyrotechnics. Then two boys from another neighborhood rode up on their bicycles and asked if they could shoot off their fireworks in an open lot next to the Mott home. The Mott siblings said yes, joined the boys, "and what would have been a disappointing day all of a sudden became a marvelous 4th of July celebration," he said.

A coincidence, perhaps. But young Bill viewed the unexpected arrival of the boys with the fireworks as a sign, an answer to an unspoken prayer. To him, the fulfillment of the dream, the feeling of fun and excitement, of doing something together, even of patriotism and love of country was much more significant than the dollar's worth of firecrackers. That incident formed a seed that later blossomed into two beliefs and a personality trait that encouraged Mott's life-long desire to build a future in which humankind appreciates nature for its own sake.

The first belief was in the incalculable value of experiencing open space in the most basic of ways, whether by enjoying a dollar's worth of sparklers and firecrackers in an open field under a blue sky on the 4th of July, thrilling to the awesome boom of a waterfall in Yosemite Valley or contemplating the age-old silence in the depths of Grand Canyon. The value was measured simply by being there, not by how much money it took to get there or what kind of fancy equipment was deployed to stay there. It was the inherent and irreplaceable existence of nature's wonders themselves that must be protected in perpetuity and made available to everyone willing to respect them and learn from them. The second belief was that given enough time, faith and hard work, dreams do come true, just the way the youthful Bill's desire to celebrate with fireworks mysteriously materialized in the arrival of the two neighboring boys. But laying the groundwork was an equally important part of this mystical process, which led Mott to a maxim he often repeated:

"A vision is a powerful thing," he said. "It is a dream based on a clear perception of the future combined with a commitment to take the necessary steps to make it happen."

The personality trait was empathy for children and their childlike wonder of nature, an involuntary response that Mott himself never lost. He loved interacting with youngsters, whether it was confounding them with the "magic" trick of producing a quarter from behind their ear that he had, of course, hidden in the palm of his hand, or leaving his official duties for a few minutes to tag along on a nature walk with them.

MICHIGAN — THE TURNING POINT

In 1925, Mathilda Mott died. With his father, sister and brother, sixteen-year-old Bill grieved deeply. Yet, in ways he could not anticipate, his mother's death marked the beginning of a very different life for him.

William Mott, Sr. continued to travel a great deal on his job, but no longer had a wife at home to hold the family together. In a decision borne of necessity, the Motts were uprooted from their eastern seaboard home. The children were sent to Jonesville, Michigan, a little town near the Ohio border, to live with Lina and Les Potter. Mott, Sr. stayed behind to continue the job that kept him on the road. The Potters were the late Mathilda Mott's sister and brother-in-law and their children were the Mott siblings' cousins. When the Motts arrived in Jonesville, Bill was a junior in high school, Lucretia a sophomore and Doug a freshman.

It was in Jonesville that Mott's love of nature, a seedling during his early childhood, found itself in nurturing soil where it began to grow. As he did chores around his aunt and uncle's house, he learned that in the country, animals like hens, cows, dogs and horses were more than pets. They were integral members of a team that enabled families to survive in a sometime harsh environment.

But there was time for fun, too. His uncle and cousins quickly introduced him to fishing, rabbit hunting, berry picking, and other outdoor pursuits. He learned to sail on the numerous lakes around Jonesville. Soon, he and another teenager bought a sailboat. But when they discovered it was slow, they sold it and bought a second sailboat. With that boat, "The Queen of Hearts," they won many informal races among friends.

Years later, sitting with friends in his living room in Orinda, Mott recalled a dawning sense of the eternal verities of the universe. "It wasn't just the hunting, or the value of paying for the gun, the license and the other equipment that went into hunting," he remembered, "but the other values. Being out of doors early in the morning, hearing the squirrels chatter..." Mott paused, groping for a way to verbalize the feelings he had. He thought about the huge oak tree in his backyard whose branches hung over his tile-roofed house. "It's like sitting here in the evening," he began again. "At certain times of year, you can hear the acorns dropping on the roof. See," he said, his eyes intent, his arm raised toward the ceiling, "that's the ripening of the acorns, signifying that fall is coming. Hearing that sound calls your attention to those values. Here those things are hitting on the tile; a *ping* over here, a *ping* over there, two *pings* down there," he said, pointing to different sections of the ceiling. "Well, that's a simple little thing," he said of the experience of hearing the acorns fall and bounce off the roof, "but it has a value, an intrinsic value." Afraid his listeners didn't quite get it, Mott said, "I can't explain it, but to me it's pretty exciting."

In Jonesville, the city boy retained his East Coast sophistication but made room in his mind and heart for bedrock midwestern mores. Looking back on the drastic alteration in his lifestyle, he said, "My whole concept of the out-of-doors changed radically because suddenly I was actually living in the out-of-doors."

And thriving in it, too. Bill's high school experience changed from big city to small town in one fell swoop. The senior class he would have graduated with at Cranford High School had one thousand-two hundred students. Jonesville High School had a graduating class of eight. Furthermore, a requirement for graduation from Jonesville High was the completion of a 4H project. Until that moment, young Bill had never heard of 4H, the young people's organization with the motto, "Learn by Doing." But Mott was intrigued by the challenge. He chose as his project the hatching of twenty-five chicks. He threw himself passionately into the assignment. So immersed was he in incubating the chicks, "I darn near slept with those eggs," he recalled. Once the eggs hatched, he monitored how much feed the chicks required, what it cost to raise them and what steps had to be taken to get them to market on time. His final report was judged best in the state and he won a free trip to a meeting of the World Poultry Congress in Canada. "This was another exciting change," he recalled, "to go to this conference and see all the people and the different kinds of chickens. It was another spin-off from rural life that you didn't get in the city. It was really quite an experience."

And a lasting one. After he moved to California, one of Mott's hobbies was to raise a batch of chicks that he got from a hatchery every year. He nurtured them in a shed in the backyard of his home in Orinda.

At Cranford High School, young Bill had shown athletic promise, participating in football despite his slight frame. At much smaller Jonesville High, Bill played not only football but also basketball and baseball and ran track. As he neared graduation, one of his coaches encouraged him to go to Michigan State University in Lansing. "Try out for the football team when you get there," he said.

After graduating in 1927, Mott did apply and was accepted to MSU. But he got injured trying out for the football team and took up tennis instead. Later, he met Ruth Barnes, a personable co-ed from Ithaca, Michigan, who was majoring in home economics.

De-emphasizing sports turned out to be a good thing. With more free time, Mott turned to his primary love, plants and animals. He decided to major in landscape architecture, took courses in seed identification and joined the intramural Dairy Cow Judging Team, on which he learned to milk cows. During summer breaks, he got work on a massive freighter plying the Great Lakes. He did tough, manual labor until one day the cook got drunk and young Bill was assigned to the galley. He learned to cook quite well. Somewhere along the line, he also learned to put up jars of jam and jelly from fresh-picked fruit. Many times in later years, he surprised people with his knowledge of milking, cooking, baking, and jam and jelly making.

Moving to Jonesville had changed Mott's outlook on life. "As a junior and senior in high school," he said many years later, "I began to realize how important land was. Not only from an agricultural point of view but from a visual point of view." Going to college only deepened that interest. Studying landscape architecture caused him to look at the land "more from [an] aesthetics [point of view] than you do with other things," he recalled. "And then, of course, you gradually begin to realize that within the land [there are] not just the forms and the aesthetics but the plant materials, the animals, the birds and the other elements that make up the total picture."

In summary, as Mott explained the genesis of his lifelong mission, "I think that's what sort of guides you in connection with the idea of developing parks."

WESTWARD BENT

When Mott graduated from Michigan State in 1931 with a bachelor's degree in landscape architecture, he found he wanted to learn about a kind of landscape different from the Midwest. "I thought I ought to take some additional work in one of the schools that was in the southern part of the United States or in the Mediterranean climate area, so I decided to go to the University of California at Berkeley." There was another reason for the decision to stay in school. "This was at the height of the Depression, and there wasn't a lot of work for landscape architects in those days," he said. "I thought I might just as well get a little more education, and maybe by that time the Depression would be solved." A third factor was also present. William Penn Mott, Sr. was now living and working in the San Francisco Bay Area. Going to Berkeley provided an opportunity for Bill Jr. to be with his father again after a separation of several years.

Mott Jr. lived with Mott Sr. while completing his master's, then returned to Michigan where in 1934 he and Ruth were married. The newlyweds' move back to the Bay Area proved permanent. Although Mott eventually held top park posts in Sacramento and in Washington D.C., he and Ruth never moved again. From 1937 on, their home in Orinda remained Mott's safe haven. He traveled constantly to win support for his mission to create, conserve, and develop parklands. He endured the adversities that came with exercising daring leadership at high levels. But he always knew that Ruth, his children, his home and his garden awaited him, offering sustenance and renewal from the rigors of the road.

NATIONAL PARK SERVICE — THE FIRST TIME

Mott's first challenge out of graduate school came in 1933 when he was hired by the San Francisco regional office of the U.S. National Park Service. Immediately he had lots to do, thanks to the massive public works programs created by President Franklin D. Roosevelt in response to the Depression. Mott supervised landscaping done by Civilian Conservation Corps and Works Progress Administration enrollees at several national parks as well as at La Purísima Mission near Morro Bay and Griffith Park in Los Angeles. He also helped plan and develop facilities in Death Valley, Sequoia and General Grant (now Kings Canyon) national parks in California, and in Crater Lake National Park in Oregon.

A third assignment was to look for possible national park sites in Nevada, which had none at the time. Nevada did have the Lehman Caves National Monument near the Utah border. Mott recommended adding a section of U.S. Forest Service land to the monument and turning the combined site into Great Basin National Park. Because the Forest Service objected, the recommendation was shelved. But as the years went by, Mott never gave up on the idea. His vision ultimately became a reality.

By 1940, the Motts were parents of two children, William III and Nancy. Mott reluctantly left the Park Service with its frequent travel and took a stay-at-home job as a public housing planner. He also started his own landscaping consulting firm and was working at both when in 1945 he became superintendent of parks in the growing city of Oakland.

A BOLD STYLE BEGINS TO FORM

This was Mott's first major leadership post. One of his initial steps was to develop "Planned Progress," a blueprint for the redevelopment and expansion of Oakland's already extensive system of parks and public landscapes. Over the next seventeen

years, the city bloomed under Mott's hand. Under his direction, Park Department staff redesigned or refurbished parks,
added flowerbeds and flowering trees, and installed new tot-
lots and playgrounds. Despite skeptics' claims that no living
thing could survive exhaust fumes close up, the staff also planted
profusions of blue Lily of the Nile (*Agapanthus orientalis*) along
street medians and traffic islands.

Equally important, Mott personally nurtured the department's
planners, gardeners, secretaries, and administrators. He began
to develop the open management style that today would be
called TQM (Total Quality Management) or MBWA (Management by Walking Around). "The real job of an administrator
is not to give orders but to inspire creative thinking in his
staff," he said early on. "Everyone is encouraged to think
creatively and offer suggestions for improvement."

Mott set the example for creative thinking through the expression of his own irrepressible imagination. No idea was too
bold to consider. To educate the public about the importance
of protecting the environment, for example, Mott hired Paul
Covel, America's first municipal park department naturalist,
or nature interpreter. It was an unheard-of idea at the time,
but quickly became standard nationwide.

Once a vision came to him, Mott lobbied city officials vigorously to get it funded — sometimes to the annoyance of other
department heads who saw money originally budgeted for their
projects diverted to parks. "This ability to squeeze water out of a
rock...not only puts Mott in a class by himself," said one local
pundit in 1947, "but has given the city living beauty and
fragrance from his blooming park system. Money so spent is
more rewarding than money poured down the funnel for surveys
and feasibility reports that bear no fruit."

FROM CITY TO REGIONAL PARKS

For all his personal modesty, Bill Mott was not one to hide
his light under a bushel. In fact, a major part of his uncanny

ability to enlist both employee and public support was the evangelism that compelled him to share his hopes and dreams far and wide. When an idea seized him, he often said he would "talk about it to anyone who will listen." Over the next fifteen years, Mott continued to introduce innovative ideas in the Oakland parks, including his all-time favorite, Children's Fairyland. He also developed an international reputation and was in demand for speaking engagements and leadership posts in the growing field of parks and recreation. So it was not surprising that in 1962, Dr. Robert Gordon Sproul, president emeritus of the University of California and president of the board of directors of the East Bay Regional Park District, asked Mott to become general manager of the district.

Formed in 1934 by the voters of Alameda County from watershed in the Oakland-Berkeley hills that had been declared surplus by the East Bay Municipal Utility District, the regional park district is one of the most extensive nature preserves in the world so immediately adjacent to a large urban area. Mott had been asked once before to take over the regional park district, but had told district officials at that time that he still had work to complete in Oakland. Now, feeling that he had accomplished much of his mission for Oakland's parks, Mott brought his long-range planning skills, sense of compassion, and infectious verve to his new post as general manager of the Regional Park District. He moved his office from Oakland Park Department headquarters to Regional Park District headquarters, also in Oakland. He was happy not to have to relocate his family, which by now included a third child, John.

Since its founding in the 1930s, the Regional Park District had fallen into a complacent, Rip Van Winkle-like slumber. Mott's first goal was to enlarge the district by buying and preserving more open space in the hills of Alameda and Contra Costa Counties before the land was absorbed by the rapidly growing East Bay suburbs. That meant convincing Contra Costa County, Alameda County's neighbor to the east, to join the district and convincing the voters of both counties to approve a small tax increase to finance land acquisition. A second goal was to develop an interpretive program to educate the public, just as he had done in Oakland, about the importance of protecting and maintaining the nature preserves. A third goal was to organize and train the first security force for the district. Times were changing, and it had sadly become necessary for rangers to also be prepared to act as peace officers. With Mott moving at a dizzying pace, these objectives were met over the ensuing five years.

By 1968, when Mott accepted Governor Ronald Reagan's invitation to become director of California's Department of Parks and Recreation, the East Bay Regional Park District had grown from one county to two and from 10,500 acres to 22,000 acres. It served a population of 1.5 million and visitors had more than tripled. Mott's leadership was key in doubling the size of the district and expanding the range and offerings of its parks. Just as important, district employees had learned from Mott that long-range planning; fiscal accountability; professional expertise in public relations, interpretation, design, acquisition and development; and creative partnerships between government, public agencies, the private sector, and the public were all necessary ingredients for success. On the first day of his new state job, Mott drove the eighty miles from Orinda to Sacramento, taking those leadership principles with him to the next level.

TAKING ON THE BIG BOYS

During his years as superintendent of the Oakland Park Department and as general manager of the East Bay Regional Park District, Mott had learned a lot about how to work with politicians. He knew, for example, that allowing elected officials to take credit for successful projects increased his chances of getting things done. This experience led to the crystallizing of one of his axioms for successful management: "Understand politics, know how politicians operate, but don't try to be one yourself."

Mott knew from having worked with state officials during his term with the regional park district that the state parks needed better management. He wanted to talk to Reagan before making a decision "to find out what his attitude and feeling was about the park system." Mott told Reagan "right from the start" that he was a park professional who wasn't interested in politics. No problem, said Reagan. "That's why I've asked you to come and reorganize the department," he said. "I'll take care of the politics; you run the department."

For the next eight years, that's exactly what they did. From 1967 through 1975, Mott brought the same high expectations and standards to the state that he had developed in the Bay Area. Among them were "a good public relations department and a good financial division so that we could present to the public a story about the parks and also be fiscally responsible, so that everybody understood exactly how we were spending their money and for what purposes."

But he didn't stop there. He also innovated, inspired and led. Using the non-profit, public-private partnership model he'd developed to create Children's Fairyland, he invited interested citizens to supplement the state's inadequate acquisitions budget by raising private money to buy and save open space. He broke precedent by hiring California's first female state park rangers. He even built unisex restrooms in the parks, which, he insisted, significantly cut maintenance costs even if they initially scandalized some campers. Also true to form, Mott's bold moves aroused criticism from detractors who thought he strategically circumvented state rules to get things done. He did, and never denied it, making sure, however, always to act within the law.

OFF TO WASHINGTON

Mott went right on "working" the system when ten years later, in 1985, his old friend Ronald Reagan, now President, tapped him to become National Park Service director. In grappling with the entrenched Washington bureaucracy in an atmosphere dominated by politics, Mott stuck by his personal and professional convictions. It was during this period that he supported park officials' handling of the Yellowstone fires of 1988 and faced down demands for his resignation in the wake of the event. Against strong opposition from ranchers and, again from some congressmen, he spurred the public education campaign that led to widespread support for the reintroduction of the gray wolf to its ancestral Yellowstone home. While that furor raged, Mott went about adding several new sites to the National Park System despite budget cuts and suggestions by some Interior Department officials that some public lands be sold to private investors.

Mott's tenure as National Park Service director ended along with Reagan's second term, but not his involvement with the Park Service itself. When he returned to the Bay Area in 1989, it was as a Special Assistant to the National Park Service. His assignment: To lead the plan to convert the historic Presidio at San Francisco from military to National Park Service use. Throwing himself into this new challenge with characteristic energy, Mott was soon advocating the Presidio as a perfect location for an international research center, an idea he had first suggested many years earlier. He was pursuing that goal and speaking out on worldwide ecological issues when he died of heart failure in 1992.

THE MOTT PRINCIPLES INSPIRE

William Penn Mott Jr.'s legacy lives in both the work his memory continues to inspire in the parks and recreation movement and in the people for whom he was a mentor, teacher, friend, parent and colleague. Many are parks leaders themselves.

Fran Mainella, Christopher Jarvi and Dean Tice, who have held leadership posts in the National Recreation and Park Association, are among them. So are Holly Miller, former superintendent of Parks and Recreation for the City of

Seattle; and Bob Barbee, National Park Service field director for Alaska and former superintendent of Yellowstone National Park. Count in Phillip Jew, former general manager of the Auckland Regional Park Service, Auckland, New Zealand, and Jane Adams, executive director of the California Parks and Recreation Society, Sacramento. But parks people aren't alone in praising Mott's major contribution to 20th century American life.

"It was a pleasure to work with a man whose dedication, optimism and cheerfulness was an inspiration to us all," said President Reagan in 1992. "We can never thank him enough." President Clinton, who as governor of Arkansas heard Mott urge the restoration of Hot Springs National Park, remembered him as "one of the most vibrant and dedicated people I have ever met. He was one of a kind."

The principles Mott offered, as he liked to say, "to all who will listen," could number in the scores. But The Six Mott Leadership Principles outlined later in this book provide a glimpse of what Mott followed and what can be practiced by anyone in a leadership position today.

*1934
Ruth and Bill Mott
on their wedding day
Mott family photo*

*1935
National Park Service
Mott family photo*

*A family photo taken in the mid 1950s
shows Bill and Ruth Mott with their three
children Bill III, John and Nancy.
Mott family photo*

Chapter 2

A City Blooms

"A rock pile ceases to be a rock pile the moment a single man contemplates it, bearing within him the image of a cathedral.

ANTOINE DE SAINT-EXUPERY

In 1946, when William Penn Mott Jr. was appointed su perintendent of parks in Oakland, he was already familiar with the city and its history. He knew, for example, that the Ohlone Indians had once occupied the land. But the gentle natives were displaced after Spain claimed California as part of the Mexican Empire. In the early 1770s, Franciscan friars were sent north from Mexico City to build missions and convert the natives to Christianity. Establishing each settlement a day's march apart, they started in San Diego and worked their way up the coast. In 1776 the friars built Mission Dolores de San Francisco and an accompanying *presidio* (fort) on the west side of the bay. They called this crude outpost *Yerba Buena* (Good Earth). Two decades later the friars founded Mission San Jose on the east side of the bay near the present-day city of Fremont. They called the East Bay *Contra Costa* (Opposite Shore). About twenty miles north of Mission San Jose, and roughly parallel to Mission Dolores across the bay, the future city of Oakland took root as two small villages called Contra Costa and San Antonio.

The priests were followed by *rancheros*, Mexican patricians awarded great tracts of land by the King of Spain. In 1820, after years of military service at the presidios of Monterey and San Francisco, one *ranchero*, Don Luis Maria Peralta, received eleven leagues, or 44,800 acres, of verdant East Bay territory. Like other *rancheros* in what would one day become Alameda and Contra Costa counties, Peralta and his family raised cattle and crops, assisted by impressed Indian laborers, and lived the genteel existence of the landed aristocracy.

By the mid-1840s, however, more and more Americans were arriving in the Bay Area. The rapacious Yankees squatted on the *ranchos*, setting up homesteads and turning many of the magnificent local redwoods into lumber. Too remote from Mexico City to get help, the *rancheros* couldn't stop the invading farmers and loggers. Peralta's *rancho* began to disappear as the town of Contra Costa grew. The final blows came in 1848, when the Treaty of Hidalgo transferred California from Mexico to the United States; in 1849, when gold was discovered in the Sierra foothills 150 miles eastward; and in 1850, when California became the 31st state to join the union.

In 1852, the fledgling state legislature incorporated the village of *Contra Costa* as the town of Oakland, a designation upgraded to city in 1854. Neighboring towns were also growing rapidly along the shore of the bay, effectively ending Mexican hegemony. Though vanquished, the Peraltas have been commemorated through several place names. And some descendants of the Peraltas still live in Oakland and other parts of the East Bay.

PARKS: AN EARLY PRIORITY

Once established, the good burghers of Oakland began transforming the frontier town into a sophisticated city. They dammed off San Antonio Slough, a marshy finger of the bay near downtown, to create 155-acre Lake Merritt. The lake became the largest saltwater lake within a city in the nation, and Lakeside

Park grew along its shores. They established a few public squares, too, with carefully manicured lawns. "Keep Off the Grass Signs," let citizens know where not to step.

As the city grew, some early estates were turned into parks. One of them was a large homestead owned by Joaquin Miller. Best known for his "Songs of the Sierras" and other literary works, Miller had built the mansion in the Oakland hills in 1886. After his death in 1913, his widow agreed to include the property in a bond issue. The estate became three hundred-acre Joaquin Miller Park, a key link in the series of parklands that occupy prominent sections of the Oakland Hills today.

"Save the Redwoods!" became the battle cry less than ten years later, when citizens mobilized to prevent the destruction of one of the last remaining groves of sequoias in the Bay Area. Majestic stands of redwoods had dotted the East Bay hills when the first European settlers arrived. The trees grew so tall that ships coming through the Golden Gate used them as navigational aids. But by 1922, very few were left. The grove in question was on land owned by the estate of Frank Havens, an Oakland pioneer who, coincidentally, had introduced the prolific Australian eucalyptus tree to the Bay Area. Developers were itching to buy the tract and cut it into lots for homes, no doubt with stunning views of the bay. But luckily the City Council approved purchase of the redwood grove and the rare sequoias reside in Oakland's Redwood Park today.

Despite, or more accurately, because of the Great Depression, park development continued in Oakland through the 1930s. In 1938, for example, Oakland won more than $1.5 million in funding from the Works Progress Administration to improve city parks. Part of the money financed preliminary blueprints for Woodminster Amphitheater, a beautiful outdoor stage planned for Joaquin Miller Park.

Work on Oakland parks was also inspired by preparations for the millions of visitors expected to attend the 1939 World's Fair on Treasure Island, the newly constructed landmark in

San Francisco Bay. After some $600,000 in improvements were completed, local officials praised the cooperation of the WPA in helping Oakland approach its goals.

Nearby, William Penn Mott, Jr. was employed as a landscape architect by the National Park Service. Working out of the Region Four office in San Francisco, Mott was assigned to develop plans for and supervise the work of Civilian Conservation Corps camps located at Crater Lake National Park in Oregon, Sequoia/Grant (now part of Kings Canyon) and Death Valley National Parks in California and at various local and state parks in the state.

Like the WPA, the CCC was one of the programs President Franklin D. Roosevelt created to provide training and work for unemployed Americans. Twenty years later, as superintendent of Oakland Parks, Mott would start Workreation, a CCC-like summer program for teenagers in Oakland, inspired by the solid values of physical labor and teamwork imparted to the youth he supervised during the Depression. Mott had been hired shortly after completing his master's degree in 1933 at the University of California at Berkeley. His decision to go West from Michigan and to get more education as a hedge against the Depression had paid off.

Mott's master's thesis gives glimpses into how his boyhood affinity for the outdoors had matured into a realization that God-given Nature could be preserved at the same time it was enhanced for judicious human use. The paper also included a discussion of another life-long interest, plants, in the form of a proposed botanic garden and arboretum.

Entitled "Report on an Alumni Club in a Park and Arboretum Setting," the paper combined plans for an alumni building, a nine-hole golf course and a botanical garden to be constructed on eight hundred acres of hilly, university-owned land. Such a development, Mott wrote, would dovetail nicely with a new regional park district already being proposed for the spine of the East Bay hills that straddled the boundary between Alameda and Contra Costa counties. "It is comparatively safe to assume," he predicted about the evolving regional park district plan, "that in the near future this vast acreage of scenic land will be developed into a continuous border of beautiful park reservation for the enjoyment and pleasure of the citizens of the East Bay."

If approved by the voters of several cities in Alameda County, the district would comprise at least ten thousand acres of virgin watershed. The land had been declared surplus by the East Bay Municipal Utility District, the local public water company. When Robert Sibley, avid hiker and executive manager of the UC Alumni Association, said, "These valuable pieces of land ought to be preserved forever," he was speaking for many East Bay residents who realized the importance of conserving fast-disappearing open space.

Though it hinted at his growing ability to combine the inspirational with the technical, Mott's grand scheme for an alumni building/golf course/botanic garden and arboretum went no further than the approving signatures of his professors. But the regional park district he anticipated was, indeed, formed in 1934 by the voters of seven cities in Alameda County. It was one of the first specially created regional park districts in the nation. He didn't know it then, but 28 years later, William Penn Mott Jr. would become general manager of the internationally known preserve that was being born as he wrote his master's thesis.

NEW AND CREATIVE THINKING

America's entry into the Second World War ended, for the time being, further expansion of Oakland parks. Developments in Mott's life also dictated retrenchment of a personal kind. Now the parents of two children, William Penn III and Nancy, the Motts agreed that a job closer to their home in Oakland

and with less travel would best serve their growing family. In 1940, Mott reluctantly gave up the work he loved with the National Park Service. For the next five years, Mott worked for the Contra Costa County Housing Authority where he designed public housing needed to accommodate some of the tens of thousands of migrants who streamed into the Bay Area to work in the rapidly established defense industries. As technical director, he oversaw the development and construction of more than $4 million in permanent and wartime housing projects.

In the late 1930s, Mott had also opened his own landscape architecture business, with an office at 2104 Addison Street in Berkeley, from which he pursued freelance park planning contracts to supplement his government income. His ability to sell his by-now-considerable skills netted him numerous jobs. Among the noteworthy projects he completed that can be seen today are the infield of Golden Gate Fields, a race track in Albany; the Embarcadero at the north end of Lake Merritt in Oakland, Thatcher Park in San Leandro and the campus of the San Francisco Theological Seminary. Mott did two freelance jobs for the Oakland Park Department during that period: In 1938, after doing a painstaking walk-through, he submitted recommendations for what recreational uses should be developed at Joaquin Miller Park. He also designed a cascading waterfall to complement the Woodminster Amphitheater, proposed earlier for construction in the park.

In 1945, the Oakland Parks Commission called for Mott's freelance consulting services once again. This time the commission asked him to survey the entire park system with an eye toward renewing the maintenance and expansion programs that had been put on hold by the war. By now, Mott knew Oakland pretty well. It took him only four months to research and write the plan for which he was paid $3,500. The commission liked what it saw. Mott proposed a "parks for use" program under a twenty-year "pay-as-you-go" expansion and improvement plan. Perhaps influenced by his work in the immense wild lands of the national parks and certainly reflecting his personal values, Mott wanted less formality and more family-friendly city parks.

"Give Oakland's parks back to her people who own them and pay for them," the proposal urged. "Remove the old-fashioned 'Keep off the grass' signs and instead let each park beckon this heartfelt invitation: 'Come, use, and enjoy your parks.' " Based on this compassionate appeal, the young consultant recommended that at least eleven new neighborhood parks be acquired and constructed, an additional mountain park be sited in the hills, City Hall Plaza be remodeled and all existing parks be modernized to include picnic tables, barbecue pits, play equipment, ball fields, and other usable facilities. After voting its unanimous approval, the commission presented the plan to a special meeting of the City Council on December 21, 1945. The gathering was a big event. Along with the council and the commission, members of the school board and the recreation board also attended.

As was becoming Mott's style, the written report and his oral presentation inspired excitement among their audience. "Oakland is on the threshold of becoming one of the greatest metropolitan centers in the world," Mott predicted with confidence. To move toward that status, some forty-eight acres of critical land, in danger of being subdivided for construction of homes, should be acquired immediately, he said. The land in question lay in hilly open space in East Oakland and was "vitally needed for the development of Dimond Canyon-Joaquin Miller-Sequoia Park and Parkways." To wait much longer, he prophesied, would be to lose this precious ground to the bulldozer.

The commission backed Mott eagerly. Implementation of the plan, one enthralled member said, "Would enable Oakland to have a park larger, more beautiful, and more available to the general public than Golden Gate Park [in San Fran-

cisco], Balboa Park in San Diego, [or] Griffith Park in Los
Angeles, and would surpass in beauty the completed parkways
in New York City." Mayor Herbert L. Beach and the city council responded more cautiously, discussing the plan for more
than two hours before declaring that further study was needed.
Judging by newspaper reports, however, initial public reaction
to the proposal was quite favorable.

"An objective 10-year plan for the development of a parkway system in Oakland rivaled by none in the west was presented to the Oakland city council today by the Oakland park
board," the *Oakland Post Inquirer* reported. "As presented by
Mott, the plan called for the improvement of existing facilities, the development of natural redwood areas found within
the limits of no other large city so that they could be used by
all, and the farsighted use of park areas for recreation purposes as well as for beautifying the city."

As was also Mott's style, the report included practical suggestions for implementation. Realization of the plan would
cost $1 million, financed through the park district's annual
budget and spread over a twenty-year period. Under no condition, commission chairman Rudy C. Bitterman assured city
fathers, would a bond issue be necessary. As the council studied the plan, Mott and the commission applied pressure for
quick action. In February 1946, Mott urged the council to buy
thirteen "critical" acres of the forty eight-acre total before private owners interested in further development near Joaquin
Miller Park snapped them up. "Five years from now there will
be 50 homes on this property and then it will be an entirely
different situation," he warned. Sometimes, he went on to counsel, it was necessary to conserve open space long before it
could be transformed into parks. Such had been the case during the late Nineteenth century, he reminded, with the land
around Lake Merritt. It had lain in public trust for twenty
years before being converted into the beautiful and popular
Lakeside Park.

By now, Mott's work had become an important part of the city's post-war concept of itself. On July 10, 1946, the commission appointed the part-time consultant to the post of full-time superintendent at a respectable salary of $7,200 a year. The dashing young visionary was ready for the new job. "It is a rare opportunity," he said, "to be able to actually remold this alluring Lady of Parks that will be Oakland. I see the possibility of helping to create one of the world's finest integrated park systems."

For those concerned that his new salary would be less per hour than he'd earned as a consultant, Mott had reassuring words: "I felt I could not stand by and idly watch so much natural beauty being dissipated by nonuse and lack of cultivation." The City Council's subsequent approval of Mott was a de facto approval of the master plan, allowing Park Commission Chairman Bitterman to announce that, "The park department is now prepared to carry out the program that was interrupted during the war." Thus, the City of Oakland entered the Mott Era, destined to last from 1946 to 1962.

THE GREENING OF PARKS AND PUBLIC PLACES

Once his appointment was official, Mott lost no time in taking his plan to the public. He was ahead of his time in realizing that to gain public support for taxpayer-funded programs, it was necessary to make sure the public was fully informed. Years later, he would refer to this process of support building as "marketing." But in 1946, that notion was anathema to most park officials, and would remain so for a long time. "The idea of borrowing the discipline of marketing from the business world and applying it to park management is risky in the minds of many park people," Mott was to say in the 1980s. "Others resist the idea of selling parks because they associate this concept with the mass marketing of products like soap and cigarettes." But properly applied, "Marketing is not a dirty word," he said. "The marketing of a park system should relate to the community or the users and their aspirations for a higher quality of life and a better environment rather than orienting the idea to the internal needs of the system such as more equipment, higher salaries, and so forth." The successful marketing approach, he explained, "is one that springs from the needs, desires, and aspirations of the people themselves, rather than from the needs and desires of the organization."

The day he uttered those words, Mott spoke from more than forty years of park management experience and as the 72-year-old president of the California State Parks Foundation. But in 1946, he was a brand new, 37-year-old municipal park superintendent. Yet, he knew intuitively the importance of good public relations. It seemed to be another trait that developed as he grew from childhood to manhood, an inborn sense of empathy with others that enabled him to see situations from beyond his own perspective. He was also a natural salesman of ideas who knew that being readily accessible to the public, including the press, enabled him to better set his own agenda.

Shortly after Mott took over the Oakland parks, a highly favorable series of articles appeared in the *Oakland Post Enquirer* comparing the city to a bedraggled maiden ripe for a cosmetic makeover. "Hard-pressed and working frantically all during the war," reporter Carl L. Houtchens wrote, post-war Oakland was badly in need of a beauty treatment. Under Mott's direction, "the treatment — broad, daring and revolutionary — may take five years, or 10, perhaps 20," Houtchens wrote. But Mott's "million dollar, cash on the line, beauty building process, which, oddly, will be comparatively painless to Papa Taxpayer, will make Oakland the belle of the ball among park and recreation developed cities in the world." And in an unusually adept way, Houtchens noted, Mott coupled a visionary look into the future with a step-by-step building program designed to make that vision a reality. As both a far-sighted seer and a highly focused doer, he recognized early in life that to make dreams come true, theory and practice had to go together.

It was that understanding that enabled him to caution other parks people that "a vision or a dream will, as soon as it is made public, face the realities of cost." As he told an Open Space Conference in Sacramento, years later, "it is very easy for developers to show that a development will increase the assessed value of the land, and that the development will provide employment and increased tax revenue. These increases," he added, "are all short term dollar values that appear to be very desirable." But "the long term intrinsic values of open space, beauty, wildlife and recreation," have worth, too, he argued. In Mott's mind there was no conflict between the essential value and the monetary value of parks. In terms of their natural worth, he explained, "neighborhood parks will be breathing spaces, furnishing a satisfying bit of fresh air, beauty and color to the gasping modern city dweller — especially his wife and offspring. They will be oases in a desert of concrete where Oaklanders may come for healthful diversion, spiritual uplift and mental ease." Their economic worth was just as easy to measure. "While the parks are enriching the souls of men, " he said, "it has been proven that they will also enrich the pocketbooks of materialists owning nearby properties." Property values, then, were positively affected by nearby parks.

To Mott's conclusions, reporter Houtchens added two of his own: That rising property values as reflected in higher property taxes would eventually pay for the parks and their improvements and that beautiful neighborhood parks led to better kept homes.

PLAN FOR PROGRESS

With the support of the Park Commission, the City Council, the press, and the public, Mott set about implementing his plan, demonstrating at the same time his unquenchable optimism, verve, and energy. Over the next sixteen years, Oakland witnessed the steady growth and development of its parks and open spaces. The city was also a willing laboratory for the kinds of daring initiatives that spilled from Mott's fertile imagination over the next several years and that continued to amaze park professionals and the public throughout his life.

By April 1947, for example, park employees were swarming around two major thoroughfares, planting fifteen thousand gladioli along the median strip of Broadway and tulips (donated by bulb growers in Holland) along MacArthur Boulevard.

That same year, the Parks Department's display at Oakland's annual California Spring Garden Show — a major exhibition attended by thousands — included two features: An exact replica of the Woodminster Amphitheater waterfall then being constructed in Joaquin Miller Park and a "sneak preview" of the flowery landscaping planned for the new neighborhood parks. The sweet tinkle of the exhibit's miniature waterfall was accompanied by the chirping of crickets and the croaking of frogs — a recorded trick that made the display all the more intriguing to families. And the neighborhood park landscaping preview showed taxpayers how their money would be used to dress up what had previously been a solid green carpet.

In addition to giving park employees a chance to show off their talents, the garden show display also enabled Mott to market the parks by creating special opportunities for Oakland citizens to see their department at work. Later, when it came time to promote the Woodminster Amphitheater's Summer Musical Series, families remembered the cheerful little waterfall with its chirping crickets and croaking frogs. Their interest piqued, they went out and bought tickets for the performances.

By 1949 more change was evident. In one case, Mott had personally redesigned several city plots, including square-block sized Mosswood Park at the corner of Broadway and MacArthur

Boulevard. The park had been a Victorian estate before it was bought by the city in 1908. Surrounded by a great iron fence, its densely wooded grounds and a creek that ran through it had become havens for vagrants. Mott removed some of the overgrowth to open up more grassy areas, installed tennis courts, ball diamonds and other sports facilities, and diverted the creek into a culvert.

Not everyone approved of this major reconstruction. Detractors called him "Willie the Gardener" and "The Glutter of Oakland". But "the minute we got the thing opened," Mott later recalled, "the critics wanted this kind of work done on every park in Oakland."

He also refurbished the Oakland Municipal Rose Garden, a favorite site for weddings and other festivities, and rejuvenated the Oakland City Hall Plaza, utilizing it for such seasonal displays as "Christmas Wonderland," Easter exhibits and a special California centennial reproduction of Sutter's Mill, the site in the Sierra Nevada foothills where gold was discovered in 1849.

In 1953, landscaping began along the enlarged 12th Street dam at the south end of Lake Merritt. Department workers laid down 7,000 cubic yards of topsoil into which they set 47,000 trees, shrubs and flowers interspersed with 150,000 square feet of lawn. Mott's thoughtful yet innovative hand could be seen in the selection of plants. Flowering fruit trees, acacias, iris and ceanothus were ranged together to produce mass color effects in the early spring while in the fall, colorful autumn foliage effects were achieved by Chinese pistachio trees and groups of red berried shrubs. Finally, incense cedars were threaded along the length of the street for overall harmony.

Why all the special effort? Mott and the park department visualized the beautified 12th Street corridor as a major approach to a section of post-war downtown where a new city library headquarters was joining the older and architecturally more heroic Civic Auditorium and County Courthouse buildings.

ALWAYS BE PREPARED

The expansion of Oakland parks took not only imagination, but also staff, money, and creative financing schemes. In negotiating all three, Mott honed a growing set of political skills that would sharpen as time passed and challenges increased. In November, 1946, for example, just three months after he started and under terms of the master plan the city had approved, Mott set up several new divisions in the parks department and won approval for twenty new positions. He hired clerks, tree trimmers, janitors and mechanics, among others. Such personnel were badly needed to re-staff a war-depleted department gearing up for expansion under the twenty-year plan.

A few months later, Mott won a trickier proposal. This time, he asked the City Council to transfer $8000 from its general fund to the park department to pay part of the costs of constructing an addition to a lawn bowling clubhouse at Lakeside Park. Lawn bowling was a popular pastime, especially for older folks. One council member didn't like the idea. "We need gyms and recreational facilities for children," said Frank J. Youell. "The idea of spending $8000 for a private club is not right." Mott was ready for the objection. First he explained that members of the clubhouse's two lawn bowling clubs had raised part of the funds to build the addition and would contribute more toward construction through increased rental payments to the city. In fact, he continued, his department encouraged private groups to lend just such financial support to projects in which they were interested. Second, Assistant City Attorney J. Kerwin Rooney said the lawn bowling clubs had agreed that anyone could join the clubs in order to use the facilities. The agreement meant the clubs were, in effect, open to the public. Third, Mayor Joseph E. Smith's initial opposition to the proposal had disappeared — perhaps after talking with Mott. "After further study I think we are getting a pretty good deal," Smith said. Mott's preparation netted him the support of the city attorney and the mayor, making it easy for the rest of the council to follow. Only Youell's dissent kept the vote from being unanimous.

This first success at acquiring needed funds through a co-operative venture led Mott to strike other agreements with private groups to contribute to projects both they and he wanted. The concept would later come to be known to all Americans as public-private partnership and would play a crucial role in the creation of Mott's signature project, Children's Fairyland U.S.A.

"EVERY CHILD'S DREAM COME TRUE"

During the length of his extraordinary sixty-year career, Mott was on a first-name basis with presidents, governors, members of Congress and titans of industry. He headed park systems from coast to coast and received countless awards, honors and other recognitions for his leadership. He traveled nationally and internationally, helping Costa Rica, Australia, and New Zealand create American-style national park systems. Above and beyond the parks and recreation movement, he inspired thousands to join him in preserving Earth's natural resources.

Yet, whenever he was asked to name the top achievements of his professional life, Mott never hesitated. The creation of Children's Fairyland, a little kingdom in a park on the shores of Lake Merritt in Oakland, California, was always at or near the top of his list. The existence of Children's Fairyland is a testament to Mott's ability to think creatively and to try new and controversial but sound ideas. He led the evolution of an imaginary kingdom into a living, working entity.

On a clear, bright afternoon, clusters of puffy white clouds sail high overhead through a deep blue sky. Wavelets on Lake Merritt dance in the sun. The translucent California light adored by painters glints off nearby steel and glass office towers. Like sunbathers lying shoulder to shoulder on a beach, Mediterranean-style homes and apartment buildings ring the lake, turning their pastel pink, white, blue, and yellow faces upward toward the warmth.

On the north side of the lake, on a pretty knoll under huge, old live oak trees, stands Children's Fairyland. Anthony, 4, and Shane, 3, skip through the entrance while 2-year-old Jackie, clutching her grandmother's hand, toddles along behind. The ticket taker sits in a tiny admissions booth built into a shoe like the one the "Old Woman" lived in, the one "who had so many children she didn't know what to do." Next to the high-topped shoe is a four-foot high tunnel leading to the magical place inside. The tunnel is tall enough for young children to traverse standing erectly, but Grandma, like most adults, has to bend over to walk through.

Once inside Fairyland, little Jackie spies a cement elf seated cross-legged atop a tall cement mushroom. A steady stream of soap bubbles floats from the elf's pipe, delighting the two-year-old who points at them and laughs. Anthony runs over to see the Three Billy Goats Gruff who crane their necks impatiently for a bit of feed being offered on the outstretched hand of another youngster. Next, Jackie climbs up a short ramp to Noah's Ark while Shane whoops as he takes several breathless turns down the long, green Chinese Dragon slide. For two hours, until they tucker out, the children explore the thirty storybook sets. Along with scores of other running, giggling, shouting youngsters, they clamor on and around Humpty-Dumpty Wall, the Jolly Roger Pirate Ship, the Crooked Man's House, the Ding Dong Well and the Lakeside Lark choo-choo train. They talk to the Three (well-fed) Little Pigs, Mary's Little Lamb, and, for good measure if not strict nursery rhyme accuracy, a resident pony and llama.

Not only are the entryway and the three-acre park scaled to kid-sized dimensions and physical capabilities, but grown-ups are allowed into Fairyland only if accompanied by a child. That rule ensures that adults and older children won't crowd out the little people for whom the park is designed. Putting small children first was one of the crucial decisions Mott made. Ensuring that Fairyland would maintain its focus on the small set has allowed the little park to retain its innocent charm over its subsequent history. Today, children enjoy gamboling in Fairyland as did the children who entered the park when it opened in 1950, many of whom are now grandparents themselves.

FIRST, THE IDEA

The spark that Mott would nourish into Children's Fairyland first ignited in the mind of Arthur Navlet, an Oakland horticulturist and civic activist. After retiring in 1947, Navlet and his wife, Alma, traveled east to see friends. They also visited places of professional and personal interest including nurseries, public gardens, zoos and aquariums.

In Detroit, the Navlets visited the Belle Isle Aquarium and its newly opened Children's Zoo. On a three-acre site, the compound featured twenty animal enclosures with houses painted in different colors to illustrate various fairy tales or nursery rhymes. At this innovative place, children were invited to do more than look. They were allowed to pet, feed and play with some of the animals. Of great interest to the Navlets was the fact that the Children's Zoo had been built with private donations. The Navlets liked the concept and decided it was something they'd love to see duplicated in Oakland. They brought the idea back to the Lake Merritt Breakfast Club. The club was an informal group of some two hundred small businessmen and women who met weekly at 7:30 a.m. for breakfast, speakers and socializing in a boathouse on the lake. One of many civic and service organizations in Oakland, the club sponsored community and philanthropic activities.

In January, 1948, the Breakfast Club appointed a committee, with Navlet as chairman, to study the possibility of sponsoring a "miniature zoo" at Lakeside Park. Soon after, the board of directors of the Oakland Parks Department appropriated $500 to pay for sketches to see how what was now being referred to as "Children's Fairyland" might look like.

THEN, THE TEAMWORK

In June, 1948, some members of the Breakfast Club argued the project was too big for the group to take on. Navlet pushed forward, however, and soon picked up an ally. Oakland Parks Superintendent William Penn Mott Jr. matched Navlet's enthusiasm for the idea. By the time the Breakfast Club splinter group lodged its protest, Mott had already used the $500 to hire Oakland artist William Russell Everitt. In November, 1948, he asked Everitt to come up with concept drawings for the first setting for Children's Fairyland, which, Mott informed Everitt, would be named The Merry Miller after the fairy tale of the same name. Mott also began to dig up ideas for Fairyland.

His single-mindedness almost got him into trouble. "I dropped by the children's room of the Oakland Public Library several times to see what the kids were reading that we could turn into sets for Fairyland," he remembered. "I didn't notice anything amiss." Years later, the late Peter Conmy, library director at the time, saw Mott at a social function. "We used to see you at the children's library all the time," Conmy recounted, "and we decided to put special guards on you to see just exactly what you were up to." The library staff had thought the man they saw hanging around in the children's section might have been a child molester. Conmy laughed at the thought. "I realize now," he told Mott, "that you were just doing research for Children's Fairyland!"

The drawing Everitt produced included a perfect replica of an English miller's cottage. But Mott wanted sets more fantastical. He imagined a place that looked like something out of Hansel and Gretel or Snow White; a kingdom with crooked lanes and thatch-roofed cottages leaning at skewed angles. He envisioned a fairyland where things were not quite real, a place straight out of the tales he'd read as a child. A realm, he dreamed, where trios like the Three Little Pigs, the Three Billy Goats Gruff, and Alice, the Queen of Hearts and the Cheshire Cat would feel right at home.

Everitt went back to the drawing board and returned with sketches more to Mott's liking. In the new version, the sides of the building sloped down under a steeply pitched roof to rest on a slightly smaller foundation, causing the cottage to lean away from the ground the way it might in a fantasy or a dream. "That's it!" an ebullient Mott told Everitt. Subsequently, all seventeen of the original sets were designed with that deftly whimsical touch.

THE HARD PART: RAISING MONEY

Although the park board had financed the drawings, the City Council declined to allocate money for construction of Children's Fairyland. "People said 'if you want to go out and do it, well, do it,' " Mott recalled. "We had to literally go out and make it happen."

Such a challenge was right up Mott's alley. One of his greatest assets was an ability to share his passion and zeal for a project and to make believers out of those who listened. He and Navlet developed a two-pronged campaign which consisted of first, alerting the community to the desirability of the proposed fairy-tale kingdom, and second, raising $50,000 to build it. That was a princely sum in 1948. A full-scale marketing campaign was in order. Mott turned again to the public-private financing strategy. With the help of the Oakland Ad Club, whose assistance Mott enlisted, the duo began to get the word out. Pretty soon, everybody in Oakland knew about the plan for the unusual theme park. As Mott and Navlet talked to scores of organizations and individuals, showing them the schematic drawings and explaining how much Oakland and the East Bay would benefit from the park, the sponsorships began to come in. The Recreation Department got the ball rolling by announcing sponsorship of the first set, The Merry Miller. The department was joined by the Lake Merritt Breakfast Club, which financed The Old Woman Who Lived in a Shoe. Quickly, the list lengthened as the Association of General Contractors chose The Three Little Pigs; Mu Chapter of Epsilon Sigma Alpha Sorority chose Mary Had a Little Lamb; The Kiwanis Club chose The Three Billie Goats Gruff; and the Women's Council of the Oakland Real Estate Board chose The Little Red Hen. Then, the Gyro Club picked up the Children's Pet Ring, and the Aahmes Temple of the Shrine chose Hickory, Dickory, Dock. Finally, the Wreath Club chose Peter Rabbit and the Oakland Rotary International picked The Humpty Dumpty Mural Wall.

Individuals also stepped forward. Funding came from Mr. and Mrs. Raymond Miller for Goosey, Goosey Gander; Lowell Berry for Rub-a-Dub-Dub, Henry Jensen for Noah's Ark, Bruce McCollum for Willie the Blue Whale, Andre Fontes for Mouse Town, and Harvey B. Lyon for Pussy in the Well.

When fifteen thousand people came to opening day on September 2, 1950, it was obvious that the delightful collection of fables brought to life had instantly captured the community's heart. Almost immediately, the friendly little installation expanded. It doubled in size to six acres as several new sets were added. Between 1951 and 1956, the original cast of characters was joined by the Walrus and the Carpenter, Little Miss Muffet, Ten Little Indians, Ching-Lung (The Friendly Dragon), a miniature but official U.S. Post Office and Robinson Crusoe, all sponsored by community groups or individuals. Eventually, a puppet theater, picnic area, and the five-car miniature Jolly Trolley rounded out the park.

WIN SOME, LOSE SOME

Mott loved recounting how he got the Robinson Crusoe set financed. He approached Vic Bergeron, the salty-tongued owner of the original Trader Vic's restaurant in Oakland, (now lo-

cated on the Bay waterfront in nearby Emeryville and the headquarters of a worldwide chain). *The* place to meet and greet in
the post-war East Bay, Trader Vic's stood on San Pablo Avenue
not far from downtown. Mott thought the restaurant's Polynesian
theme, decor and menu made it a great candidate to finance
the Crusoe installation, based on the 18th Century Daniel Defoe
novel about a sailor shipwrecked on a tropical island.

"Trader Vic, can you help us out with the Robinson Crusoe
set?" Mott asked several times on the telephone or after dropping by the restaurant for lunch. Bergeron refused to say yes
or no. He just grumbled.

Finally one day, the crusty proprietor got fed up with Mott's
persistence. "Oh, go ahead and build the damn thing and
send me the bill!" he shouted.

Mott bustled about and got the Robinson Crusoe set constructed. It featured a thatched roof cottage, three spider mon-
keys shipped in from Florida, two five-foot alligators, and a
parrot. Soon after, Mott sent Bergeron a bill for $20,000.

The old guy hit the ceiling. "Mott!" he hollered over the
phone. "What's this goddamn bill for?"

Answered Mott with some trepidation but with a sly twinkle
in his eye: "Mr. Bergeron, you told me to build the set and
that's what I did. You didn't tell me how much I could spend!"

Mott relished such successes, noting that Trader Vic for-
gave him after reaping the public relations windfall from the
well-received Crusoe set. Mott also remembered inspirations
that didn't work out in the execution.

"I had the idea of 'little people' running Fairyland and I
wanted to hire a couple who could represent Mother Goose
and her husband," he recalled. "Well, I learned there were
quite a number of midgets and dwarfs living in the Bay Area.
Some had been skilled workers in the defense industries during World War II," he continued. "They could get into tight
spaces during the construction of ships and airplanes, for example, that more average-sized people couldn't squeeze into."

Mott found a husband and wife team he thought would fill the bill. "The couple I hired was really great," he said. But he found their small size made it difficult for them to handle the crowds that poured into Fairyland. He reluctantly replaced them with full sized personnel.

By 1952, Children's Fairyland had been featured in national magazines including *LIFE,* the *Saturday Evening Post* and the *Rotarian.* By the end of 1952, Mott reported to an approving Park Commission that more than 750,000 visitors had paid nine cents admission if 12 or under and 14 cents if over 12 to pass through the Old Woman's Shoe. An article in the October 1953 issue of *National Motorist,* written by Helen A. Kennedy, president of the Oakland Ad Club, added to Fairyland's growing national reputation.

Families flocked to see Fairyland's live animals and carved figures and its man-made creek bubbling alongside a winding path. In a small pen next to the Three Little Pigs eight-foot-high red brick house with white trim were the little porkers in person. Nearby were some miniature straw houses which, of course, had been blown down by the Big Bad Wolf. The overall effect of this and other installations was charming to children and adults alike. So fresh and original, in fact, that a well-known Hollywood entrepreneur came up from Southern California to take a look.

DISNEY DROPS BY

Walt Disney was in the process of creating his own "dream come true" when he arrived in Oakland for a visit in 1954. His much larger theme park, Disneyland, was under construction in Anaheim and due to open in 1955. There was no comparison in scale between Mott's modest little installation in a shady corner of a city park and Disney's sprawling, nine-million-dollar extravaganza. Nonetheless, Disney was impressed enough by what he heard about Fairyland to meet and talk with Mott.

"Disney said he'd been toying with the idea of building a

children's theme park (as part of Disneyland)," Mott recalled. "I said I thought that would be very popular." Mott informed Disney that until Fairyland there had never been such a theme park built especially for children. "But even if it's just for children, it will also attract adults," he predicted. About six months later, "Disney asked me to come down and look at some of the designs they'd created for his children's theme park," Mott continued. The installation was to be a section of Disneyland called Fantasyland. "So I went down, looked at their designs and said I thought they were going about it the right way."

As it turned out, Disney was impressed with more than just the concept and construction of Children's Fairyland. In 1956, after Disneyland had been open for a year, he hired Dorothy Manes to be director of Youth Administration at the giant theme park. Manes had been Fairyland's first director and an instrumental part of its founding.

So it was that Navlet's original idea for a theme park scaled for children and Mott's ability to carry the thought through struck a responsive chord. Between 1955 and 1961, other cities created their own special places for children. In California alone, Pixie Woodland opened in Stockton, Storybook Fairyland in Martinez, and Storyland in San Francisco. Although not quite the same concept, children's zoos opened in Pittsburgh, Pennsylvania, and New York City during that same time period.

When Mott pursued the private funding that financed the seventeen original sets for Children's Fairyland, the concept was new and daring. True, he had successfully pursued the idea in developing funding for the addition to the lawn bowling club at Lakeside Park, but it was not uniformly defined, understood or appreciated by all concerned. Mott refined and expanded upon the technique as he climbed the ranks of leadership from city parks to regional parks to state parks to the National Park Service. Other leaders followed suit. Nowa-

days, public-private partnerships are an accepted way to raise
money for public programs and institutions that cannot come
into being based on tax monies alone. Long ago, Mott used
them as a way of getting things done, creating models that are
emulated today.

Not long after Lake Merritt was created in 1869, local bird
lovers discovered that the in-town inlet served as a rest stop
for birds migrating up and down the Pacific Flyway. In 1879,
Oakland activists asked the California State Legislature to de-
clare the 155-acre lake an official wildlife refuge — the first of
its kind in the nation. And in the 1920s, the U.S. Biological
Survey added Lake Merritt to its chain of bird banding stations around the country so the annual travels of the water-
fowl could be documented for scientific purposes.

In 1934, the Lake Merritt Breakfast Club hired Paul Covel,
a young nature lover, to supervise the tagging activities and
serve as a guide on winter weekends at the Duck Feeding
Station at the lake. Covel could point out the visiting migra-
tory birds including pintails, widgeons, canvasbacks, scaups
and ruddies. The job was part-time and low paying. But for
Covel it was the first step toward his long-held goal of becoming a full-time, salaried naturalist.

That dream came true thirteen years later in 1947 when
Superintendent Mott called Covel into his office. Covel had
heard about Mott who had, in Covel's words, "exploded on
the Oakland scene" a year earlier. Now, much to Covel's surprise, the bright, new parks boss was offering him a full-time
job as a naturalist with the Park Department. But Mott didn't
have an opening for a naturalist, he told Covel, because such
a position didn't exist on the city's civil service list. Covel
would be hired as a ranger, Mott explained. After Covel did
the naturalist job unofficially for awhile, Mott would have the
ammunition to show the park board why the classification should

be officially created. Covel absorbed all this with amazement. Then he said yes. "Bill Mott possessed extreme confidence and infectious enthusiasm," he wrote later. "I took his offer on the spot and never regretted it."

The hiring of a full-time naturalist had long been a dream of Mott's. One of his strongest and most enduring beliefs was in the importance of education through interpretation. To Mott, interpretation meant not only educating people about the natural, cultural, and historic values of parks and what was in them, but also inspiring people to look further into a subject on their own and to learn what it meant to them and to society. Mott began to formulate that belief during his early years with the National Park Service when he supervised CCC workers and saw raw city youth evolve into pretty good woodsmen. For example, the CCC camp at La Purísima Mission in Southern California was made up of teenagers from Brooklyn, New York. They knew little about the outdoors when they arrived. But as they did all the work to reestablish the Mission they learned about natural values. So influential was the experience that for many years they held annual reunions at La Purísima. Added to the spiritual revelations of his youth in Michigan, Mott's observations of other young people in similar circumstances helped put interpretation near the top of his list of priorities.

With no uniform and no office, Covel immediately plunged into the job. With little precedent and only part-time experience behind him, he was nervous at first. "But with the ingenuity and persuasion of Superintendent Mott [and] the generosity and understanding of park staff friends, the starry-eyed visions of a nature man with a mission worked wonders," he said of himself. Soon, demand for Covel's services soared. He was giving nature talks at the lake, at city-sponsored day camps that had sprung up after the war, to students on field trips, at school assemblies, to the public at parks and at meetings of civic and service organizations. "Forty hour weeks didn't have much meaning for me in those days," Covel recalled. "My working examples were guys like Bill Mott [and others] who never had worried about the lengths of their working days and weeks."

(There were other details Mott didn't worry about, either. At one point, according to an oft-repeated story, some domestic ducks got into the Lake Merritt wildlife area and began to multiply. A nearby merchant began to bag the ducks for purposes of sale. Mott knew about it, the tale continues, but did nothing to stop the merchant — as long as he did his "hunting" under cover of darkness.)

After Covel had been several months on the job, creating a stir in the community, his boss was true to his word. Pointing out how warmly Covel had been received by the public, Mott asked the city to approve a new job classification called park naturalist. Covel was afraid there would be adverse reactions on the part of a few dour taxpayers: "What? A naturalist's job for us to support along with all [Mott's] other costly wild plans! What will that man Mott come up with next?" But the Park Commission, the Civil Service Commission and the City Council now saw the value of the job. The classification was rubber-stamped and Covel became the first full-time municipal park naturalist in the nation.

Covel had adapted a ranger's uniform to his new job. Now, all he needed was an office. The death in 1950 of Brighton C. "Bugs" Cain, founder of the Oakland Ornithological Club, the bequeathing of Cain's bug collection to the park department and Mott's ability to turn an opportunity to his advantage paved the way for its construction.

After a proper period of mourning for Cain, Mott got things moving. First, he organized a citizen's committee to raise money toward building, in Cain's memory, a nature center in Lakeside Park. With those pledges in hand, he persuaded the Oakland Rotary Club and the City Council to cover the remaining construction costs. The Oakland Rotary Club was the third oldest in the world. Chicago, where Rotary was founded, was the oldest, followed by San Francisco, then Oakland. Mott had a close relationship with the Oakland Rotary Club. He was an active participant, turned many times to his fellow Rotarians for help with worthwhile projects, and served as president of "Oakland No. 3" from 1982 to 1983.

A local contractor offered to build the nature center at cost. Soon, a new Rotary Natural Science Center was going up next to the Duck Feeding Area in Lakeside Park. Covel moved into the new center in September, 1953. Still, Mayor Clifford E. Rishell wasn't enthusiastic about the progressive but costly ideas Mott kept throwing out for what the mayor considered "frills", such as park naturalists and nature centers. The arrival in 1955 of an envelope from the U.S. Fish and Wildlife Service changed the mayor's attitude.

Inside the envelope was a band dated November, 1953. It had been removed from a male pintail shot in Anabyr, Siberia, in September, 1954. Awed naturalists concluded the fowl had left Lake Merritt, flown up the pacific flyway to Alaska, then crossed the Bering Strait into the Soviet Union. In the name of science, the Cold War notwithstanding, the Soviets had mailed the band back to its point of origin — Oakland.

Sensing the potential public relations coup of this unusual occurrence, Mott immediately explained its import to the mayor. Rishell was no dummy. The international recognition the high-flying duck brought to Oakland was not lost on the city leaders. "It did wonders," Covel reported, "for the political support of the park department."

THE LEGACY

By the mid-1950s, Mott's promise to make Oakland parks more beautiful and usable was well on its way to fulfillment. At mid-decade, total parks attendance hit 2.2 million, more visitors than in any year in the department's forty six-year history. The Rotary Natural Science Center and the duck feeding area clocked 600,000 visits, while adults and children entered Fairyland through the Old Woman's Shoe 444,000 times. The Peralta Playground, a smaller tot-lot Mott had set up next to the Oakland Municipal Auditorium, logged 414,000 visitor rides on a miniature steam train called the Oakland Acorn, a merry-go-round, a Lil' Belle sternwheel boat, and a stable of mild-mannered ponies. Another 150,000 people attended the free exhibitions of cineraria, begonias, dahlias, and chrysanthemums at the Trial and Show Gardens in Lakeside Park. Mott had a direct hand in creating all of these attractions.

The Oakland Park Department enjoyed a national reputation for excellence, a perception enhanced by Mott's election twice during that decade to the presidency of the American Institute of Park Executives. In 1960, he was asked by the Institute of Inter-American Affairs to serve as a consultant to Costa Rica. There, he spent two months helping that nation set up its now highly regarded system of nature parks and reserves. When Mott accepted in 1962 the call to become general manager of the East Bay Regional Park District, his record of accomplishment in Oakland was staggering. According to records kept by department publicist Burton Weber, Mott redesigned every park in the city, established more than fifty miles of median strip plantings, installed cement tubs of flowers and bushes in business and residential areas, put in many small planting beds that he called "exclamation points of beauty," constructed aviaries in several downtown locations and commissioned young sculptors to provide works of art for the parks. With the help of the sixty-five clubs and societies that belonged to the Oakland-East Bay Garden Center, Inc. (which he founded), Mott "encouraged homeowners throughout the city to turn to the club members and to the [park department] staff for ideas, help, and materials in making their own yards and gardens more beautiful," Weber recorded.

Under Mott's master plan, the Oakland Zoo was established in its present location in Knowland Park in the Oakland hills.

Dunsmuir House and Gardens — created from another nine-teenth-century estate — emerged as an important new visitor attraction after Mott acquired it in 1960. In addition to purchasing existing buildings, six rustic lodges were built in various parts of the city for citizens to rent for meetings, programs, parties and other festivities. A trout pond and casting pool emerged as a national leader in its specialized field — and as a producer of world-caliber flycasters.

But Mott's impact on the community extended far beyond the boundaries of park operations. Along with the greening of the city, the cultural traditions he conceived elevated the level of social and civil discourse among its citizens. After landscaping the Woodminster Amphitheater, for example, he launched the annual summer series of Broadway musical productions that continues today. He originated Oakland's annual Mother of the Year program, which still takes place every Mother's Day in the Municipal Rose Garden. The concert seasons of the Oakland Municipal Band almost tripled in length during his tenure and were broadcast for several years on a West Coast radio station.

How fortunate for the Bay Area that Mott's new job would keep him at home. He would continue to have an impact on its growth and development as he took his creative ideas to the wider arena represented by the East Bay Regional Park District.

1962 - William Mott, w/Lake Temescal Boathouse in background,
Oakland, California
Oakland Tribune Photo

Chapter 3

Creating a Regional Greenbelt

"If all the beasts were gone, we would die from a great loneliness of spirit...All things are connected.
Whatever befalls the earth befalls the children of the earth."

CHIEF SEATTLE

When Mott bustled into the Oakland Hills offices of the East Bay Regional Park District on July 1, 1962, he was intent on jump-starting a slow-moving jurisdiction. The district, which had been in the making when Mott was getting his master's degree in 1932, consisted by the early 1960s of five woodland parks totaling 10,500 acres in the East Bay hills. Tilden, above Berkeley, shared part of its border with the wooded University of California, Berkeley campus. Sibley, Redwood, and Lake Temescal ranged above Oakland, the industrial and commercial center of the East Bay. Anthony Chabot backed up San Leandro, the bedroom town just south of Oakland. While the district had popular facilities, including a merry-go-round, a "Little Farm" with barnyard animals that children could feed, camping and equestrian activities and Roberts Recreation Area — named after Tommy Roberts, an East Bay labor leader — its pace was sleepy enough to earn it a kind-hearted comparison to a place in which the mythical Rip Van Winkle would have felt comfortable.

The previous general manager, Richard Walpole, had run the district a bit like a personal fiefdom. The five-member board of directors, representing the seven Alameda County cities that had voted the district into existence in 1934, was content to maintain that status quo. Operations and maintenance took precedence, with land acquisition occurring when extra funds were available. The budget was financed by the levy of 5 cents per $100 assessed valuation approved by the voters when the district was formed.

Under this system, the district bought in 1952 some 959 acres of land from the East Bay Municipal Utility District (referred to as EBMUD and known familiarly as "East Bay Mud"). The land, called Grass Valley, surrounded an EBMUD reservoir called Lake Chabot. While no swimming, fishing, or boating were allowed in or on the water, families could camp out in the park, the first regional park in southern Alameda County. Getting their own park had persuaded residents of two southern Alameda County communities, Eden Township in 1956, and Washington Township in 1958, to annex themselves to the district, joining the original seven north county cities that had formed the district in 1934. Their membership broadened the district's tax base, providing funding for future acquisition of additional open space. The name of the new site was later changed to Anthony Chabot Regional Park, commemorating the East Bay engineer who in 1892 built the dam that created Lake Chabot.

Informality under Walpole's management had its advantages. Maintenance workers did whatever had to be done with little concern for official divisions of labor. Carolyn Thatcher, one of the few women on staff, not only kept the books but also developed sketches for a new headquarters building on Skyline Boulevard in the Oakland hills, and drew up plans for two Regional Recreation Areas, Cull Canyon in Castro Valley and Don Castro in Hayward. An important development during Walpole's fifteen-year term of office came in 1959 when employees, led by Robert Blau waged a successful campaign to create Local 414 of the American Federation of State, County and Municipal Employees. Before inauguration of the union, employees belonged to the East Bay Parks Association, an in-house organization without real power. Dues were one dollar a year and the money collected usually went to buy an annual gift for the general manager.

The atmosphere at meetings of the district board of directors was equally informal. Clyde Woolridge, an Oakland merchant appointed to the board in 1958, recalled the low-key proceedings. "When I first went on," he said, "we met once a month and looked at whatever problems we had. Our general manager [Walpole] really ran the district. We set the policy, and that was basically what the board was about. Nobody had much preparation for the meetings," Woolridge continued. "Walpole would come up with some ideas or problems that we'd need to solve and the board sat down and solved them."

Mott's impact on that relatively placid environment was like the sudden appearance of a tornado on the horizon. "Bill Mott turned the whole thing around," said Woolridge. "Before he came we were just coasting along with no real big plans." Mott "had an idea a minute," said Woolridge. When Woolridge introduced Mott at speaking engagements, he'd kid the new general manager by telling the audience, "The only trouble with Bill is that nobody can afford all those proposals!" But Mott's exuberance was unquenchable. "The beautiful part about it," said Woolridge, "was the fact that you'd turn him down and it didn't dampen him. He'd turn around and work on another idea."

It was this spirit that had led to Mott's hiring in the first place. The process began in 1960 when Walpole resigned. Dr. Robert Gordon Sproul, the distinguished president emeritus of the University of California, Berkeley and one of the founders of the Regional Park District, was an influential member of the board. "We were sitting there with Dr. Sproul," said Woolridge, "and he said, 'Let's get Bill Mott.'"

"Bill's got a job," Woolridge replied. "He's not going to leave that."

"How do you know?" Sproul retorted. "We haven't asked him."

Sproul and Woolridge invited Mott to lunch at the Athenian-Nile Club, an exclusive gentlemen's retreat in downtown Oakland. Mott agreed to the meeting. "I was kind of excited about it," he recalled of the prospect of dining with the former president of his alma mater.

However, when Sproul asked if he would accept an appointment as general manager of the Regional Park District, Mott respectfully demurred. "I'm right in the middle of completing some of the work in Oakland," he explained. "We've gone through every park, and redeveloped them and I won't be able to take the position because I don't want to leave the department without completing what I have set out to do. I have put together a good organization that I feel can carry forward," he added, "but sometimes even a good organization doesn't carry forward unless you are there to push."

Sproul asked when Mott might be willing to reconsider. "I think it will take another year for me to do what I want to do and then I will be interested," Mott said, "but I would not want you to consider holding the job open for a whole year."

"Let me think about that," Sproul replied.

The next day, he called Mott and said the board was willing to wait a year. Mott again reacted cautiously. "I've got an idea," he said. "About a year from now, let's get together and see how you feel and how I feel about the position at that time," he suggested. "We may both have changed our mind during this period."

"No," said Sproul, "we're not going to change our mind. We want you."

Mott promised to talk again the following year.

With hopeful hearts, the board appointed Wesley Adams, a Walpole assistant, to the post of acting general manager. Adams had had the distinction of being the first field employee hired by the district back in 1937. While Adams was competent, he did not innovate. "There was no aggressive program," Woolridge said. "If you read some of our minutes (taken during that period) they say: 'This ditch was cleaned out, and this trail was repaired.' Wes did a good job and held it together."

By 1962, after almost seventeen years with Oakland parks, Mott was ready to make the move. When he met again with Sproul, he asked what the board thought needed to be done. The board wanted Mott to modernize the district's financial and administrative structures, expand its tax base by annexing Contra Costa County, plan for growth, and buy land before developers got to it, Sproul replied. Mott said he'd take the job if among the people he could hire would be specialists in Interpretation and Public Relations. Two areas of operation he had pioneered and used well in Oakland, he wanted to bring them along to the next level. The board gave him the green light and he accepted the appointment.

PROFESSIONALIZING THE PARK DISTRICT

Mott chalked up an amazing series of accomplishments during the nearly five years he held the post. One of his first moves was to reorganize, expand and update the district's administrative staff and procedures. He created separate departments for finance, planning, acquisition, equipment, interpretation, park operations, and public relations. Then, over the next two years, he hired the best people he could find to run them. These included Robert Herman, Controller; Irwin Luckman, Plans, Design, and Construction; Perry Laird, Chief of Parks, and Robert Clark, Equipment and Fire Operations. To head Interpretation, he hired Christian Nelson away from the Sacramento Children's Museum in 1963. And in 1964 he asked Richard Trudeau to become director of Public Relations. As head of PR for the Bay Area United Way, Trudeau had worked previously with Mott on several projects, including Children's Fairyland, and also brought experience in parks work from his home town of Seattle.

Herman tightened financial procedures and personnel policies that had been administered rather loosely before. Staff
members had lived in district-owned cabins and cottages rent-
free, for example. People were hired, as Nelson later liked to
say, "by the one-foot-on-the-running-board method. You put
your foot on the running board of a district truck, asked the
driver if there were any openings and were told to report the
next day." In another informal practice, outside suppliers routinely gave liquor, fruit, hams, and other gifts to district employees at Christmas time.

Some years later, longtime staffer Eddie Collins expressed
the doubt and resentment many long-time employees had about
the tighter, more highly organized ship Mott ran. The general
manager started collecting rent from employees who occupied district housing, Collins complained, and "everybody that
had any position at all started doing a lot of paperwork." Also,
Collins recalled, Mott "wanted to know what you did and how
you did it." Collins considered these reports nothing more
than "tattle sheets —you tattle on yourself, and you don't have
any choice but to do it."

As for the suppliers holiday gift habit, Mott stopped that
one personally. "I wrote to all of them and told them I was not
interested in those kinds of things and if they brought them
we would return them," he said later. What the district wanted
instead, he told the suppliers, was reliable goods and services
at the best possible prices. The gifts stopped flowing. Services
and prices improved.

Before Mott's arrival, the district's interpretive program had
consisted of a Junior Ranger program of modest scope that
took a few kids out for hikes on Saturday mornings. Run by
the district's first resident naturalist, Jack Parker, the program
was so limited, the story went, that mothers would call from
the maternity ward to sign their newborns up for a spot on the
roster six or seven years later. Within that limited scope, however, Parker and another ranger, Josh Barkin, did a marvelous

job. Barkin, who had joined the district in 1960, brought nature to city children in new and imaginative ways. He created puppet shows on energy conservation, and his famous "gutter tours" showed kids what kinds of natural life they could find under their feet. Taking along youngsters who thought milk came in bottles instead of from cows, he toured local supermarkets, explaining the origins of every-day foods. Barkin, Trudeau said in later years, was "the foremost interpretive teacher in our time anywhere in the country," constantly in demand, state and nationwide, to train other naturalists as the concept caught on elsewhere.

Some employees were shocked, therefore, when Mott set up an entire interpretive department and put Nelson in charge. As good as the program was, Mott demanded more. "He wanted the most innovative, creative interpretive program ever devised," Nelson said, along with "an innovative, creative interpretive center that would set new standards in program and exhibition for the park field." Nelson eagerly accepted Mott's challenge. He understood what the boss had in mind: "That you get the support of the public by making them a part of the system and making them recognize the value of the resources." But, while Barkin stayed on, some of the senior staffers had trouble adjusting to Mott's higher expectations. The general manager had to educate them about what interpretation meant, why it was worth financing, and why an informed and involved public would pay dividends in the future.

MANAGEMENT BY COLLABORATION

While Mott was putting his new management team together, he was also getting acquainted with the secretaries, landscapers, truck drivers, mechanics and other district staff. One morning, he asked a group of employees to meet him at the flagpole in front of the new headquarters on Skyline Boulevard in the Oakland hills. When the employees arrived, they noticed a U.S. Marine in full dress standing at attention next to the general manager. Mott astonished the group by asking the Marine to demonstrate the right way to hoist the American flag. The flag was being improperly raised, Mott informed the group. He wanted to make sure that from then on it was correctly flown — and it was. "He insisted on excellence," remembers one retired employee who was among those gathered. "He didn't just mouth it — he demanded it."

But as he had in Oakland, Mott tempered his demanding management style with a disarmingly common touch. While Collins griped about Mott's insistence on employee accountability, he conversely appreciated Mott's interest in his employees. It was not unusual, for instance, for Mott to drive a Regional Park District car along the winding, wooded roads of the parks, stopping to chat unannounced with drivers, tree trimmers, carpenters, or golf course groundskeepers. A man could be working deep in a ditch, shoveling dirt or fixing pipe, only to see the tips of a pair of shoes at the rim. Glancing up, he'd see Mott standing there, that unfailingly cheerful ear-to-ear smile on his face. "Good morning, I'm Bill Mott," he'd say, as if the startled worker didn't know. "How're things going?"

"He wanted to know all about us, what we'd done, the whole case history of our tenure," recalled Collins, the crusty old-timer. "He had this big mass meeting and he wanted all the ideas. You could come into his office any time. You could do a lot of dreaming, because he said, I'm a big dreamer myself, and we want big ideas. We want to start thinking big. This outfit has thought little long enough, he'd say. Now we're going to do things and we're going to expand."

When Mott put his arms around his workers, professionally and emotionally, some, like Collins, stiffened at first, as if they were children squirming in a father's overpowering embrace. Some were so unsettled by this sudden change of atmosphere that they left. But once others realized that Mott's interest in them, their ideas, and even their families, was sincere, they responded with affection and, in many cases, a devotion to him during his tenure with the park district and to his memory since. "Mr. Mott always stopped and talked to you," recalled retired worker Bob Daskam. "He knew everyone who worked in the parks." Added Bud Scott, another veteran, "Mr. Mott would stop to talk to you wherever you were to ask about you and your family."

Nor did Mott have a problem with the union. "In fact, he did something extraordinary," said Blau. "He gave us permission to have dues check off. For the first time dues were automatically deducted from our paychecks. Suddenly, instead of having to chase down people to collect their dues, the money came right into the treasury. That procedure gave us enormous strength." Blau was surprised that Mott agreed so readily to this boost for the union. "He could have put up a fight but he didn't," he said. "I'm not sure he realized what he was doing. He was not some soft-hearted pinko, you know."

Indeed not. Mott was a life-long Republican. But in the mold of Theodore Roosevelt, Laurance Rockefeller and other Republican naturalists, he was nonpartisan when it came to nature. He was also a republican in the classic sense: A man who believed that the people he managed were equals and should share the collective goal of growing and developing the park district.

Mott's attitude toward the union may have sprung from the conviction that individuals should be paid fairly for their labor, a principle based at least partially on his own experience. He had been a galley cook on those freighters plying the Great Lakes. He had pitched in on his uncle's farm. He had worked up a sweat alongside the CCC crews he'd supervised in the national parks during the Depression. He had labored over his drawing board as a freelance landscape architect. As superintendent of Oakland parks, he had, Burton Weber recalled, even rolled up his sleeves one time and dug ditches with a construction crew.

Another experience had also influenced Mott's attitude toward management-employee relations. In the late 1940s, shortly after he became superintendent of parks in Oakland, the city had held up his paycheck while it disputed whether a freelance landscaping job he was finishing for another city meant he was improperly working for two jurisdictions at once. The city council didn't accept Mott's explanation that he'd started the job before knowing he was going to be appointed superintendent. For over a year, Mott worked without salary until his case was won in court and he received back pay. Throughout that period, friends and relatives sustained the Mott family while Mott refused to give in. He stood on principle and was vindicated. "That's when I began to learn about politics," he said. "You have to know how politicians operate but you don't have to be one yourself."

Upon reflection, Blau wasn't surprised after all that Mott allowed the dues check off. If belonging to the union meant employees would make a living wage, put in a solid day's work and feel loyal toward the Regional Park District, that's what counted. "Mott was interested in parks — period," said Blau.

Mott's collaborative management policy soon paid dividends. "I was amazed this Christmas by one of the employees who had been in the district for many, many years," he recalled during a speech in February, 1964. "In this process of developing a creative dynamic organization, some of the employees found that the former way of just going along was what they liked, and obviously there were many resignations. But some of the older employees, and some of the younger employees, began to get the spirit of this new kind of action — and the day before Christmas, one of the older employees came into the office, the door of which is always open, and put on my desk an accumulation of forms which we used to indicate overtime. Now, I assumed that when he put them on my desk that he did this because he, like some of the other employees, just couldn't take it," Mott continued. "They had been in a rut too long. The employee said, 'I'm giving these to the East Bay Regional Park District.' And I said, 'I'm sorry that you've decided to leave the district, you've been a faithful employee for 20 years.' He turned to me and said, 'I'm not leaving the district — This is my Christmas present *to* the district. I now am finding this an exciting experience. I can't wait to get to work in the morning. My kids are doing better in school. We don't quarrel so much at home any more. So this is my present *to* the East Bay Regional Park District.'"

The employee had found going to work so gratifying that he decided not to charge overtime. To Mott, the man's joy was simply "the way people react when they're given an opportunity to do the things that most normal people want to do" —work hard, think creatively, and make decisions.

EXCEPTION TO THE RULE

But Mott didn't get along well with every employee. And when he followed his own principle of taking a "calculated risk," he sometimes got into trouble. That was the outcome early in 1965 when he attempted to dismiss James Roof, the long-time supervisor of the Botanic Garden in Tilden Park. Mott wanted to expand the botanic garden, home of the world's most extensive collection of native California plants, and move it to Anthony Chabot Regional Park — without taking Roof along. Roof filed a grievance and was able to marshal support for his position from members of the University of California, Berkeley faculty and hundreds of botanic garden aficionados from Berkeley and surrounding cities.

An overflow crowd attended the district board meeting on March 3, 1965 to protest Mott's attempt to retire Roof and relocate the garden. Under the banner of "Friends of the Botanic Garden," UC Berkeley Professor Leo Brewer described the garden as "one of the finest in the world, an asset that can not be duplicated for a million dollars." The board reversed the dismissal and Roof returned to tend the garden.

But Mott rarely dwelled on a setback for long. He seemed to be able to absorb the disappointment and move on. Whether he maintained an inviolate inner peace based on his spiritual foundations or whether he simply wasn't by nature self-pitying, he acknowledged the loss and then quickly turned his attention to the next priority on his list.

GROWING PARKS THROUGH PARTNERSHIPS

As soon as he was appointed in 1962, Mott initiated a flurry of activity aimed at creating new park and recreation facilities in rapidly urbanizing southern Alameda County. Despite the presence of 4,972-acre Anthony Chabot Regional Park in San Leandro, which had opened for hiking and camping under the Walpole administration in 1952, residents still felt slighted because most of the regional parks were concentrated at the northern, more heavily-populated end of the county. One of his first opportunities came in November, 1962, when a San Leandro advisory committee asked Mott to support its proposal to open the 315-acre Lake Chabot, the centerpiece of the park, to water activities. Mott joined the commission for an inspection tour of the lake and came away favoring the plan. In 1964, at the completion of protracted negotiations, the Park District signed a lease with EBMUD to initiate boating and fishing at the lake. When a fishing derby was announced in 1966 to celebrate opening day for angling, such was the pent-up demand for the sport that by three o'clock that morning some twenty-thousand persons were lined up at the gates, waiting impatiently to throw in their lines. "When the signal was given, they all surged forward," Trudeau recalled. "It was scary, but wonderful."

The collaboration was a win-win situation for both the agencies and the public. It allowed the Regional Park District to do what it did best — manage nature facilities and programs — and the utility district to do what it did best — own and manage public water supplies. And it gave the public additional recreation and leisure-time choices. The opening of Lake Chabot was another example of Mott's ability to forge imaginative and successful partnerships between public agencies. But when Mott decided to build a golf course called Willow Park on part of the leased land near the lake, his zeal went too far. He awarded the construction contract without competitive bidding. He also granted a 25-year lease to the course operators although the district's lease on the land was good for only thirteen years. Once built, the construction company went broke and the course, situated on low-lying acreage, suffered repeated flooding. The Alameda County Grand Jury and State Assemblyman John Knox, a Democrat from nearby Richmond, launched investigations to look for potential illegalities. Adopting the motto that discretion is the better part of valor, Mott took a sudden two-week vacation leaving public relations expert Trudeau and the rest of the staff to cool the controversy. They did this by marshalling support for the Regional Park District and by pledging to quickly correct the mistakes Mott made. No illegalities were found among the irregularities. But EBMUD general manager John MacFarland, already hostile to Mott over a development issue they had previously fought about in Orinda where both lived, decided that from then on the water district would run its own reservoir-based recreation programs. Regional Park District proposals to run recreation facilities at EBMUD's Lafayette Reservoir in Contra Costa County were shelved. Although the Park District's lease at Anthony Chabot became permanent, EBMUD "didn't like Bill Mott, they didn't like his lease on Chabot, and they didn't like what he did at Willow Park," said Trudeau.

Relationships went more smoothly with a third public agency, the Alameda County Flood Control and Water Conservation District. As mentioned earlier, Cull Canyon and Don Castro Regional Recreation Areas were created through partnerships between the park district and the flood control district. In the early 1960s, the flood control district announced it would create two reservoirs by damming two creeks in southern Alameda County. Mott made an agreement with the flood control district to lease and manage land around the new reservoirs, then turned the planning over to his staff of architects and engineers. Regional Park District staff built hundred acre parks surrounding Cull Canyon Reservoir in Castro Valley and Don Castro Reservoir in Hayward. In both parks, designers did something unprecedented: They created inner swimming lagoons separated from the main reservoirs. The 1.5-acre lagoons, surrounded by beaches of trucked-in sand and filled with water pumped from the reservoirs, remained unaffected by the reservoirs' seasonal fluctuations or the activities of anglers and boaters on the reservoirs. The lagoon design won the 1966 Governor's Design Award for Exceptional Distinction for Recreational Development in the landscape category.

CITIZENS DONATE LAND

Private citizens made historic agreements with the Regional Park District, too. And Mott's ability to shape these agreements resulted in enormous gains. Instead of seeing each individual acquisition separately, Mott saw them as pieces of a larger puzzle. That was the case with three parcels of land near Hayward that became part of a much more significant whole. Bud Garin, a rancher, owned land just over the crest of the East Bay hills from the campus of the brand new California State College at Hayward. When the Regional Park District found out the land might be for sale, Mott paid a visit to Garin.

"We talked at considerable length about parks and open space," he later recalled, remembering that Garin was already predisposed to his property becoming a park. And "because the land was adjacent to Hayward College," Mott said, "I felt that it would be a very good acquisition. We could relate our interpretive program to some of the class work at Hayward State and have a joint operation." The district also needed more parkland in Southern Alameda County. Adding another site to Anthony Chabot, Cull Canyon and Don Castro would go a long way toward quieting criticism. When Garin and his lawyer, Jack Smith, made it possible for the district to buy the land at less than its appraised price and — for the first time ever — on an installment plan basis, Mott returned the favor. "We agreed to call it the Garin Ranch Regional Park," he said. "We felt that was a proper way to handle the matter." The ranch became a vast, 1,520-acre sanctuary of rolling hills and grasslands, which, with hiking and riding trails for humans and protected habitat for wildlife, remains largely in its natural state. Although Mott's hoped-for collaboration with Cal State Hayward never materialized, a strong partnership of another kind emerged from the deal. Jack Smith later became a highly successful developer who remained loyal to the concept of retaining open space in the region. He became a staunch ally of the Regional Park District, giving generously of his time and money in subsequent years.

At about the same time, Mott had negotiated an agreement with another Southern Alameda County landowner, Charles "Chet" Soda, that if the Garin parcel became available so would an adjacent parcel Soda owned. And a little farther to the southeast, in an even more rural part of the county, stood the Dry Creek Pioneer Ranch, owned by three sisters who were drafting their wills against future inevitabilities.

Mott entered into discussions with Mildred, Jeanette, and Dr. Edith Meyers about the possibility of deeding their land to the park district. Before meeting with the three ladies, he — as always — did his homework. "I remember the first time I went down there to talk with them," he told oral historian Mimi Stein. "I took some of my jelly and gave it to them as a gesture of goodwill and a basis for talking. They were very much interested in plant materials. I'd had a number of [earlier] conversations with them, and I told them that I had a hobby of making jelly out of the fruit of wild plants. I had just come back from Nevada and I had collected some special fruit from some plants at one of their state parks — I think it's called Ichthyosaurus State Park [actually Berlin Ichthyosaur State Park just southeast of Reno]— where they'd found some fossil remains and that sort of thing. I brought these berries back and made some jelly, and I gave the Meyers sisters some of that jelly as a conversation piece and to keep them interested in making their land a gift to the regional park system."

But negotiations stalled when the California State Department of Transportation proposed putting a highway through the middle of the property. Progress was delayed while the Regional Park District backed the Meyers sisters in their successful fight to block the proposed roadway. Eventually, after Mott had left the district, negotiations for the property were renewed and the Meyer Sisters donated 1,200 acres to the district. That land became the bulk of the 1,563-acre Dry Creek Pioneer Regional Park. When added to the adjacent 1,520-acre Garin Regional Park, and the adjoining Soda property, more than 3,000 acres of East Bay agricultural land were preserved just minutes from the city of Hayward—perhaps with the help of a little homemade wild berry jelly.

ANNEXING CONTRA COSTA COUNTY

Meanwhile, the tireless Mott was moving forward on the other major charge given him by the Regional Park District board of directors: To develop a master plan for future parks in Contra Costa County enticing enough to convince the voters of the county to join the district. Ironically, two Contra Costa cities, Richmond and El Cerrito, had been among the original group of nine cities willing to vote on whether to form the district back in 1934. The other seven cities, Oakland, Berkeley, Emeryville, Albany, Alameda, Piedmont and San Leandro, were all in Alameda County. But the Contra Costa County Board of Supervisors, lobbied by farmers and ranchers who didn't want to annex at the time, refused to sanction the election, forcing Richmond and El Cerrito to back out. But now, post-war suburbanization was gobbling up that agricultural land. Tract developments were fast obliterating the fruit and nut orchards, the crops of vegetables and the grazing lands that had once stretched all the way to the California Delta. Still, the burgeoning population had rejected several county park bonds. Contra Costa was in the strange position of having a county park department but no county parks.

Sproul and Mott weren't alone in their desire to bring Contra Costa County into the fold. In the spring of 1963, Robert Kahn, a member of the Contra Costa County Grand Jury and of a wealthy East Bay retailing family, joined with other county leaders to support the annexation drive. It took a year, but other than one small area near the Delta where asparagus growers refused to join in, Kahn and the others managed to get an annexation measure on the June, 1964 ballot. The measure included a request for a five-cent tax (the same levy Alameda County paid) for operations and maintenance of the park district, plus an additional five-cent tax, lasting only for five years, in Contra Costa to be used only for land acquisition in the county.

But when Trudeau joined the district in April, 1964, there was no campaign organization in place. Despite a master plan for park acquisition that Mott had developed, voter support for the proposed annexation was conspicuously absent just as it had been for county park bond measures in the past. Trudeau had two months to pull off a public relations miracle.

"I'm not going to be able to do anything else," he told Mott.

"That's all right," Mott replied. "You don't even have to show up at the office. Just get the situation organized."

With the support of Kahn, Trudeau pulled together a team that swung into action. Community activist Doreta Chaney organized pro-annexation citizens committees. Contra Costa resident and Sierra Club activist Hulet Hornbeck voluntarily stumped the campaign trail. Mott gave breakfast, lunch, and dinner talks to service clubs, garden groups, newspaper publishers, youth organizations, and to as many other opinion makers and potential voters as he could squeeze into the day — or night. The best bet for passage was to educate the public about the importance of saving portions of the county's wooded hills, deep canyons and tumbling creeks before developers obliterated much of that natural beauty. And the best transmitter of that message was Mott.

Often quiet and soft-spoken off-stage, Mott came forcefully alive before an audience. A gifted speaker, with clear enunciation and a raspy, light-timbred voice, he had the natural rhythms, extemporaneous humor and emotional epiphanies of an evangelist. He would start a typical address by cracking a joke to relax his listeners. Then, he would begin addressing his topic in casual, conversational tones. As he continued, his body language grew more intense until, voice raised and fist pounding lectern, he held the group transfixed. As he ended, always on a positive note, the audience usually erupted into loud, spontaneous applause. Invigorated, they often broke into an animated buzz, eager to discuss with each other the points they had just heard. Said one listener after a Mott speech, "The air had a sudden charge to it. You could almost feel it through the hair on the back of your neck. Was I the only one who felt like this? No, others began to talk excitedly about what had just transpired."

Mott's message was almost always a variation of his life-long theme of reverence for nature, adapted to the particular needs of the situation — in this case the crucial need to save some of Contra Costa's best land in the form of regional parks. Mott carried out his round-the-clock speaking blitz, talking to "anyone who will listen." Trudeau cultivated favorable editorials in the newspapers and along with Chaney organized supportive citizens to educate their neighbors. Dr. Clark Kerr, who had succeeded Robert Gordon Sproul as president of the University of California at Berkeley, and his wife, Catherine, known as "Kay," were residents of El Cerrito, one of the two originally

supportive Contra Costa County cities. Avid environmentalists, they agreed to serve as honorary co-chairs of Citizens for
Regional Parks NOW. State representatives John Knox and
George Miller of Contra Costa County also supported annexation. Esteemed environmentalist Laurance Rockefeller donated
$25,000 to cover the cost of campaign materials. With no time
to spare, the tide turned. In June, the annexation measure
won by 54 to 46 percent. The vote was in no way a mandate,
but it was a triumph in a county that had turned down previous bond issues for parks and tax-generating annexations.

Mott's willingness to demonstrate complete faith in trusted
associates — as he had in delegating the election tactics to
Trudeau and later the land acquisition strategies to Hulet
Hornbeck, who joined the district after annexation — formed
one of the most enduring and endearing components of his
leadership style. So did his respect and affection for the public he served. "The citizen groups who got behind us made the
difference," he asserted. "In fact, I don't think we could have
done it without them." Most of the time, Mott realized where
his greatest strengths lay. He was the visionary, the researcher,
the planner, the agenda-setter, and the communicator who
"thought big," acted decisively and was not afraid to take risks.
He was quite willing to lead the charge while counting on
proven associates to carry through on the details. Sometimes,
as in the controversies with James Roof over the Tilden Park
Native Plant Botanic Garden and with EBMUD over the Willow Park fiasco, the details got messy. Both EBMUD and James
Roof sued the Regional Park District in legal battles that went
on for years. "If you're a leader like Bill was, you have a lot of
friends," Trudeau reflected later. "But you make a lot of en-
emies in the course of doing that, too, because sometimes you
run over people to get where you're going. When people liked
Bill they were fond of him; when they didn't like him their
dislike went back a long way."

MAKING GOOD ON THE PROMISE

Once Contra Costa County was part of the park district and its tax revenues began to roll in, Mott went to work on his master plan. But just before launching it in January of 1965, he took a little break from Regional Park District matters to go Down Under. The government of Australia asked him to consult with them on matters of national park planning. More specifically, the director of the Department of Parks, Ministry of the Interior, based in Canberra, asked Mott "to examine the work, policies, and methods of park administration now underway...as well as to suggest policy improvements, report on the adequacy of recreation and playground facilities as compared with American and overseas trends and make suggestions for future development and recreational changes." During five weeks of unpaid leave in December 1964 and January 1965, Mott traveled through Australia, viewing parks and recreation sites. When he returned, he said Australia reminded him of California 25 years earlier. "Although open land is plentiful there now," he said, "this will not always be so." As was his wont, he added what he believed so strongly: "There is a need for long-range planning." His report, sent back to Australia some weeks later, made that recommendation.

While in Australia, word reached Mott that he was once again being considered for a higher post. His name had been suggested to California's second-term Democratic governor, Edmund G. "Pat" Brown, as a candidate for director of state parks and recreation. But just as when the regional park district tried initially in 1960 to woo him away from Oakland, Mott turned the offer down — and for essentially the same reason he cited then. "I think I owe it to the people of Alameda and Contra Costa Counties to stay with this job and get done what we set out to do in our five year projection," he said.

Mott's integrity showed through, but he wasn't insensitive to political realities. Perhaps to make clear he wasn't turning Brown down because the governor was a Democrat, Mott took the first opportunity available to praise the "America the Beautiful" program that Brown's fellow Democrats had launched in Washington. Lyndon and Claudia "Lady Bird" Johnson's beautification project, Mott said, "is in keeping with the kind of program we're attempting to carry out" in the Regional Park District. And since "There is a big job to be done here and our plans are well under way," Mott preferred to remain in his present job. Three months later, from May 23 to May 25, 1965, Mott attended the White House Conference on Natural Beauty at LBJ's invitation where he served as chairman of a panel on Landscape Reclamation.

Whether from a sense of honor or from a desire not to get too cozy with a Democratic administration, Mott's decision not to go to Sacramento greatly benefited the East Bay Regional Park District and the people of the Bay Area. That same year, new tax revenue from Contra Costa County joined that already coming in from Alameda County. The district's budget nearly doubled to $3 million. For the next two years under Mott's leadership and with the herculean work of his talented staff, the groundwork was laid for several new parks in Contra Costa County.

In 1967, Kennedy Grove Regional Recreation Area became the first regional park in the county. A lush 95-acre eucalyptus grove near San Pablo Dam Road, which runs between Orinda in central county and El Sobrante in west county, Kennedy (named after the assassinated president) was deeded to the district by the county shortly after annexation. The district needed several months to build picnic areas, horseshoe pits, volleyball courts and a central lawn for ballgames.

Briones Regional Park also came into being in 1967 with a preliminary gift from the county of grazing land. Continued acquisition over the following years enlarged the park to its ultimate size of 5,756 acres of high hills and steep canyons surrounded by the cities of Lafayette, Walnut Creek, Pleasant Hill, Concord, and Martinez. Hospitable to hiking, jogging, bicycling, horseback riding, archery, bird-watching, and wild-flower studying, Briones, named after the Spanish family that once grazed cattle on it, became the second largest park in the entire district. It shelters a profusion of wildflowers, native madrone, manzanita and oak trees, black-tailed deer, coyotes, red-tailed hawks, turkey vultures and an occasional eagle as well as a myriad of smaller mammals and birds. Its two highest points are Briones Peak at 1,483 feet, and Mott Peak at 1,424 feet.

Another Contra Costa County park begun during Mott's tenure was Las Trampas Regional Wilderness. Mott had hiked that stretch of ridge land forming part of the boundary between southern Alameda and Contra Costa counties and thought it would make a marvelous regional park. He envisioned hikers, backpackers and equestrians sharing the territory with a variety of wildlife including occasional mountain lions and golden eagles. The district acquired a basic unit in that area and, as Mott's successors took over, continued to buy adjacent lands until a total of 3,638 acres was preserved. And not a moment too soon as that part of Contra Costa County's I-680 corridor boomed in the 1980s with sprawling housing developments, shopping centers and business parks.

FROM THE RIDGE TOPS TO THE BAY

While developing parks in the interior of the East Bay, Regional Park District officials realized they needed also to begin looking down from their aerie high atop the Oakland hills toward San Francisco Bay shimmering below. "We need to begin to acquire bay shore frontage as a part of the whole regional concept," Mott said. That dawning awareness was heightened when his friend, Kay Kerr, helped found the Save San Francisco Bay Association and he later chaired the organization. Alarmed by increasing amounts of fill going into the bay, the citizen group lobbied for protection of the very resource that defines the Bay Area. Their work eventually led to formation of the state-run Bay Conservation and Development Commission, which thereafter began monitoring and regulating shoreline fill.

Mott's major move on the shoreline was Alameda State Beach, a stretch of bay front in the island city with a long and colorful history. The beach, originally a resort area, became Neptune Beach, an amusement park, from 1917-1939, then a training center during World War II. Finally, under a bill sponsored by Robert Crown, state assembly member from Alameda County, the beach was acquired by the state in 1967 and turned over to the Regional Park District to manage. When the fine-grained sand used to create the beach kept eroding, the district embarked on a fifteen-year struggle to save the facility. Finally, with the help of the U.S. Army Corps of Engineers, installation of medium grained sand dredged from the bottom of the bay stabilized the situation. Rededicated in 1982 and a favorite with families, it quickly became the largest and most heavily used swimming beach on San Francisco Bay.

THE LEGACY

By the time Governor Ronald Reagan asked Mott to become director of California's Department of Parks and Recreation in mid-1967, the East Bay Regional Park District had grown from 10,500 acres to 22,000 acres and from five to twenty parks, serving a rapidly expanding population of 1.5 million in two counties. It was seeing triple the number of visitors that had been counted before Mott's tenure. And though Irwin Luckman, chief of planning, held the post of general manager until 1968, it was Trudeau's promotion from acting general manager to general manager in 1969 that enabled the Mott tradition not only to continue but to expand.

Unlike the pristine watershed lands in the hills, waterfront lands often had multiple owners, histories of ground and water pollution and other complications that made them more difficult to convert into parks. As a result of sometimes difficult and strenuous negotiations beginning in the late 1960s under Trudeau and land acquisition manager Hulet Hornbeck, however, and backed by the recommendations of an 83-member Citizens' Task Force chaired by Alameda County Supervisor Joseph Bort, the district initiated a push for more shoreline parks.

In Contra Costa County, there was Miller/Knox Regional Shoreline, named in honor of the late State Senator George Miller and former Assembly Member Robert Knox, who, after the Willow Park flap was resolved, became a strong supporter of the Regional Park District. Another was Brooks Island Regional Shoreline, and a third was Point Pinole Regional Shoreline, formerly owned by Bethlehem Steel which had acquired the land from Atlas Powder Co., a manufacturer of gunpowder and dynamite for almost one hundred years. In Alameda County, plans got underway for Oyster Bay Regional Shoreline, just south of Oakland International Airport, and Alameda State Beach was renamed Crown Memorial State Beach, in memory of the State Assembly member whose bill created the popular facility. Impetus was also given to the acquisition of regional trails, the most important at the time being the Alameda Creek Trail, dedicated in the early 1970s by former Interior Secretary Stewart Udall, who had served as a consultant to the district.

As one of Mott's closest confidantes, Trudeau had learned a great deal from the charismatic leader. But Trudeau brought his own enormous talents to the job. While his administration, including the indomitable Hornbeck, continued to enlarge and diversify the district, Trudeau gives Mott credit for inspiring much of its modern evolution.

It was Mott who talked "to all who will listen" about the urgent need to save the land and who devised acquisition strategies that turned seemingly unattainable goals into done deals. Although not above pique and short-lived outbursts of temper when he was frustrated, Mott rejected destructive competitiveness in favor of collaborative relationships either to acquire land and water for the district or to develop and manage recreational facilities on land and water owned by other public agencies. He was also relentless in encouraging private parties to contribute to the saving of natural resources for the use and enjoyment of generations to come. The development of much of the East Bay Regional Park District from the 1960s through the 1980s "would not have happened," said Trudeau, "without Bill's vision and daring."

*Mott on the
San Francisco Bay
with close friend
and supportor
Bill Lane, 1974.*
Mott family photo

*William Mott, Gov. Ronald Reagan,
and Bill Lane, Jr., when Mott was director
of State Parks and Recreation.*

Chapter 4

From Seashore to Mountain Tops: A Statewide Crusade

The vision must be followed by the venture.
VANCE HAVNER

M ott had never met the movie star turned governor when he got a call from Ronald Reagan's appointments secretary in January of 1967, asking if he'd be interested in becoming director of the state Department of Parks and Recreation. Reagan had earlier heard from Norman "Ike" Livermore, newly appointed Secretary of the State Resources Agency, of which the Parks and Recreation Department was a division. Mott's claim that he didn't know why Reagan tapped him for the job was typically self-effacing. After all, Pat Brown, Reagan's predecessor and a Democrat, had wanted Mott. It was not far-fetched to assume that Reagan, a Republican, would also recognize a fellow Republican's political pedigree, professional stature, and thoroughly nonpartisan qualifications. ●

Ike Livermore and his brother, Putnam "Put" Livermore, are fourth generation Californians. Born in San Francisco, they grew up in Marin County, just across the Golden Gate Bridge to the north. Their mother, Caroline Sealy Livermore, was an early member of the Save-the-Redwoods League. Their father, Norman, Sr., was a businessman who also belonged to the League. Before becoming State Resources Secretary in 1966, Ike was a logging-firm treasurer who, in a seeming paradox, belonged to the Sierra Club. Put, a lawyer, helped the San Francisco-based Nature Conservancy buy millions of dollars worth of privately-owned land which the Conservancy later resold at reduced prices or donated outright to the state for parks. Republicans in the environmentalist tradition of Theodore Roosevelt and John D. and Laurance Rockefeller, the Livermores were apolitical when it came to preserving open space. Reverence for the state's rugged coastline, flowered meadows, and snow-capped mountains ran deep in their veins.

Although Ike Livermore lived in Marin County, directly across the Bay from Alameda and Contra Costa counties, he had never heard of Mott. On the other hand, Put Livermore had. "They were trying to figure out who should head state parks," Put Livermore recalled. "I told my brother, 'You should meet William Penn Mott. He's already internationally known and he's right over in Oakland.' " Ike asked Put to arrange a meeting. "It took awhile to get together because Mott had a good job that he liked over there," said Put. "But eventually the three of us got together in my office at 111 Sutter Street in San Francisco."

"I immediately liked him," Ike remembered of the meeting. "When he said he'd like the job, there was no other applicant as far as I was concerned. He was well known in the East Bay. He was a wonderful guy." Livermore sought approval for the Mott appointment from the Reagan camp. He got no opposition from Tom Reed, Reagan's Northern California campaign chairman and short-term appointments secretary. Reagan "wanted guys who couldn't be bought for lunch," Reed later told Reagan biographer Lou Cannon, department heads with "ability, integrity and a basic philosophy not antagonistic to the governor."

Mott, with his proven record in parks management, insistence on quality operations, national and international reputation for honest and hard-hitting open space advocacy, rock-like integrity and belief in partnerships between the public and private sectors, filled the bill. The fact that he was also a visionary, given to looking many years into the future and to proposing ideas others sometimes considered little more than flights of fancy, didn't bother the Reaganites. Professionally, he was the best qualified for the job. Politically, he was a known quantity and a team player who would not embarrass the governor. The appointment was offered.

Before Mott accepted it, however, he warned Livermore he would not be able to assume the new post before March 1. He had some work to finish up at the regional park district. He also said he wouldn't be able to make a final decision without meeting Reagan personally to assess his views on parks and recreation. Livermore set up an appointment.

After Mott was ushered into the governor's ornate office in Sacramento, Reagan asked Mott what plans he had for the department. Before answering, Mott marshaled his thoughts. Six years earlier, in 1961, Governor Brown had merged the old Division of Beaches and Parks with the Division of Recreation and the Division of Small Craft Harbors to form the new Department of Parks and Recreation. But the gubernatorially appointed commissions, one for parks and one for recreation, continued to operate separately. "It's inefficient to have a recreation commission and a park commission overlapping in many cases and sometimes in conflict," Mott said in his straightforward manner. "The two commissions should be combined into one parks and recreation commission. No longer do we think of parks and recreation as two separate identities. The department needs to be reorganized to meet the challenges of the next 25 years." Mott added he would "support a total balanced program" between the need for unsullied wilderness, as traditional campers and climbers wanted it, and the demand for more recreational facilities coming from the masses of Californians who knew little about the outdoors. He would not, he said, "favor one group over another" but would try to accommodate everyone. Without getting into specifics, he also suggested that changes were needed in the department's personnel and operational policies, as well as in its land acquisition and development programs. Then Mott paused.

"There is one more thing I need to mention," he said after a moment.

"What's that?" asked Reagan.

"If I take the job, I thought you should understand that I will be operating on a strictly professional basis only."

Reagan "looked me straight in the eye," Mott later recalled, "and told me, 'That is the reason you have been chosen. You run the department. I'll handle the politics.' "

UNEXPECTED ALLIANCE

Conservationists were fascinated by the apparent contradiction embodied in Mott's membership in an administration neglectful of if not downright hostile toward the environment. But at least three reasons lay behind the governor's easy approval of Mott's appointment. First, Reagan, who had never been a public official before being elected governor and who was never, in any event, accused of being a workaholic, developed a management style that leaned heavily on trusted subordinates. In this case, Livermore wanted Mott, and Reagan trusted Livermore. Second, Mott, whatever his ideology, was eminently qualified for the job. Third, the governor was not so much against as generally indifferent to the environmental movement. He did not actually say, "If you've seen one tree, you've seen them all," but came close to it during the 1966 campaign. In apparent bafflement over conservationists' efforts to protect as many of California's redwoods as possible, Reagan, according to biographer Lou Cannon, had declared, "a tree is a tree — how many more do you need to look at?"

Unnoticed by most observers at the time, there was a fourth explanation for the warm welcome Mott received in Sacramento. Edwin Meese, a close Reagan advisor, had grown up in Oakland when Mott was superintendent of parks. Meese's mother had participated in garden shows sponsored by Mott's department. Meese had worked during the summers immediately after World War II at Tilden Park, flagship of the East Bay Regional Park District. And like Mott, Meese was an "Old Blue," as alumni of UC Berkeley called themselves. Meese had graduated from Cal's Boalt Hall of Law before going to work for the Alameda County District Attorney's office where he eventually caught Reagan's eye. Meese thought Mott would be a "sparkplug," who would re-energize the state Parks and Recreation department under the incoming administration.

So it was that on February 14, 1967, Governor Reagan made the announcement in Sacramento. Confirmation by the State Senate of the 57-year-old parks man to the $22,500-a-year job occurred without incident. Mott gave two weeks' notice at the East Bay Regional Park District. His last day would be February 28. He would assume his new duties in Sacramento the following day.

MIXED FEELINGS

Reaction in the Bay Area to the news was swift. Acknowledgment of Mott's achievements mingled with regret at his leaving. "Under his leadership the regional park district nearly doubled in size, with the annexation of Contra Costa County and Pleasanton Township," the *Oakland Tribune* reported on Feb. 14. "The land holdings available for open space also have grown to twice their size at the time he took over. The present park system embraces some 16,000 acres, and more acreage is about to be added. His often-stated belief that 'parks are for people' has been carried out in fact, and last year more than 4 million persons used regional parks facilities. Two days later, repeating a statement by Interior Secretary Stewart Udall, who had called the East Bay Regional Park District "one of the finest inter-county park systems in the Nation," the *Tribune* editorialized that "while (Mott's) departure will be a distinct loss to the East Bay, his elevation to the state post is a deserved honor."

Personally, Mott was not leaving the East Bay totally behind. For several reasons, he and Ruth decided not to move seventy-five miles up Interstate 80 to the state capital. Ruth didn't relish the idea of a domestic upheaval. As a member of local chapters of the Republican Party and Daughters of the American Revolution, she was also active in community affairs. While Bill III had finished college, married Zee Zee Talbot, and established his own home and Nancy was planning a September wedding to Dan Pichler, John, the youngest child, was only in eighth grade. The Motts did not want to take the boy away from his school and friends. Mott would be traveling so much, both on park matters and for speaking engagements, that there was no point, after twenty years in Orinda, in establishing a new home only ninety minutes away. Besides, his position was appointive. He served at the pleasure of the governor, which meant he could be fired at any time. And, finally, his heart spoke. He loved his oak tree-shaded home, its garden where he cultivated flowers, gathered wild fruit for his homemade jams and jellies, read, puttered, and thought. He did not want to move and found no good reason for doing so.

Still, his departure from his professional posts and volunteer positions in the Bay Area sparked a round of farewells, public and private. At one event, hosted by the park district, over three hundred civic, government and business leaders feted Mott's prodigious energy and spiritual commitment to the environment, a record of service that had garnered him a national reputation of legendary proportions.

Officiating at the reception were six women representing five outdoor entities and one charitable organization with which Mott had held leadership positions. Two of the outdoor agencies were, of course, the Oakland Park Department and the East Bay Regional Park District. The other three were Citizens for Regional Parks, an early model for the principle of pub-lic/private partnership that Mott enunciated at every level of his career; the California Roadside Council, of which Mott was vice president and had been president; and Save San Francisco Bay Association, of which he was then president. The charitable organization was the Bay Area United Crusade. Mott was president of two of that umbrella organization's member agencies, the International Institute, and the Metropolitan YMCA of Alameda County.

Save the Bay, as it was informally called, had formed to stop rampant filling that began in earnest after World War II. At 550 square miles but with an average depth of only 18 feet, the Bay Area's eponym was in danger of being reduced to a sluggish shipping channel. Members of the board of directors included Paul Covel, the man Mott had named as Oakland's — and the nation's — first urban park naturalist. Other old friends on the board included Kay Kerr, wife of Clark Kerr, the man who had succeeded Robert Gordon Sproul as president of the University of California, and Mrs. Newton Drury, wife of one of the major founders and developers of the State Park system in the 1920s and 1930s. Newton Drury had gone on to serve with distinction as National Park Service director from 1940 to 1951 and as state parks director from 1951 to 1959.

But those were not the only East Bay civic organizations to which Mott lent his influential name and on whose behalf he dipped deep into a seemingly inexhaustible reservoir of time, energy, and spirituality. Those he also served as president, chairman, vice president, or board member included Goodwill Industries of Oakland, Diablo Valley United Crusade, Oakland Council of Churches, Booth Memorial Hospital, and Rotary Club. He had also been made honorary life member of the Lake Merritt Breakfast Club, Hillside Gardeners of Montclair, California Congress of Parents and Teachers-28th District, Oakland Advertising Club, and West of Market Boys. State-

wide he had been president of the California Conservation
Council and board of directors member of Save the Redwoods
League.

In recognition of his tireless commitment a steady stream
of local and statewide plaudits dotted his office walls. He had
received the Oakland Junior Chamber of Commerce Good
Government Award, Oakland Service Clubs "Man of the Year"
award, Orinda's "Man of the Year" award, California Landscape Contractors' Association's "Daisy Award" for Beautification and the Honor Award, California Council of Landscape
Architects.

'THOUSAND POTS' MOTT

Bill and Ruth were members of Oakland's First Presbyterian
Church, where he held numerous lay leadership posts and
occasionally delivered the sermon. Early one year, during his
Oakland parks director days, Mott was put in charge of deco-
rating the building for an upcoming convention First Presbyterian was to host that April. The congregation feared that the
cost of engaging a florist for so large a church would require a
round of out-of-pocket donations.

But Mott had other ideas. He asked his committee to meet
at the church one Saturday morning. When they arrived they
found a large pile of geranium prunings from the Oakland
Park Department's refuse dump, a pickup truck load of pot-
ting soil and a thousand six-inch clay pots he had persuaded a
manufacturer to donate. "In a few hours the prunings were
trimmed by those with green thumbs and planted in pots by
everyone," recalled committee member Will Styles. "They were
then rapidly purchased by the church members for the low
price of five plants for a dollar with the provision that they
would nurture them and then loan them back in April to
decorate the church." When the convention took place, "the
many varieties of geraniums made a very colorful display and,
of course, the flowers were as fresh on the last day of the

convention as they were on the first," Styles said. Not only that, the $200 raised from the sale paid for supplementary plants and flowers.

For years afterward, when his name came up in the news, church members laughed about "Thousand Pots Mott," the man who taught them how to reuse natural resources, a concept he spread to others throughout his life.

FOR THE LOVE OF THE Y

A month after starting his new job in Sacramento, Mott was named "Man of the Year" by the Metropolitan YMCA of Alameda County, where in addition to being president and director he was chairman — not surprisingly — of the Long Range Planning Committee. Mott's work with the YMCA was typical of his devotion to causes he believed in. Fred Stickney was one of his proteges. When Stickney graduated from Northern Arizona University in 1961 with a major in education, he interviewed for jobs in Cheyenne, Wyoming; Kansas City, Kansas and, in California, Los Angeles and Oakland. Through courses he'd taken in parks and recreation he learned about Mott's exemplary management as superintendent of parks in Oakland. When it came time to choose from among the jobs he was offered, what he had heard about Mott tipped the balance. Stickney accepted an entry-level job as assistant physical director at the downtown Oakland headquarters of the Metropolitan YMCA of Alameda County. What he didn't know was that Parks Superintendent Mott was also president of the board of directors of the "Y." And there, at the first board meeting Stickney attended, was the man himself. "To meet your 'guru' right out of college – well that was really something," said Stickney. Even more amazing was the fast friendship that quickly developed between the new employee on the lowest rung of the ladder and the board president at the top.

Mott immediately put Stickney in touch with Jay M. Ver Lee, the outstanding director of the Oakland Recreation De-

partment. Due to the collaborative nature of their two leaders, the parks and the recreation departments, still separate
entities at that time, enjoyed productive and cooperative relationships. "Instantly, I was able to set up recreation programs
between the Y and the recreation centers, a process that would
have taken much longer without that direct contact," Stickney
said. The next summer, after Mott had moved from Oakland
Parks to the East Bay Regional Park District, he asked Stickney
and "Y" General Secretary John Thune to drive up to Redwood Regional Park and look over a site where he planned to
put a day camp. "When you get there, look around and give it
a name," he requested.

"Well, we went up and started looking around," Stickney said,
"and just then we saw a hawk fly over the ridge. We told Bill
we'd like to name the day camp Hawk Ridge and he said,
'Fine' – just like that. So within less than a year, I met the man
I had come to Oakland to be near, gotten off to a good start
on my job and named a ridgeline in a regional park. It was all
quite a thrill."

So committed was Mott to the Oakland YMCA that he remained a member of the board even as he prepared to take
the new job in Sacramento. He also kept his membership in
many of the other organizations he had served. No wonder, as
the *Tribune* noted, that he embarked for the state capital "with
the best wishes of his many friends in the East Bay."

FERTILE SOIL FOR ENVIRONMENTALISM

Mott's participation in so many ecological organizations re-
flects their abundance in California. With a landscape more
varied than any other state, California's spectacular geogra-
phy stimulates such interest. Thundering surf, sandy beaches,
rugged sea cliffs, wooded hills, lush valleys, vast deserts, deep
gorges, primordial mountain ranges, even volcanoes — de-
scriptions of California inspire superlatives. Within a hundred
miles of each other are the lowest and highest points in the

contiguous United States. Some 1,500 plant species are native to California alone. And among California's treasures are the largest (the giant Sequoia Redwood) the tallest (the Coastal Redwood) and some of the oldest (Cypress pine) living things on Earth.

California hugs these astounding assets to an immense bosom. Trailing only Alaska and Texas in size, the Golden State shares 215 miles of state line with Oregon on the north and 140 miles of international border with Mexico to the south. Its eastern boundary touches Nevada's for 610 miles before following the Colorado River that separates it from Arizona to the southeast. A plumb line unfurled at the Oregon border would drop 780 miles down the middle of the state to Mexico. The 1,100- mile Western boundary doubles as the edge of the continent.

Location works as another major attraction for naturalists. Despite the admission of Hawaii and Alaska to the union, California still represents the figurative last chance in the push westward from America's Eastern core. People "start over" in California, believing it capable of granting them a new persona. "More than any other state, probably, California represents — at least to those of us who have spent our lives elsewhere — the promise of a new and better life," said writer Joyce Maynard after moving from New Hampshire to Marin County in 1996.

The Bay Area, with its easy access by land or sea, its burgeoning literary, cultural, and academic communities, its dramatic scenery, its tolerance of quirky individuality, and its relative lack of social stratification, has had a special lure for environmentalists. Along with the organizations Mott belonged to, the Nature Conservancy and the International Rivers Network also called the Bay Area home. Long-time Bay Area residents have included Ansel Adams and David Brower, while writers Jack London, Bret Harte, Joaquin Miller, and Ina Coolbrith and photographers Peter Stackpole and Dorothea Lange have sung its praises. And for one and all, then and now, the haunting grandeur of Yosemite Valley, less than two hundred miles away, has been the symbol of statewide natural wonders worth preserving.

In 1864, the decision by the Congress and President Abraham Lincoln to turn over to the state of California twenty thousand acres of federal land, including Yosemite Valley and the nearby Mariposa Grove of Big Trees, was mightily influenced by the eyewitness accounts of Eastern visitors such as Frederick Law Olmsted, Thomas Starr King, and Ralph Waldo Emerson. A few years later, John Muir found his way to Yosemite Valley.

Yosemite was initially operated as a state park. But Muir's unceasing advocacy led to the congressional transfer of Yosemite to the federal government as a national park in 1890. Nearby Sequoia National Park and General Grant National Park (later incorporated into Kings Canyon National Park), were established at the same time. In 1892, a group of Bay Area business, professional, and educational leaders formed the Sierra Club. With Muir as charter president, the club's purpose was to provide public support for the new national parks. Its scope gradually expanded to embrace environmental causes nationwide.

In 1903 Muir accompanied Theodore Roosevelt on a camping trip to Yosemite National Park. Muir lobbied for its protection from careless private development and ultimate ruination. Already a naturalist who loved the West, "TR" needed little coaxing. A supporter of the fledgling national park, national forest, and national monument-movements, he proclaimed eighteen of the latter before leaving office, including a magnificent stand of redwoods in Marin County named Muir Woods.

THE RISE OF STATE PARKS

If Yosemite inspired California's first national park, the ancient redwood trees of Northern California and the crumbling Spanish and Mexican-era missions in Southern California prompted grassroots movements for state protection of these and other treasures. The subsequent evolution of the state parks system is brilliantly told by Joseph H. Engbeck, Jr. in his definitive history, *State Parks of California: From 1964 to the Present.* In brief, the movement started with the founding in 1902 of the Sempervirens Club (taking its name from *Sequoia sempervirens,* the scientific designation for coastal redwoods) which helped establish the first state site, Big Basin Redwoods State Park near Santa Cruz. It continued with the establishment by the California Historic Landmark League, also founded in 1902, of several historic sites around the state. The formation of the Save-the-Redwoods League in 1918 provided extra momentum toward preservation of California's natural and historic heritage. The lobbying of these and other citizens led to approval by the State Legislature in 1927 of a State Park Commission, a State Park System and a state survey of likely park sites. The survey, conducted by pioneering landscape architect Frederick Law Olmsted, Jr., provided a chart for the future. In 1928, the voters passed a $6 million bond issue to fund additional state parks.

From that point forward, legislative appropriations, bond issues, and federal funds from the Land and Water Conservation Act of 1965, among other sources, provided additional financing for park acquisition and development as well as recreational facilities and park lands around State Water Project dams and reservoirs. The state continued to produce outstanding park leaders, among them Newton Drury. And private donations of land and money from enlightened individuals helped the system evolve into one of the finest in the nation. By 1966, its 180 units, representing scenic and natural wonders, outstanding recreation areas and historic sites, were receiving 38 million visits per year. Recognition of recreation as a state responsibility came when the Legislature founded the State Recreation Commission in 1947. The commission was asked "to consider the whole problem of recreation for the people" and to "formulate a comprehensive recreation policy for the State of California." The commission responded, publishing in 1960 the California Public Outdoor Recreation Plan, the first of its kind in the nation.

TROUBLE IN PARADISE

Yet, while park and recreation facilities continued to expand during the 1960s, California's population grew far faster. New families, including those formed by veterans, defense workers, and other migrants attracted to the mild climate and "second chance" mentality, fueled the boom. From the 1950s through the mid-1960s, rapid growth forced increased tax-generated spending for such governmental services as public schools, two- and four-year colleges and universities, hospitals, and parks.

Many Californians expressed a willingness to see their property taxes fund such cutting-edge public institutions, and California entered what, in hindsight, came to be viewed as a "Golden Era." The state became a national model, for example, for a vast network of institutions of higher education. While the California State College system educated hundreds of thousands of students through the master-degree level, existing campuses of the University of California at Berkeley, Davis, San Francisco and Los Angeles expanded in unprecedented fashion. Brand new UC campuses were added at Riverside (1954), Santa Barbara (1958), San Diego (1959) and Irvine and Santa Cruz (1965). Berkeley continued to lead the way, home to more doctoral candidates and Nobel-Prize scientists than any other campus, public or private, in the nation,

At the same time the nationwide civil rights movement spun off related phenomena that were to rage on through the late 1960s and peak in the mid-1970s. Among them were the equal opportunity and black power movements, the women's and gay liberation movements, the anti-poverty and welfare rights movements, the anti-pollution movement, and the anti-Vietnam War movement.

Now, as the human landscape grew more complicated, some Californians began to resent their tax dollars going to respond to such stunning social upheavals. As property tax rates kept rising, public support for spending began to veer from the generous levels of the 1950s and early 1960s toward a more parsimonious attitude. More trouble was introduced when Governor Edmund G. "Pat" Brown decided to remove offshore oil royalties as a source for park funding, throwing parks back on the mercy of the general state budget. Suddenly, parks and recreation had to compete with other state priorities. When compared with education and law enforcement, leisure services were viewed by some voters as luxuries. Tapping into that rising sentiment, Ronald Reagan was able to sweep into office in November, 1966, by pledging both to reduce state spending and restore social order. Still, demand for parks and recreational facilities showed no signs of abating. During peak periods hundreds of thousands of people were turned away. Passage of the 1964 California Recreation and Parks Bond — during the "Golden Era"— had helped. But creation of just two new parks, Sugar Pine Point at Lake Tahoe, and Point Mugu near Los Angeles, committed about half the bond funds available for state park acquisition. By 1966, writes Engbeck, "parks director Fred Jones indicated that $500 million would have to be spent over the following 20 years, if the state was going to solve the turnaway problem and adequately meet the growing demand for park and recreation opportunities."

Mott was well aware of these trends when he took over as director of State Parks and Recreation in 1967. He often addressed the effects of overpopulation on parks and society in general, and, in the wake of riots after the assassination of Dr. Martin Luther King, Jr., the need to make park and recreational opportunities available to the urban poor. But he tried to avoid partisan gamesmanship. He simply wanted to reorganize the Parks and Recreation Department so it could better "face these new realities." He wanted to create and expand parks and recreational facilities. And — as always — he wanted to espouse "to all who will listen" his philosophy of "parks for the people."

While Mott threw himself into running the state parks, he stayed closely involved in what was happening at home. 1967 was an eventful year for the family. Ruth's mother, Madge Ethel Barnes, who had come out from Michigan to be close to her daughter, died in May. In September, Nancy married a young man named Dan Pichler and moved to Mountain View, south of San Francisco. Bill III and Zee Zee returned from a two-year stint living and working in Japan, and John rapidly grew into young manhood.

BETTER ORGANIZED, MORE PROFESSIONAL

By late 1967, as Mott had promised, the Park Commission and the Recreation Commission, both seven members strong, had been replaced by a new, nine-member Parks and Recreation Commission. This move was made not only for efficiency's sake but also for philosophical reasons. Mott thought the two fields gained strength by working together. Back when he was superintendent of parks in Oakland and Robert W. Crawford was superintendent of recreation, the two had agreed on "mutual planning of parks and playgrounds," and "had coordinated building and remodeling activities" to avoid duplication and to save money. Twenty years later, Mott still urged cooperation between the two disciplines, and with an even greater sense of urgency. He'd read about a psychiatrist who questioned the need for more open space on the theory that most people felt "fear" not "freedom" in the out-of-doors. To counteract that line of thought, Mott said more research into the psychology of the parks and recreation user was needed.

"You and I believe without question that man gets inspiration and his whole being is improved by beauty and open space and the opportunity to go out-of-doors," he told the Texas A&M Recreation Management Institute in 1967. But,

"We have not done the necessary research to prove our contentions." Who knows, he continued, "we may find that some of our ideas and plans are not right and we should be doing something else as we plan today for the year 2000. We must know that we are proceeding in the right direction and we must have sufficient basic research data to support our planning efforts."

As state parks director, Mott put that philosophy into practice. A new research division joined existing operations and maintenance divisions. In 1968, his researchers produced the California State Park System Plan, a twenty-year master blueprint. Such far-sighted projections were needed, Mott reasoned, in order to make a case for spending money on resources increasingly regarded by the voters as "frills."

Management was another area that Mott wanted to improve. "There are still too many parks and recreation departments administered by political appointees who are not qualified to creatively and professionally carry out the responsibilities of their highly specialized government service," he said. Parks and recreation needed administration "by qualified professionals who are well-trained, skilled managers with imagination, who are aggressive and creative, and who have a deep sense of personal integrity.

BREAKING THE GLASS CEILING

When Mott discovered that women had never been allowed to take exams to become state parks rangers, he reclassified the job — to grumbling from many old-timers. In 1972, after completing a ranger training class with nineteen men, Paula Peterson became California's first, full-time female state park ranger. With a baccalaureate in recreation administration from Chico State University in Chico, California, Peterson was clearly qualified for the job. Hired by Area Manager Curt Mitchell, she went to work at Big Basin State Park near Santa Cruz. Was there something symbolic about the first woman ranger work-

ing at the original state park? No, said Peterson, it was more
that "I was hired by a very progressive manager, who was open
to the idea that maybe a woman could do this job." During
the hiring process, Peterson never saw Mott directly but assumed correctly that he was behind the new policy. "When I
did meet him after I started working at Big Basin, he was
positive, inspirational, and welcoming," she said. "I think it is
appropriate to credit him with the change." By 1997, Peterson
had advanced to chief ranger for the Monterey District of the
State Department of Parks and Recreation. "Whenever I get
frustrated with either what I am doing or how things are being done — which, of course, happens occasionally -- I draw
strength and inspiration from the memory of William Penn
Mott. Whether you agreed with him or not, and I usually did,
he was goals- and value-directed. With him in charge, you
knew where you were going."

Mott's decision to add interpretation and law enforcement
to rangers' duties and to transfer their maintenance tasks to
park employees trained in that area were other changes that
sparked controversy. Many of the seasonal interpretive employees were graduate students, teachers, and others who earned
extra income during the summer. But as always, Mott believed
interpretation important enough to be elevated to a full-time
professional responsibility, even if it meant stepping on toes
to do it. As for law enforcement, the social upheavals of the
period required the presence of police officers in the parks.

TRAINING CENTER

Mott needed a centralized location for all this new training.
In 1967, he determined that Asilomar would be such a location. The story of how he spearheaded construction of a modern training center is worth a brief digression. A conference
center and summer camp that had been founded by the YWCA
early in the 20th century, Asilomar was located in the town of
Pacific Grove on the Monterey Peninsula. When the state parks

acquired the center in 1956, Governor Goodwin Knight thought it would be a drain on the state treasury. He said it could become a state park but would have to operate independent of the state parks budget. If it ever needed a bail out, it would have to go to the city of Pacific Grove.

However, the nonprofit concessionaire hired by the state managed the center so skillfully that it became self-supporting and amassed an operating surplus. Meanwhile, as the only state park unit that had meeting rooms, Mott asked if he could set up the new training center there. The concessionaire gave him the use of a small cottage. The training sessions proved so popular that by 1971 they had outgrown the little cottage. Mott asked the concessionaire to use some of the operating surplus to acquire private homes across the street when they came on the market. By 1972, space was available for construction of an expanded training center. On February 28, 1974, the Asilomar East Woods, Center for Continuous Learning, was dedicated.

While the monies to buy the nearby properties and build the center were technically state funds, they never went through headquarters in Sacramento. Some observers thought Mott's financing plan was improper or even illegal. It was never found to be either — just creative. In November, 1975, in a rare tribute to a sitting director, the State Park and Recreation Commission renamed the facility the William Penn Mott, Jr. Training Center. They acted in recognition of Mott's "courageous leadership and vision in establishing the training program and providing for its physical needs at no cost to the taxpayers."

Land acquisition and park development also occupied much of Mott's attention. When he found out two months into office that less than $25 million of the $85 million in the parklands acquisition portion of the 1964 bond issue had been spent, he said, "I am going to spend the rest of the money by October 1 of this year or know the reason why." He set hard deadlines

for surveys, appraisals, negotiations, and purchase on all properties. "We are not going to lose opportunities," he vowed,
"because of internal delays." He also warned landowners not
to try to bid up the selling price to the state. "I'm going to
pull the plug on them," he said. "When I see this happening,
I'm going to withdraw from the market. We'll put the money
aside and wait for a reasonable, businesslike offer."

TOP PRIORITY: BEACHES

Based on the low acreage of parklands per capita in the
densely populated Los Angeles region, Mott put acquisition of
Southern California beachfront at the top of the list. Beaches
didn't come cheap. Adding 12,140 feet of beach at Bolsa Chica
State Beach, Orange County, cost $11.8 million; 6,300 addi-
tional feet at Topanga State Beach, Los Angeles County, cost
$6 million. Some 5,950 feet at Refugio State Beach in Santa
Barbara carried a price tag of $4 million, while 2,201 feet at
Leo Carrillo State Beach, Ventura County, cost $2.6 million.
But some shoreline became available through other financial
routes. Mott leased San Onofre and Border Field beaches in
San Diego County from the U.S. Navy at low or no cost. Most
of the $2 million price tag for adding 16,630 feet of beachfront
to Will Rogers State Beach in Los Angeles was covered by gift
funding of $1.5 million.

The *California Journal,* a respected monthly that critiques
state government, asked skeptically in 1971 whether Mott was
emphasizing beaches over other kinds of land because beaches
helped pay for themselves through heavy use. "We do feel as a
first priority that the acquisition of the warm water, gently
sloping sand beaches of Southern California should take precedence over other acquisitions, and beach development is
important to us," he replied. "But basically it is because most
of the recreation deficiencies are in Southern California where
we have the tremendous volume of people, and we can get a
lot of people on a beach without destroying the resources."

Mott reiterated his commitment to a "balanced" statewide recreation program. "The fact that we concentrate on some beaches doesn't necessarily mean that we don't do [anything] else," he said. "We are just as concerned about Point Lobos and its development for 2,000 people [a state reserve on the rocky Central Coast] as we are Huntington Beach [in Orange County where] 600,000 people [go to swim, surf and sunbathe]." And, sure enough, the state over the next several years acquired thousands of feet of precious oceanfront up and down the coast.

When the chance arose to grab a worthwhile parcel before it met some other fate, Mott was capable of moving quickly, worrying less about procedure than capturing the opportunity. In the late 1960s, Howard Bailey, a rancher who owned 6,400 acres of land in Riverside County, north of and adjacent to Anza-Borrego State Park, decided to retire. He offered to sell the land, worth $640,000, to the state Parks and Recreation Department. Months later, when no action had taken place, Bailey's patience wore thin. "I can't wait any longer," he told park superintendent Bud Getty. "I'll give the park department until the end of the week. If they don't come through, I'm going to give my land to the Boy Scouts."

Ordinarily, Getty contacted state park leadership through channels. This time, Getty broke the rules. "I picked up the phone and called Bill Mott."

The next day, Mott called back and asked Getty to meet him at the San Diego Airport the following day. On the way from the airport to the park, Mott explained his strategy. Under the federal Land and Water Conservation Act, the U.S. Bureau of Land Management would put up a matching grant of $320,000, if California Parks and Recreation covered the other half of the purchase price. Just one problem, Mott continued. As state director, he was empowered to spend no more than $300,000. He had a check in his briefcase for $320,000. "What do you think Bailey would do if I ask him to donate

$20,000 back?" he asked. "Bill . . . explained the situation and charmed Howard, who was a neat old fella. Bill handed Howard the check for $320,000 and Howard handed Bill a check for $20,000. 'Let me make this check a donation,' Howard said, and that's how we got 6,400 acres, an area of land bigger than most state parks, to add to Anza-Borrego."

Years later, Getty was still amazed. "I would never have called most directors like that," he recalled. "But I could call Bill and he was able to react. What he did showed the way he operated. He scurried to get the paperwork done. He just believed in it and knew it was a significant piece of land. He knew that Howard was serious about settling his affairs and would have given that land to somebody else."

SPARE ROUND VALLEY

In 1968, as part of the massive State Water Plan that had begun during the Pat Brown administration, the U.S. Army Corps of Engineers proposed construction of a 730-foot high dam on the middle fork of the wild Eel River in far Northern California. The Dos Rios Dam would have become part of the massive system of dams and aqueducts that captures and transports water from Northern California to Southern California. The dam would also have flooded Round Valley, where the descendents of seven California Indian tribes eked out a living by farming. As director of State Parks and Recreation, Mott would be in charge of building recreational facilities along the shoreline of the reservoir the dam would create. But when Resources Secretary Ike Livermore indicated he did not want to see the Eel River compromised and Round Valley flooded, Mott spoke out against the proposal.

In testimony before the Joint Assembly-Senate Committee on Water Resources, he said the thought of building recreation facilities at Dos Rios was not "a particularly attractive prospect." First, the reservoir would be at least a four hours drive from the nearest metropolitan center. Second, the department was committed to building reservoir-type recreational facilities within two hours of major metropolitan centers. Third, the shoreline would advance and recede, depending on demand for the water, stranding boat docks and other facilities. Fourth, these factors would make the cost per visitor day of recreation use high when compared to other areas of the State

"I am concerned," he testified, "that a beautiful and unique mountain valley would be flooded, destroying the present scenic and ecological values as well as removing Round Valley from agricultural production and dispossessing its inhabitants. The archeological values of the reservoir area are extensive, unique, and poorly studied at present. The remains of the Yuki Indian culture here represent the only surviving field evidence of an extinct group of native Californians."

Still, pressure from pro-dam, pro-water, and pro-construction industry forces weighed heavily on Governor Reagan. So Ike Livermore invited Reagan to take a trip to Round Valley for a look. When the governor saw the valley for himself, and the homes and farms the Indians would lose, he had no trouble making up his mind. "We're not going to build a dam there because we've broken enough promises to the Indians," he said. The following year, plans for the dam were dropped.

Reagan's reaction "was like a movie role come to life," recalled John Zierold, the Sierra Club's Sacramento lobbyist from 1965 to 1984, in an oral history conducted with him by the Bancroft Library at the University of California at Berkeley. It was as if the governor were playing a part in a western, Zierold said. Getting Reagan out of the office and up to Round Valley allowed him to deal with the concrete rather than the abstract. Connecting reality with the fantasy industry he identified with so strongly seemed to enable him to see issues more clearly.

Livermore saw Reagan's decision to oppose the dam in a wider context. "I think it was the combination of the bum park proposal [Mott's insistence that the reservoir would not

be a good place for recreation], the question of arithmetic
[the cost-benefit ratio], some bias that the governor had toward the Corps of Engineers [it was one of those "big government" agencies], the [plight of the] Indians, and then, last
and most important of all, the general political climate [in
favor of preserving natural resources]," he said years later in
his own Bancroft Library oral history. "I think it [the political
climate] was favorable to his decision." Yet, even after taking
all that into consideration, "The main help was Director Mott,"
Livermore said. "I'm talking about within the state government and [in response to] all those outside influences." Mott
was the one who "knew the dam would be like a huge bathtub
[as the water level rose and fell depending on demand] with
no guarantee of a shoreline".

The 1968 master plan had put Southern California beaches
at the top of the list, followed by "continuing acquisition of
lands of historical significance, preservation of and development of recreation projects for the coastal sand dunes, and
completion of major redwood parks acquisition along the north
coast." Mott used a variety of mechanisms to make progress
toward those goals:

- When Governor and Nancy Reagan opted to live in a
  modern home in a residential neighborhood of Sacramento rather than in the old-fashioned Governor's Mansion downtown, Mott turned the quaint Victorian and its
  grounds into a state historic park.
- When the Parks and Recreation Commission accepted a
  gift deed of 556 acres of land in the Santa Cruz Mountains from by the Sierra Club and the Varian Foundation,
  the acreage became the nucleus of Castle Rock State Park.
- A study by the Advisory Board on Underwater Parks and
  Reserves, initiated by Mott, resulted in the designation of
  state underwater reserves at Salt Point State Park on the
  north coast, Julia Pfeiffer Burns State Park on the central
  coast and Torrey Pines State Park on the southern coast.

- When a group of African American citizens asked the department to turn Allensworth, a Central Valley town founded in 1908 by black settlers, into a state historic park, Mott supported development of a preliminary plan in 1972 which led to designation in 1976 of Colonel Allensworth State Historic Park.

CLASH AT POINT MUGU

The supporting documentation for the 1964 State Parks bond issue had included a study that advised voters that because of the high demand for state parks, it would be necessary to buy land at sometimes uncomfortably high prices. New parks purchased with bond money would, wherever possible, include a variety of recreational facilities to appeal to as many different users as possible.

In 1965, after the bond measure passed overwhelmingly, Gov. Pat Brown asked the Legislature for approval to use $16.7 million of the money to create Point Mugu State Park in the Santa Monica Mountains. The site, Brown said, represented California's "last chance to preserve a major natural area of state park quality near the densely populated Los Angeles area." Not only that, ecologists considered Point Mugu's 6,500 acres of grasslands and 3.7 miles of ocean frontage an "irreplaceable resource. In keeping with the "something for everyone" plan, the department developed a master plan that envisioned a variety of uses for the park. The Sycamore Canyon part of the park was "the last remaining untouched coastal canyon of significance in the entire Santa Monica Mountain Range," the department said, "and should be preserved as a typical example of the southwest mountains and valley landscape province." Recreational facilities, on the other hand, would be concentrated in the La Jolla Valley, a meadow area of the park.

For several years, Mott had been espousing the principle that nature had to be accessible to more than just the traditional corps of outdoors people — a largely white, adult, middle-class group. Younger, older, poorer, and minority-group Americans needed to feel just as comfortable away from the cities, he believed. If senior citizens preferred beds in a hotel to sleeping bags on the ground and urbanites wanted active recreation when they went camping, such amenities should be available within reason and without hurting the intrinsic values of parks. He had mentioned these ideas as far back as 1964 when, as general manager of the East Bay Regional Park District, he had hosted a meeting in Berkeley of the State Parks and Recreation Commission. "One might conclude," he had acknowledged at that meeting, "that the two ideas [more urbanized facilities within regional and state parks] are not compatible, but they can be if imagination is utilized in developing the parks so that the total environment, including the people who will be using the facilities, is considered and recognized. This would seem to suggest that those developments which are to be used intensively be clustered together, allowing extensive wild, unspoiled areas in between to be simply used by hikers, horseback riders and cyclists."

Mott saw Point Mugu as an opportunity to put these concepts into practice. After several public hearings unearthed little opposition, he approved a plan to create a Point Mugu Recreation Area within the larger state park. The proposal called for a shopping complex, camping facilities, two small amphitheaters, a dormitory-hostel for 500 persons, sleeping cabins, an administrative center, picnic units, a conference lodge for 240 persons, recreational pavilions and game areas, a series of parking lots, multi-use meadows, a swimming pool, and a 12-acre play area. A golf course would also be built, not only to provide that popular form of recreation but also to reuse wastewater reclaimed from the other facilities and to provide a "green zone" firebreak.

North of the meadow area, the department proposed sites for a rifle range, a motorcycle course, and a model airplane field with a landing strip, control tower, and 45-car parking lot. Meanwhile, plans for the beach portion of the recreation area included a hotel/dormitory/restaurant complex with a multi-story parking lot for two thousand cars. The state would spend about $14 million on the development with private investment, including concessionaires, contributing another $9.3 million. Except for the Sycamore Canyon section, the plan said, "Point Mugu is not intended to provide a wilderness experience. It is rather to provide non-urban outdoor recreation to satisfy a family's total recreation needs in a pleasant and expansive natural setting. The area is designed primarily to satisfy recreation needs of people in the Los Angeles area and provide convenient and pleasant relief from the congestion of a metropolitan complex."

But the size and scope of the facilities seemed too great for many open space advocates. They reacted strongly. On December 15, 1970, at a public hearing held in Oxnard, objections were heard from the national board of the Sierra Club and the League of Women Voters of Ventura County, among others. After that meeting, Mott struck the golf complex, marksmanship range, model airplane area, parking structure, motel building and much of the La Jolla Valley parking from the plan. He added a 150-acre natural preserve for native grasses and four 50-person group camping areas. Still, opposition continued. On February 2, 1971, at a public hearing attended by 350 people in Santa Monica, 27 of 32 speakers objected. They included not only Sierra Club Southern California spokesman Murray Rosenthal, but also representatives of the Federation of Western Outdoor Clubs, the Audubon Society, Friends of the Santa Monica Mountains Park, Santa Barbara Beautiful, Friends of Point Mugu, Los Angeles Zero Population Growth, the Earth Action Council and — though oil had nothing to do with it — two anti-offshore oil drilling organizations, Santa Barbara's Get Oil Out and No Oil Inc. of Pacific Palisades. Rosenthal spoke for many attendees when he pinpointed the proposed five miles of motorcycle trails for special criticism.

"Those who like that form of recreation deserve a lot more than just that token area which is in fact a fire danger," he said. "And it would be a detriment for those of us who do not like that form."

Not since his attempt to fire James Roof, curator of the Botanic Garden in the East Bay Regional Park District, had Mott faced such an agitated crowd. He was forced to speak, in effect, against his own plan by assuring that the proposal, if passed by the State Parks and Recreation Commission, would still need the approval of the state Environmental Control Council. "They can tell us to remove anything they determine is environmentally detrimental," he said. Rarely had Mott's environmental credentials come under such fire. "This plan has already been adjusted to meet the comments made at Oxnard," he said. "We feel it is a balanced plan which will meet the recreational needs of the area as well as protecting the natural beauty of Point Mugu." But he saw the writing on the wall when he added, "There may well be more changes as a result of this meeting." Eventually, both the Commission and the State Legislature trimmed financing for Mott's plan until the money allocated paid for little more than an access road and a water system. Over the years, the park has expanded to 13,300 acres but is still virtually undeveloped.

Later in 1971, Mott concluded that public opinion had shifted at some point after the recreation plan was first proposed. "Between that time and the time we finally got ready to go there was this tremendous change in people's attitudes and feelings about the out-of-doors," he told the *California Journal*, "and so we had to shift from a recreation concept to a park concept and eliminate certain things that we thought were desirable as part of the recreation development." One thing he'd learned, he admitted wryly: "When you mention motorcycles, people get all shook up."

PROTECTING THE COASTLINE

Strong disagreement between Mott and other members of the environmental community was rare, however. That same year, his department issued a wide-ranging California Coastline Preservation and Recreation Plan that warned, as did other conservation groups, that the California shoreline was in danger. Of the state's more than 1,100-mile coastline, some 61 percent was privately owned with another 14 percent owned by the military. Only 25 percent was owned by the taxpayers and access to that was limited and diminishing. Regardless of who owned it, the entire coastline was in danger of degradation from pollution, erosion, and unthinking residential, recreational, commercial, and industrial development. The report outlined a number of recommendations, including the enlargement and expansion of state parks and underwater reserves that would protect the environment, provide increased recreational opportunities, and preserve historical resources. The department agreed with those organizations that were calling for creation of a governing body to protect the coastline. A year later, in November, 1972, the voters of California passed Proposition 20, the Coastal Conservation Initiative. The initiative required development of a California Coastal Plan that was subsequently adopted in 1975 by a newly appointed Coastal Commission. Based on that preliminary work, the California Coastal Act was enacted in 1976 to provide long-term protection of the seashore.

THE IDEA-A-MINUTE MAN

At the risk of rare miscues like the Point Mugu episode, Mott's imagination and earnestness generated proposals for state programs and projects that went above and beyond the basic charge of good management, competent personnel, more parks, and more recreation. No idea was too big, too small, too lofty, or too corny to consider. In the words of one em-

ployee, "He had a certain fearlessness about him." That fearlessness led those he worked with to believe that together they
could find ways to achieve their goals. "To him, nothing was
unattainable," the co-worker said. "And, if one idea didn't
work, he'd just throw out another one that did."

- **Citizen Advisory Groups.** As state funding for parks
  dwindled, Mott concluded that the personal involvement
  of interested citizens was important to the development
  of the system. He appointed advisory groups of activists
  and volunteers who willingly contributed their time to
  the development of individual parks. By 1969, he had
  twenty such groups in place and hoped to expand the
  program so that every park had an advisory group of its
  own.

- **Computerized Reservation System.** As demand for recreation outpaced supply, families would arrive at campground
  entrances only to find cars backed up for miles. Mott
  thought that if a family were going to be turned away,
  they should know that when they were planning their
  outing, not well after they were on the road. In 1968, he
  established a telephone reservation system, handled separately by each park. By 1970, the program was centralized
  and computerized so that campsite reservations could be
  made through commercial ticket outlets in cities throughout the state. The computerized reservation system for
  California state park campsites was the first of its kind in
  the nation.

- **Coffee Fund.** Here was a small idea that boosted employee morale. Beth Walls, a secretary at headquarters in
  Sacramento, was one of two who kept a coffee fund in
  the Resource Management division office. "One day, Mr.
  Mott came by and stopped to chat, as he did every now
  and then," she recalled. "He happened to mention that
  he needed $50 to file a fee to obtain a small piece of
  land, probably an inholding at Anza-Borrego Park. There

were many such small privately owned parcels within park boundaries that the state was gradually acquiring. Without a specific appropriation in the park department budget, he had no authority to spend other funds for that purpose." On an impulse, Walls and the other secretary dipped into their coffee funds and came up with the $50. Mott later publicized the gesture in both the departmental newsletter and the local newspapers, emphasizing the need for all Californians, even state park employees, to come to the support of their parks. He bestowed a Quail and Poppy Award on Walls, a certification of recognition that offered its own bit of interpretation by picturing the state bird and the state flower. The certificate, signed by the director, remained on the wall behind Beth Walls' desk for the rest of her tenure in Sacramento. Further contributions from the Coffee Fund — and a division bake sale or two — enhanced Mott's reputation as "one of the best nickel-and-dime men around," according to one admiring colleague, and actually helped finance the acquisition of additional small parcels of land.

• **Equal Access Potties.** One of the traits that made Mott so unusual was the way he combined poetic, far-sighted vision with practical, quite earthy sensibilities. One day, while flying on a jetliner to one of his innumerable speaking engagements, he noted that the lavatories on the plane were marked "occupied" or "unoccupied" instead of "men" and "women." People seemed to use them without embarrassment. Why couldn't comfort stations in the state parks adopt the same model? If one building consisted of several walled-off stalls with occupied or vacant signs on the doors leading directly to the outside, then the building could serve both genders. When Mott mentioned the proposal in some newspaper interviews, public reaction ranged from amused to horrified. The change was made, however, and despite early fears, the public accepted it.

Since then, consolidation of restroom facilities has reduced state parks construction and maintenance costs in
that category.

* **A Dollar Per Pooch.** For many years, dogs were not allowed in state parks. When the public began to demand
  permission to take pets camping with them, the department resisted. Then, in 1968, Mott decided he'd allow
  people to take their dogs in. But to finance the cost of
  clean up, he'd charge one dollar per pet. After initial
  complaints, the public accepted the small fee as a reasonable price for bringing Fido along. "I got $90,000 from
  the dogs last year," he quipped to one reporter as he
  campaigned statewide for Proposition 1, the $250 million
  State Park Bond Act on the June, 1974 ballot.

The bond measure passed, incidentally, with support not
only from Mott and Livermore but also from Reagan. Much to
the surprise of many environmentalists, the governor made
"three highly publicized appearances," according to Engbeck,
during which he "praised the State Park System for the job it was
already doing and asked the voters to make it possible for the
state to preserve more of California's heritage and provide still
greater recreational opportunities for everyone." Anyone amazed
by Reagan's advocacy of more spending for parks and recreation
just didn't know how extensively he had been influenced by
Livermore and Mott.

THE CALIFORNIA STATE RAILROAD MUSEUM

Except for vast land acquisitions, the California State Railroad Museum was the biggest vision that Mott helped turn
into a reality during his tenure as State Parks and Recreation
director. The story of how Sacramento got a renowned museum that was originally proposed for San Francisco is worth
telling if only to clarify what one indignant San Francisco newspaper called "The Great Train Robbery."

The Pacific Coast Chapter of the Railway and Locomotive Historical Society was founded in 1937 by Gilbert Kneiss. Its members, most of whom lived in the East Bay, collected vintage steam locomotives and railroad cars. By the late 1950s, the chapter was storing more than forty pieces of equipment in borrowed warehouse space in Oakland and Richmond. Among the passenger cars in the collection was the *Gold Coast*, the 1906, Savannah, Georgia built coach that San Francisco writer Lucius Beebe had bought in 1947 and later given to the Society. Beebe had the car's interior refurbished to reflect its plush Victorian origins, including crystal chandeliers, smoked glass mirrors and a faux fireplace. Society members were lovingly restoring other cars and engines in the collection to their original condition and badly needed a permanent home for the assemblage.

Meanwhile, in 1951, Karl Kortum had founded the non-profit San Francisco Maritime Museum at Aquatic Park near Fishermen's Wharf in San Francisco. In 1955, the *Balcluthea*, an historic sailing ship berthed at the Hyde Street Pier, became part of the museum. That same year, when two million dollars became available to San Francisco from the State Division of Parks and Beaches, Kortum proposed expanding the museum into a state-run maritime park that would also display other forms of historic transportation. He and Kneiss envisioned housing the Pacific Coast Chapter's outstanding train collection in the Haslett Warehouse, a building near the museum.

But several ensuing debates between and among San Francisco and state officials stalled forward progress of the park, including whether the state money should go for the maritime park or another city-sponsored park project, how the park should be configured, whether a subterranean parking garage should be built under it, and who would provide police protection. Once those issues were settled, the state constructed Victorian Park, one of the features of the expanded maritime park, and opened it in 1962. That same year, the state bought the Haslett Warehouse from its private owners. But progress slowed again when estimates for converting the warehouse into a railroad museum came in variously at $1.5 million and $4.5 million and museum planners realized that the entire collection — which Kneiss wanted kept intact — was too large for the building. "As a result," wrote Michael Jenkins in a Museum Seminar paper, *A History of the Hyde Street Pier*, (1977) "nothing was done with the warehouse for several years."

The San Francisco Maritime State Historic Park opened in 1963 — without the railroad collection. Eventually, the state leased part of the Haslett Warehouse to a developer who turned its third and fourth floors into office space. After a court battle in 1971 over the renewal of the lease, the state ousted the developer — but not his tenants — and took over operation of the warehouse. The state continued to run the historic park until 1988, when it was transferred to the National Park Service. The upshot of the state's unwillingness to convert the building, Jenkins wrote, "was the loss of the Kneiss collection. When Kneiss died, the Railway and Locomotive Historical Society no longer felt bound by his wish that the collection be displayed in San Francisco. They were concerned by the Haslett situation and decided to donate the collection to a state park in Sacramento."

What kind of museum did the railway society envision? Chapter members Brian Thompson and Marshall MacDonald met with Bob Uhte and Bill Fahey of the State Department of Beaches and Parks one day in 1964. "That day, we worked out the basic philosophy of what we'd want to see in a railroad museum," Thompson recalled: Such a museum should not be narrowly focused on the mechanics of railroading, the foursome agreed, but broadly interpretive so that ordinary people could understand the pivotal role of the railroads in the wider context of Western economic and social history. As time passed, the chapter grew anxious to find a permanent home for the collection. Some of the members knew Bill Mott, then general manager of the East Bay Regional Park District. "One day in 1966, Louie Stein, a Berkeley pharmacist, MacDonald and myself met with Bill in his office on Skyline Boulevard in Oakland," Thompson said. "He got all excited. He thought that perhaps the collection could become part of the Regional Park District. He asked us to work up a proposal." But before the chapter members could complete a plan, Mott became director of California Parks and Recreation. So much for parking the historic locomotives in the East Bay Regional Park District.

Up in Sacramento, that city's Redevelopment Agency had plans to clean up and convert the rundown Sacramento River waterfront into an Old Sacramento historic district. When Mott heard that one part of the plan was to build a small museum to commemorate Sacramento's pivotal role in Western railroading history, he thought about the Railroad Society's collection in the East Bay. He got together with the Redevelopment Agency and other Sacramento city and Sacramento county officials to talk over the possibility of incorporating the collection into Old Sacramento.

It was a fitting idea. The history of the Sacramento riverfront and of the western railroads were intimately intertwined. Two of the antique locomotives in the collection, the *Governor Stanford* and the *C.P. Huntington*, had actually been fired up for the first time in Sacramento after having been built in the East; disassembled, boxed, shipped around Cape Horn and ferried up the Sacramento River from San Francisco Bay. The Sacramento Valley Railroad, built in 1855, was the first railroad constructed west of the Mississippi River. The offices of Theodore Judah, whose design work sparked the western section of the transcontinental railroad, and of the "Big Four" barons, C. P. Huntington, Charles Crocker, Mark Hopkins and Leland Stanford, who financed the line, had been located in Old Sacramento. The Embarcadero (the wharf along the Sacramento River) had been a major stop on the short-lived Pony

Express and a disembarking point for prospectors during the Gold Rush of 1849. A railroad museum also fit in well with three of Mott's basic principles. First, it would emphasize interpretation, the concept he loved most of all. Second, it would preserve an important facet of California history and culture, a responsibility he strongly believed to be part of the department's mission. Third, the museum itself would be financed through a combination of private-sector initiative and public-sector funding, a partnership of the sort Mott was renowned for and which had contributed to his appointment to the state post in the first place.

By 1968, when the locomotives and cars appeared headed for a section of Old Sacramento now designated a State Historic Park, the San Francisco newspapers accused Mott of stealing the collection from the City by the Bay. Fred Stindt, president of the Pacific Coast Chapter, begged to differ. With little movement on the Haslett Warehouse, "we presumed the issue was dead," he said. "That's why we designated the collection for the new state park in Sacramento where the state has already bought the historic land where the Central Pacific Railroad started operations."

On May 7, 1968, a cartoon captioned "The Great Train Robbery" ran in the *San Francisco Chronicle.* The drawing showed two bandanna-masked bandits hijacking a steam engine and chugging toward Sacramento. The desperadoes throw the engineer, labeled "San Francisco," off the train. The accompanying editorial, entitled "Highballing Down the Wrong Track," said the *Chronicle* was "astonished and deeply angered" at the news "that some quiet-behind-the-scenes plans" had produced "the greatest train robbery since the 1963 sidetracking of the Glasgow-to-London Royal Mail at Cheddington." The "until-now hidden talks" had removed the invaluable collection even before it reached its long-announced Haslett warehouse destination. That Mott had other plans for the collection came as a "startling surprise."

The "hidden" talks, however, had been reported for several weeks in the *Sacramento Bee*. "We feel a railroad museum housing our collection can do the Old Sacramento project a lot of good and vice versa," Denny Anspach, a Sacramento radiologist and chapter member, told the *Bee*.

Sacramento fired off a few shots of its own. "I, for one, would like to turn the [Sutter's Fort] Cannon on San Francisco if they try to get [the collection]," a newspaper quoted V. Aubrey Neasham, consultant to the Sacramento Historic Landmarks Commission, as vowing. "Sacramento is girding for battle with its old enemy, San Francisco" added R. Burnett Miller, commission president. As spokesman for the railroad society, Anspach had the last word. "We own the equipment and the final disposition is up to us and us alone," he said. When some San Francisco politicians accused Mott of "playing favorites," the director got a spirited defense from State Parks and Recreation Commission chairman Harry E. Sokolov of Beverly Hills. "I resent very much attributing politics or unfairness to Mr. Mott," he said. "I've never met anyone more fair or honest." As for Mott, his opinion was that the Haslett warehouse should become part of the maritime park, which in the intervening years had become a state preserve. He considered that course of action "logical, possible and germane." On the other hand, Sacramento, as the state's first intercontinental railroad terminus, "logically should have the railroad museum." In a ceremony on March 1, 1969, in a warehouse next to the toll plaza at the Oakland end of the Bay Bridge, where some of the precious rolling stock resided, Mott signed the papers formally conveying the collection over to the state. But animus among some San Franciscans toward Mott's alleged "Great Train Robbery" lingered for many years.

DINNER ON THE *GOLD COAST*.

After chapter members moved the collection to Sacramento and secured its most fragile pieces in warehouse space donated by Safeway, the State Department of Parks and Recreation made the proposed railroad museum a focal point of the historic state park. Now came an even bigger challenge: raising money to finance its construction. In 1970, Mott asked a private group, the Sacramento Trust for Historical Preservation, how this could be done. In February 1972, the Trust, composed of ten museum proponents, presented a 197-page document, most of which had been written on Anspach's kitchen table.

The museum, the study said, would serve to "interpret for the public and historian alike, in a way different from most other such museums, the railroad as it affected the Western Movement and the development of California, taking advantage of the historical railroad sites in geographic proximity to the museum location, and the extensive collection of appropriately-historic rolling stock of the Pacific Coast Chapter. Included in this goal," the report continued, "are the stories of the western portion of the Transcontinental Railroad and its competitors, and the manner and feeling of the railroad as it entered the lives of generations of Californians." The study further recommended the museum be built primarily with public funds but operated under contract to the State Department of Parks and Recreation by a private, nonprofit organization whose employees would know a lot about both railroading and fund raising. They would simultaneously develop and run the facility while establishing an endowment to cover continuing acquisition and restoration programs. Such a plan would mean bypassing some aspects of the bureaucracy, a course not usually welcomed by bureaucrats. But Mott supported the public-private concept.

Circumstances helped the proposal gather steam. Sacramento State Senator Albert S. Rodda was chairman of the Senate Finance Committee, and his brother, Richard "Dick" Rodda, happened to be political editor of the *Sacramento Bee* and another railroad aficionado. Stories in the *Bee* and its rival daily, the *Sacramento Union*, piqued public interest. Over the next two or three years, the Sacramento City Council and the Sacramento County Board of Supervisors climbed aboard.

But how to win Reagan's support for legislation to provide planning and construction funding? Trust members had a bright idea: Why not invite the governor to a dinner on the *Gold Coast* just as it would have been served during the 19th century? That might be the best way to demonstrate the historical and educational interest of the collection. A date was set and Mott sent a formal invitation to Reagan. When the governor accepted, the *Gold Coast* was taken out of storage and pulled to the Old Sacramento Embarcadero. A kitchen car was coupled to one end and a lounge car to the other.

On the evening of July 13, 1972, Ronald and Nancy Reagan were ushered onto the train. After cocktails in a coach car where schematics of the proposed museum were on display, the Reagans were guided to the table set for ten in the *Gold Coast*. Joining them were Denny and Caroline Anspach, Ed and Ursula Meese, and Bill and Ruth Mott. Carolyn Slobe, a leading member of the Trust, and Larry Hoyt, a representative of Southern Pacific, which was supporting the railroad museum proposal with in-kind services worth millions of dollars, rounded out the group. The table was set with Dresden china lent by Slobe, crystal ware from the nearby Crocker Museum, silverware from the Sacramento Society of California Pioneers, long, wooden matches in burnished silver containers and menus delicately silk-screened on linen. A waiter, a veteran of the Southern Pacific dining car corps, provided impeccable service.

Years later, when Mott recalled what transpired, his eyes lit up:

> The governor was sitting directly across from me, and we talked about the railroad museum, the history and importance of railroading and the pieces that had been restored. He didn't seem to be real excited about it and I thought, well, we aren't making much headway. After dinner was

cleared away, we passed around these big cigars and some kind of rum drink, whatever it was. Then the governor spied the little silver container with the wooden matches in it. 'I learned in the movies,' he said, 'that at a society dinner like this it wasn't polite to strike a match under the table. No,' he continued, 'you had to strike it with your thumbnail.' Well, he showed us how to do that, and with that, he began to talk about how as a boy he'd always wanted to be a tramp on the railroad. He even said he'd talked to a tramp one time about including the man's story in a picture. He got onto this subject and talked for maybe an hour about this sort of thing. After the dinner, he said, 'I think you've got a good idea here. I will support it.' Back at the office the next day, I wrote him a letter to remind him. Well, needless to say, we got the money.

Reagan put preliminary planning funds into his budget and the Legislature put preliminary construction funds in its. By 1976, the first phase of the museum, the reconstructed Central Pacific Passenger Station, opened. Five years later, in May of 1981, the California State Railroad Museum opened, a magnificent 100,000 square foot, three-story glass and brick edifice with forty interpretive exhibits, and a breathtaking display of twenty-one pieces of authentically and meticulously restored rolling stock. Also opening was the Big Four Building, with a replica of the original Huntington and Hopkins hardware store, a fully staffed railroad library and archives and a re-creation of the Central Pacific's boardroom. By the time the museum welcomed eager crowds that first day, it represented a $22 million investment of public and private funds. A high price, to be sure, but worth it, according to the glowing reviews it got as an aesthetic, historic, and cultural landmark.

To Mott, the dinner on the *Gold Coast* was living proof of the value of advance preparation. But it was also evidence of the serendipity of life and the reality of the force for good that often worked beyond one's control or knowing. Mott and Anspach didn't know the setting would appeal to Reagan's sense of drama in the same way that the trip to Round Valley had reminded the governor of films about broken treaties with the Indians.

"You can plan from hell to breakfast," Mott said about the event, "But it's the little spark that occurs and off you go. That kind of thing always interests me," he mused years later, "because it was just one little incident and things opened up completely. If it hadn't been for the matches, we probably wouldn't have made it. And that happens over and over again, I've found." Was he remembering the two boys with the fire-crackers on that long ago Fourth of July? The unexpected move to Jonesville that changed his life? The pintail duck that had flown from Lake Merritt to the Soviet Union and been returned to Oakland in a bag? Whatever it was, he said, "You've got to watch for these little situations that make it possible to win rather than lose."

THE LEGACY

It has been said that the acreage of the state park system nearly doubled during Mott's tenure. But figures vary according to who's doing the reporting. A story in the *Oakland Tribune* on March 30, 1975 ("Rhodes, Mott Differ as Parks Chiefs"), for example, asserted that park holdings had increased from 750,000 to 1,300,000 square acres during the Mott years and that state coastline ownership jumped from 170 miles to 270 miles of frontage.

Records kept by Ken Mitchell, a landscape architect and park designer during Mott's administration and Land Acquisition Chief from 1982 to 1992, tell a different story. "The Mott years were dynamic," he said, "but he did not double state park lands." What were added between January, 1967 and December, 1974 to 800,000 acres of existing park lands, according to Mitchell, were an additional 153,735.8 acres — an astounding accomplishment by any measure. Other acquisition projects that Mott had started were still in progress and were finalized after his departure.

A total of twenty-four new parks, historic parks, reserves, beaches and recreation areas were begun during Mott's tenure. These included facilities developed on the shores of immense reservoirs created by dams built by the State Department of Water Resources, the Army Corps of Engineers, and the federal Bureau of Reclamation.

In addition to new units, thousands of acres were added to such existing state parks as Anza-Borrego Desert, Big Basin Redwoods, Calaveras Big Trees, Humboldt Redwoods, Mount Diablo, Mount Tamalpais, Robert L. Stevenson, Smithe Redwoods, and Topanga state parks, among others. In an administrative decision in 1968 that Mott did not particularly favor at the time, three, noncontiguous state parks in Northern California, Jedediah Smith Redwoods, Del Norte Coast Redwoods and Prairie Creek Redwoods, were authorized by Congress to become part of a new, 110,000-acre Redwood National Park. Today, the three state parks comprise almost half of the national park. The remainder is composed of formerly privately owned redwood groves and thirty miles of Pacific Ocean coastline. Although Mott thought the parks should remain in state hands he was gracious when President Nixon and former First Lady Claudia "Lady Bird" Johnson flew out to dedicate Lady Bird Grove, a part of the park near the small town of Orick, 330 miles north of San Francisco. At $1.5 billion — including the cost of compensating private timber owners and loggers — Redwood was the most expensive national park ever created. Whether the trees came in under state or national management, however, Mott gratefully acknowledged that the hard-fought campaign, pressed primarily by the Sierra Club, meant protection in perpetuity for one of the greatest natural wonders of the world.

Other expansions during the Mott era included establishment of state historic parks at Bodie, a mining ghost town in the high Sierra; Downtown Columbia, a Gold Rush town; El Presidio de Santa Barbara, a Spanish fort dating back to 1782; Fort Tejon, 1854 home of the U.S. Army's First Dragoons; Indian Grinding Rock, near Stockton where the Miwoks once lived; Jack London, a country home the author kept north of Sonoma; Malakoff Diggins, where Nineteenth-century hydraulic miners stripped away whole hillsides in a frenzied search for gold; Will Rogers, site of the humorist's estate in Los Angeles, and the Mendocino Headlands and Historic Preservation District in the quaint, Northern California coastal town that is now a popular artists' colony and tourist mecca.

Mott's quick action at Anza-Borrego was in keeping with his overall intent to capture quality land, wherever possible, whether for existing or future parks. "While a lot of land was brought into the system during that period, including some larger, major state parks, Bill was more interested in supplementing the system than in individual parks," remembered Les McCargo, chief of land acquisition. "Bill was better than most at maximizing land soon after acquisition," recalled Ken Mitchell. "We had a fairly coherent system of acquisition, development, planning, and capital outlay during his administration. He made a lot of things possible, and planted a lot of seeds that came to fruition after his tenure was over."

William Penn Mott Jr. stands as one of the most outstanding directors in state park history. He enjoyed a supportive relationship with his immediate boss, state resources director Ike Livermore, and had superb assistance in working with the Legislature from Robert Meyer, his Parks and Recreation Department deputy. The *California Journal*, leery of Mott's motivations in 1971, had gotten to know him a little better by 1973. "Mott," it said, had "developed a reputation as something of a magician with projects, a master manipulator of elected officials, a hard nosed negotiator for park property and a fighter to preserve the state's natural resources."

Two years later, the *Journal* graded nine departments on what they had accomplished during the Reagan Administration just ending. Only two of nine headings got A's: Water Resources and Park Development. Under Park Development, "California conducted an aggressive property acquisition program over the past 10 years," the *Journal* said. "[Sierra Club lobbyist Larry] Moss calls it 'probably the best in the nation;' and [John] Zierold credits this to William Penn Mott Jr., Reagan's director of parks and recreation, and especially to Robert Meyer, Mott's deputy."

In his 1985 Bancroft Library oral history, Zierold called Livermore and Mott "the two pluses in the Reagan administration." The administration was basically unsympathetic to environmental issues, he said. "Nonetheless, we put together, during Reagan's second term particularly, more park acquisitions than had been made in a long, long time in the State of California. We were able to do so primarily because of Bill Mott," he said, "and Bob Meyer, who was a bright young man from Santa Monica, an insurance executive, who really was aggressive but in a skillful way. Bob Meyer did nothing that Bill Mott hadn't directed." Therefore, Zierold said, despite administration resistance and "because of public concerns and because there was a Democratically-controlled legislature, we were able to make some of our most significant gains at that time, which is an anomaly, really."

Twelve years later, in a 1997 interview, Zierold held firm to his views. "Mott did the best he could," the now-retired lobbyist said. "You have to remember that for the most part the parks department had to be very skillful about taking positions that they were not allowed to take, so that if the Reagan administration was opposed to an acquisition — as it almost uniformly was —it was difficult for the parks department to support it. Yet, though there might be a veneer of opposition, the parks department, in the way it described a property, made clear its desire to acquire it. The Sierra Club was cozy with the Democrats in the Legislature and Meyer was able to get Republicans to support some of the acquisitions. Mott was very good about 'looking the other way' [rather than supporting an administration position he didn't agree with]. He was a first class man. A man of integrity."

Mott's appointment was, by its nature, political, and he couldn't entirely avoid conflicts between the environmental community of which he was a part and the Reagan administration to which he owed professional loyalty. Whenever possible, he came down on the side of "protecting the resource". He was often ahead of his time, taking criticism for launching unpopular ideas. Some of those, such as off road vehicle parks for motorcycles, dune buggies and other motorized recreational vehicles, later became accepted concepts and full-fledged members of the California State Parks System. Like a running back in the football contests he loved as a youth, Mott barreled straight through some bureaucratic barriers and adroitly sidestepped others. Of course, he sometimes fumbled the ball. Still, his uncanny ability to see all sides of a strategy resulted in gains for the people of California that are cherished today.

When Reagan decided not to run for a third term in 1974, Democrat candidate Edmund G. "Jerry" Brown, Jr. defeated Republican nominee Houston Flournoy for the governorship. Brown replaced Mott with Herbert Rhodes, a Vietnam War veteran from East Palo Alto. Mott would be "a tough act to follow," commented the *Oakland Tribune.* He was known for his ability to "squeeze more park land out of a dollar than anyone else." The *Tribune* hoped that "another challenge" could be offered, "perhaps at the federal level. The talent of William Penn Mott shouldn't be wasted."

At age sixty-five, having worked nonstop for parks for forty years and seen his children grow up to be fine adults, Mott could understandably have retired to his garden. But as he headed home to Orinda, new opportunities already awaited that would keep him very much in the game.

1975
Moraga Mayor
William G. Combs and
William Penn Mott, Jr.
Contra Costa Times photo

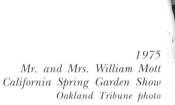

1975
Mr. and Mrs. William Mott
California Spring Garden Show
Oakland Tribune photo

Chapter 5
Public-Private Partnerships for Parks

"At my feet lay the Great Valley of California, level and flowery, like a lake of pure sunshine — forty or fifty miles wide, five hundred miles long...And from the eastern boundary of this vast golden flower-bed rose the mighty Sierra, miles in height, and so gloriously colored and so radiant it seemed not clothed in light but wholly composed of it, like the wall of some celestial city."

JOHN MUIR

Soon after he returned home to the East Bay in March 1975, Mott received two national honors in recognition of his splendid work as state parks director: the 1975 Award for Excellence from the National Society for Park Resources and, a year later, the Department of the Interior's annual Outdoor Recreation Achievement Award. But rather than sink into a reverie about what he'd accomplished in the past, the master motivator now took on three new "part-time" jobs which were to occupy him more than full-time for the next ten years.

MORAGA PARKS AND RECREATION AUTHORITY

The first was as director of and consultant to the Park and Recreation Authority of the town of Moraga. Together with its neighbors Orinda and Lafayette, Moraga comprises the affluent "Lamorinda" area of Contra Costa County. The three towns serve as upscale bedroom communities for professionals who commute to Oakland and San Francisco.

The citizens of Moraga had voted the park and recreation authority into existence only fifteen months earlier. After holding the job for a short time, the authority's first director, Gordon Vinther, had resigned in February, 1975. As soon as it was known that Governor Jerry Brown was replacing Mott, talk began to circulate over the latter's potential availability to fill the vacancy in Moraga. The buzz grew louder early in April when the *Contra Costa Sun* reported that while Mott had received job offers in many states, he did not want to leave California. In that case, the paper commented, "It is hoped that he will find the right place to expend some of this boundless energy in Lamorinda."

The long-time Orindan was well known in the area, commuting home from Sacramento on weekends, often fulfilling speaking engagements. "Mott gave talks on ecology before most people ever heard of the word," the *Sun* noted. He often warned that the earth was in danger of running out of the natural resources that we all take for granted. On one occasion, at the Orinda Community Church, he explained in easily understandable terms humankind's charge to be good stewards of the land. Humanity "had to pay the rent for the short time we are Earth's tenants," he said, "and leave it ready for occupancy by the next generation." During his eight years as California parks and recreation director, Mott had been "one of the greatest stewards of them all," the *Sun* said, adding that the policies and programs he had developed at the state level should be "carried forward indefinitely." It didn't take long for speculation to become fact. "A Coup for Moraga," the paper announced on April 18. As of May 15, "Mott to Head Parks." And a coup it was, according to Hazel McClearnen, president of the board of directors of the authority, who said the mere possibility of hiring a man of Mott's "caliber, experience and stature" had at first "flabbergasted" the board. But after some negotiating, Mott had agreed to take the position on a part-time consulting basis at a pro-rated salary of $9,600 per year. A large part of the job would be to develop a master plan for the authority's future development.

Why would a former state director, who had had an enormous impact on the vast California landscape, want to bother with a small-town park authority that was so tiny it had only one property to oversee? Certainly, he wanted to supplement his retirement income and to stay active in the field in a location close to home. But Mott always looked at the bigger picture. The post, he said, offered "a great challenge and opportunity" to set up a prototype of a local park jurisdiction that could be copied nationwide.

Progress began immediately. Hacienda de Las Flores, the town's first community and recreation center, opened in June, 1975. Fifteen hundred people showed up for the event, which included as one of its attractions a welcoming reception for Mott. In 1976, a caretaker's cottage on the grounds was re-modeled into an arts and crafts building, named La Casita del Arte (Little House of Art). That same year, a series of Bicen-tennial programs at the Hacienda featured such nostalgic and genteel Americana as "Songs of the Gilded Age," ice-cream socials and Sundaes in the Park, illustrating how parks and recreation programs could reflect community mores and tra-ditions and meet community needs for leisure-time fellowship and cultural re-creation.

Despite pleasant fellowship all around, Mott occasionally got into minor scrapes with his open space colleagues. In March, 1976, he threatened to withhold Moraga's share of the cost of a new Lafayette-to-Moraga hiking trail unless the entire trail was built at the same time. This differed from the plan his old friends, Dick Trudeau and Hulet Hornbeck of the East Bay Regional Park District, who wanted to complete Lafayette's portion of the pathway first. When the dust settled, the dis-pute was resolved in favor of the regional park district's plan.

Mott's playful side found expression, too. In 1975, when the parents club of a local school found it had some pumpkins left over from a Halloween fund raising event, he dreamed up a Thanksgiving-themed "Great Pumpkin Pie Bake-Off Contest." The idea was to see who could "Bake a Pumpkin Pie Best Like Grandma Used To." He worked an element of interpretation into the project by providing directions for how to cook the pumpkins — as grandma would have done in the days before pureed pumpkin was available in cans from the grocery store.

Some fifty pies were judged by three home economists, with a Moraga woman winning first place and an actual grandmother from Orinda snagging runner-up. The pies were then auctioned off with proceeds going to the school. During the festivities, Moraga Mayor William Combs was presented with a cream pie because it was his birthday. He was told he could throw it at anyone in the room. Selecting Mott, to no one's surprise, the mayor calmly put the pie to the director's face. Laughing, Mott produced a second cream pie and returned the favor, to the amusement of all. Everyone had such a good time that the pumpkin pie-baking contest was held again in 1976.

Despite fond memories of the pie contest, the attributes those who worked under Mott recalled most were his ability to attract good people (and let them do their jobs) and his ability to market the authority to the community. "When we were developing Hacienda de Las Flores," remembered Josephine "Jo" Mele, who was a recreation supervisor at the time, "Mott was able to hire college-educated landscape gardeners because they knew of him by reputation and wanted to work for him. Employees soon found out why Mott had a reputation for successful organizational leadership. "He was the best manager I ever worked for because he didn't micro-manage," Mele said. "He'd ask us how we wanted to handle the job, we'd tell him, and he'd say, 'Go for it.' Then, you'd knock yourself out because he'd given you the opportunity to do your best. You wanted to show him how well you could do to prove you deserved his confidence." Mott's management style didn't mean that he shirked authority. On the contrary, he remained closely involved in day-to-day operations and liberally shared his philosophical and leadership principles with his co-workers. Whenever a staff meeting was called, one of the gardeners would typically whisper to the others, "Uh-oh, it's little-acorns-into-giant-oaks time again!" They may have chuckled about the boss's fervor, but a little bit of his creative approach rubbed off on them nonetheless.

Mott encouraged staff members to use their imaginations to solve problems or create new programs. One day, Mele wondered how the authority could get more use out of the Moraga school district's playing fields. Staff members suggested the authority offer to maintain the fields year round in exchange for being allowed to use them after school, on weekends, and during the summer. Mott applauded, and the idea worked. When Mele suggested a similar joint use agreement for auditoriums and other indoor school facilities, the authority scored again. "When we'd ask how to approach another agency with such a request," she said, "he'd just say, 'tell the truth.' And he was usually right. He was a good person to have as a mentor."

Mott treated his employees kindly, too. "When some staff member finally annoyed him too greatly, he'd finally pitch a fit," Mele said. "But he always took the person into his office to spare them the humiliation. And once he'd exploded, he was done. He'd come out of his office with that familiar grin on his face." Mele was echoing what Burton Weber of the Oakland Park Department (changed in 1969 to the Oakland Office of Parks and Recreation) remembered from thirty years earlier. Back in the 1950's, Weber had witnessed an unusual act of compassion. In those days, employees with cancer — a disease for which there was little effective treatment — were often shunned or even dismissed. One such Park Department employee had no family and would have had no financial support and nowhere to go had he been let go. Mott quietly directed a department regular to put a bed in a back room of a storage building. There the man lived, remaining on the payroll, until it was time to go to the hospital and die.

THE LEGACY

Mott's strong guidance and cheerful smile made a lasting impression in Moraga. So did the ideas originating during his tenure. Besides those Mele mentioned, the Moraga agency also:

- Mailed its quarterly recreation brochure to each home, another Mele inspiration. Now almost every recreation department does so routinely.
- Determined class fees by dividing class expenses (salaries and supplies) by the minimum number required for the class to run — another new idea that enabled classes to be self-supporting. By late 1977, the steady growth in the number of classes and registrants was indicative, Mott wrote, "of the fine job our recreation staff and instructors are doing in planning and presenting programs that are of interest to this community.
- Formed a private, nonprofit Moraga Park & Recreation Foundation with family and business memberships, another way to involve the community and to raise needed funds.
- Supported joint ventures with community groups.
  In all these activities, Mott had the help of his familiar allies from the private sector, the women's and the fraternal organizations, who gave money and devoted countless hours of volunteer time to the betterment of facilities and programs. They included the Moraga Junior Women's Club, Kiwanis Club, Rotary Club, Service League, Historical Society, Garden Club, and Women's Society, among

others. Among the enduring programs developed are the annual Artists Faire, a major fund raiser for the Women's Society, the annual Egg Hunt of the Moraga Junior Women's Society, the Moraga Youth Summer Theater, now an award-winning, year-round theater program for all ages, the Moraga Hacienda Seniors, grown from 50 to 500 members, and the Amigas de La Hacienda, a volunteer group especially for the community center.

While not on a list anywhere, another legacy is the whimsical sense of humor that Mott brought to so much of what he did. At one Tulip Festival, an annual springtime event he started, "The hundreds of bulbs our gardeners had planted some months earlier were in glorious bloom, we had games and food evocative of Holland, and loads of volunteers showed up to make sure everything went smoothly," Mele recalled. During the planning process, staff members had even called the Dutch Consulate in San Francisco to make sure they were getting the cultural aspects of the festival right. Mott had worked with the consulate before, charming them out of bulbs for planting in Oakland parks. So when they heard their old pal was in charge of this festival, they sent over some traditional Dutch outfits for women staffers to wear. "Lucky me!" said the usually unflappable Mele, still blushing at the memory. "I had to walk around all day in clogs, a lace apron and a cap." While she felt a bit chagrined, her boss took it in stride. "Bill," she said, "thought the outfit was most amusing."

THE CALL OF THE NOT SO WILD

Despite his involvement in Moraga, Mott still had energy to burn. During the two years he spent helping the Moraga authority get up and running, he also provided consulting services to the East Bay Zoological Society in Oakland. The zoo was located in the 465-acre Knowland Park on a verdant East Oakland hillside. It was owned by the city, with the non-profit zoological society acting as a volunteer auxiliary. The society's members worked steadfastly to keep the zoo open. They sponsored fundraisers, sought grants, and encouraged families to patronize the homey animal park with its adjoining kiddy rides and picnic tables. But with paltry funding from the city and few attempts to market the attraction, the zoo failed to keep up with rapidly rising national standards. Its primates huddled in small, barren cages. Its adolescent elephant was rapidly outgrowing her cramped enclosure. Its two lions shared a small concrete platform surrounded by a moat. No wonder concerned citizens periodically called for the whole thing to be shut down.

By 1977, with Mott as consultant, the zoological society had developed a last-ditch but ambitious 25-year improvement and expansion plan. Now, the society needed "an experienced planner and designer" to negotiate with the city to start the proposal toward reality. They knew exactly whom they wanted for the job.

In June, 1977, Mott resigned his Moraga post in order to become part-time general manager of the zoological society. At the zoo, Mott once again raised his — and everyone else's — sights daringly high. He declared that the Oakland Zoo "has the potential of becoming the finest zoological garden in the United States." Once again, he insisted such a goal could be reached by combining the support of the public and private sectors. Once again, he turned to the wide network of people he knew in the business, political, philanthropic, social and service club sectors. He asked them to help turn the zoo from a minor attraction into a "first-class" facility of which the East Bay could be proud.

Mott's self-confidence was catching. The people responded, although with mixed success. Ten years had passed since he'd been top man at the East Bay Regional Park District, fifteen years since he had run Oakland's parks. During that time, the political power structure had changed in the East Bay. It was harder to raise money through the old personal networks.

The contributions he had been able to garner in the past from largely Republican businessmen and women, agreements based on a phone call and a hand shake, were not as easily obtained anymore. Still, with the help of Doreta Chaney, his old fund-raising colleague from East Bay Regional Park days, Mott and the Zoological Society raised over $1 million in corporate, foundation, and individual gifts. The funds enabled improvements to be made to the zoo's physical plant. Structures were rebuilt or repainted. New picnic, barbecue and bathroom facilities were installed. Drainage systems were improved to keep water used to wash down cages out of storm sewers. Termite-infested shelters were replaced The funding also bought increased staffing, new enclosures, modern record-keeping systems, attractive interpretive signs, and other upgrades that offered the animals a better standard of living and visitors a more pleasant and informative experience.

In 1981, Mott made one of the most astute hiring decisions of his career. He engaged Dr. Joel Parrott from nearby Castro Valley to serve as on-call veterinarian. Soon, Parrott had improved the care and feeding of his charges and had worked with the veterinarian societies of Alameda and Contra Costa counties to establish an on-site animal hospital. Mott made another smart hire when he brought Martha Smith, a bright, young public relations expert, on board. Smith (later Bauman) launched highly effective marketing programs designed to create a more positive image for the zoo. One of her most successful gambits was to schedule photo opportunities for the newspapers whenever an irresistible baby animal was born. A picture of a cute kid cuddling an even cuter kid — or cub, lamb, or chick — had surefire appeal. In keeping with Mott's lifelong belief in interpretation, an excellent wildlife education program was established, run by Arlyn Christopherson, a master teacher from the Oakland Unified School District. Elementary school classes attended weeklong sessions on site while a "zoo-mobile" visited those classes unable to schedule field trips. With a veterinarian named Parrott, an imaginative marketing campaign, and a teacher who introduced animals to kids, the zoo began to get more favorable notices in the press.

Mott brought his characteristic energy to the job. He loved to take a brisk turn around the large facility, inviting co-workers to go along as they talked over ideas and laughed about life's foibles. One of his favorite stops was at the children's petting zoo, a small enclosure at the bottom of a long hill. At age sixty-seven, he strode down and hiked back up the slope with ease. "He had quite a gait on him," Bauman remembered. "He could outwalk all of us."

Mott treated his subordinates with his usual measure of respect and trust. "He'd ask you what your ideas were and after you told him, he'd let you run with them," Bauman said. Mott also had "the most charming way of making suggestions," she recalled. "Well, what if you tried this, he'd say diplomatically, and by the time he finished outlining his approach, he'd get you all revved up about doing it that way." Parrott responded to Mott's more forceful side. "He had tremendous values," he said. "Whatever he was involved in, he was never neutral. He was very intolerant of incompetence and indecision. He wanted to get moving, even if it meant taking a risk." Parrott and Bauman laughed as they recalled how they knew when Mott was really fired up. "He'd bang his fist on the desk and say, 'Let's get going on this!' " they said. As for Parrott's feelings about his boss? "I loved him!" he said, his eyes sparkling at the memory.

Mott's aggressive approach didn't always net him what he wanted. In one instance, a part of the zoo master plan that called for the installation of five new outdoor habitats for the larger, hoofed animals was shelved after nearby homeowners' associations vigorously objected. Stretching to the top of a steep hill behind the zoo, the habitat areas would have come too close to surrounding houses, said leaders of the homeowners' associations. After heated discussions, Mott backed down, as he usually did in the face of strong opposition. He acknowledged without lasting rancor that the zoo would not try to have its way if it meant encroaching on the very people it was intended to serve.

In 1981, when the society offered to take over full responsibility for the financing and operation of the zoo and park, city officials were willing to consider this unusual proposal. After delicate negotiations, the shift of responsibility took place in July, 1982. "We're taking kind of a gamble," one city official said. "They (the society) thought they could do it, and we're giving them a vote of confidence." The zoological society's one thousand-five hundred members were gung-ho about the new set-up. "It's kind of a neat challenge," Mott agreed.

But not long after the changeover, the zoo received two damaging blows to its improving yet still-fragile reputation. First, the American Association of Zoological Parks and Aquariums refused to grant accreditation, despite the upgrades that had taken place. Then, *Parade Magazine*, the Sunday newspaper supplement, published an article in February, 1984, that listed Oakland's as one of the ten "worst zoos" in the nation, according to an analysis by a representative of the Humane Society of the United States

"The Oakland Zoo provides a good example of the effects of weak community support," the article charged. "Here the zoological society has a management contract with the city under which the society has responsibility for both the zoo and the surrounding park. However, it receives no tax revenues to help run either of them. The result is a zoo that can neither properly care for nor exhibit its animals nor serve the public." Adding insult to injury was the photo that ran with the story. It showed what were now two elephants, Smokey and Lisa, crammed into their inadequate enclosure. The pachyderms, the caption said scathingly, "Would be better off serving five to 10 years in Leavenworth." In the ensuing media maelstrom, Mott fired back, enumerating improvements both completed and pending. It didn't matter. The society was unable to raise enough money to meet its budget. There was no choice but to go, hat in hand, to the City Council. About then, Mott discovered he was under consideration for a high-ranking post in the second term of President Ronald Reagan. If the appointment came through, it would fall to Parrott, whom Mott by that time had promoted to assistant general manager, to carry on the fight for the survival of The Oakland Zoo.

CALIFORNIA STATE PARKS FOUNDATION

Some of the sniping that came Mott's way in the wake of the zoo's problems stemmed from the perception that perhaps he had accepted too many responsibilities. For the third "part-time" job he had taken after leaving Sacramento in 1975, was as president and chief executive officer of the nonprofit California State Parks Foundation. This was the most challenging of the trio.

The California State Parks Foundation had opened for business six years earlier, in October 1969, with high hopes and a zero bank balance. Its purpose was to raise money for the purchase of land and other environmental and historical assets throughout the state. Once acquired by the foundation, the assets would be deeded to the California Parks and Recreation Department. An important principle of the foundation's operating procedure was that it would cooperate fully with the department. Though not financed or run by the state in any way, the foundation would raise money primarily for projects first approved by the State Parks and Recreation director.

Mott himself had created the foundation during his second year as director of State Parks and Recreation. Based on his successful experience with Citizens for Regional Parks, he hoped a similar organization would work equally well at the state level. After checking with state officials to make sure there was no conflict of interest in working "on company time" toward establishing a private sector entity, he obtained $5,000 in seed money from three friends, Lowell Berry of Oakland, Margaret Owings of Big Sur and Harold Zellerbach of San Francisco. He deposited the money in a department contingency fund for the purpose of incorporating the foundation. In July, 1969, after the state approved the corporation, he used some of the seed money to hire Robert Howard as executive director. A veteran of nonprofit work, Howard set up a desk in borrowed space in a San Francisco office out of which the foundation worked for its first two years.

Once everything was in place, including a five-member board of trustees Mott had recruited, the director asked Governor Reagan not only to approve the new organization but to announce it, take credit for its establishment and personally place his imprimatur on the concept. It was a perfect example of the powerful partnership Mott had been able to develop with Reagan in support of environmental causes the governor normally would have ignored or opposed. Because the foundation was a private, non-profit organization it seemed to tie in with Reagan's theme of less government. Ironically, of course, the work of the foundation, if successful, would lead to a bigger and better state parks system.

So it was that in ceremonies in the governor's office on October 28, 1969, Reagan unveiled the new entity with Mott respectfully standing by. "It is my pleasure today to formally announce the culmination of two years in the formation of the California State Parks Foundation," the governor told assembled members of the public and press, in remarks that had, to the ear of those who knew Mott, the mark of the director's philosophy written all over them. "As of today," Reagan continued, turning toward the board of trustees, "you and the Foundation are open for business, and I want to thank each of you, for myself and on behalf of the people of California, for taking on this very important job."

In his warm and intimate speaking style, the governor explained how the foundation would be able to accept gifts of land, stocks and bonds, and other forms of real and personal property and use them to acquire and develop state parks in ways that state law prevented the parks and recreation department from doing. "And the foundation will have the flexibility to act in a matter of days or weeks, whereas now, through normal governmental procedures, it takes the state years to act," he said. "Through the foundation," he said, "funds can be provided for such important tasks as interpretation, publications, research, planning, and experimentation. There never seems to be enough state money available to do as much in these areas as we would like to do." In conclusion, Reagan said, "The foundation is an important step forward for state government, for the Department of Parks and Recreation, and for present and future park users." With a friendly nod toward the trustees, he said, "I predict we'll be hearing great and good things about you and the foundation from now on."

Reagan then accepted the first gift to the infant foundation — a six-minute home movie called "The Golden Years," made and donated by Ken Murray, his "good friend" and fellow Hollywood actor. The film consisted of priceless footage of William Randolph Hearst and some of the movie stars who frolicked at Hearst Castle during the 1920s and 1930s. The late newspaper baron's fabulous estate in San Simeon, California was now the Hearst San Simeon State Historical Monument, a unit of the state park system. The film became part of the public-tour program and Murray was asked to serve on the board of trustees.

A few days later, in a thank-you letter to Murray, Mott explained the thinking behind the foundation. "For a number of years, I recognized the need for such an organization," he said, "one that could make funds available to the Department without the normal budget restrictions; a fund that could creatively do the many things that we are unable to do to improve the environmental quality and the personal experience enjoyed by users of our State Park System. I believe that the achievements of this foundation will have a dramatic effect on the development of the State Park System and foresee exciting new concepts in park operations."

Murray was only one example of the strong link Mott established with Reagan's base of support among wealthy Southern Californians. Along with Murray, who lived in Beverly Hills, other trustees included real estate executive John P. Elsbach, also from Beverly Hills, business owner Arthur J. Kates of Pacific Palisades and banker W. Allen Perry, of San Diego. Helen Shirley, the only woman on the board, lived in Pomona and was president of the State Board of Lawyer's Wives. Balancing the L.A. star-power were Northern Californians Joseph M. Long, longtime Orindan and owner of a drugstore chain; Robert H. Power, owner of the popular Nut Tree restaurant in Vacaville; Carl McConnell, a rancher and commercial developer in Redding; and Robert Nahas, a successful builder and developer from Piedmont. Regardless of where they lived, however, all the trustees agreed to serve three-year terms without compensation and most reached into their pockets to provide funds to keep the foundation going.

The advisory board — a largely honorary group invited to show a wide base of support and to attend an annual meeting — included such prominent figures as Ansel Adams, the great nature photographer; Walter Haas, the philanthropic-minded chairman of the board of Levi Strauss & Co.; George L. Killion, chairman of the board of Metro-Goldwyn-Mayer Inc.; and Dr. Edward Teller, famed professor of physics at the University of California at Berkeley. Along with several industrialists, other members of the advisory board included William F. Knowland, publisher of the *Oakland Tribune*, former governor Edmund G. Brown, who had moved to Los Angeles to practice law; and Robert Cummings, who listed his affiliation simply as "motion pictures."

Under the spirited leadership of Long, the board of trustee's first chairman, and with the sure guidance of Mott, who attended all meetings and presented a report that became the de facto agenda, the foundation got off to a fast start, especially in making itself known to California's financial upper crust. Social events were planned to introduce potential donors to the idea of contributing to the foundation. To pull them off, park devotees, more accustomed to camping out than dressing up, sometimes needed a little schooling in the finer things of life.

Foundation patron Margaret Owings helped plan an introductory cocktail party at the Larkin House, an historic building in Monterey, for October 30, 1970. She provided a guest list heavy with Monterey, Carmel and Pebble Beach socialites, including Leo Firestone of the tire company, Nicholas Roosevelt of the presidential clan and Justin Dart of Dart Industries. Ansel Adams, Harold Zellerbach and noted landscape architect Harry Dean were lined up as official hosts.

Anticipating an overflow crowd, the planning committee set the party up in two shifts, one from 4-5:30 p.m. and the other from 5:30-7 p.m. Mrs. Owings intervened, advising that the event take place in one shift from 5-7 p.m. "The reason is," she counseled in a handwritten note to the committee on her personal stationery, "that 4:00 is too damned early — and not very fashionable." Afterwards, pronouncing the party a hit, she predicted it would be a model for similar soirees around the state since it had been successful in "informing a select group of people about the purpose of the foundation."

Mrs. Owing's hunch proved accurate. More social events were held, including annual meetings and banquets to which trustees, advisory members and guests were invited, followed by personal visits, lunch and dinner meetings, letters and telephone calls from Howard, Long, Mott and members of the board of trustees. The foundation gained rapid notice among both prominent citizens and parks and recreation activists. By 1971, after only two years of operation, the foundation received the National Conference on State Parks award for Meritorious Service for its contributions toward expansion of the California State Park system. "Perhaps more states will follow your fine example," the citation said, "in expanding and strengthening their park systems."

That same year, the foundation moved to its own office in the Bank of America headquarters building at 315 Montgomery Street, San Francisco. And in 1972, when the foundation celebrated its third anniversary with "An Evening at San Simeon," the glitterati streamed to the mountaintop aerie at $200 per couple to soak up the luxurious atmosphere immortalized in "Citizen Kane." One of them, State Parks and Recreation Commission member Harry E. Sokolov, who was a lawyer in Hollywood, invited Debbie Reynolds and Cary Grant. William Randolph Hearst Jr. and his wife came out from New York for the gala, after which Hearst joined the advisory board and served for many years.

Despite the rich and famous present that night, it was Mott who was chosen to give the keynote address. Introduced by Long as the man "whose vision, energy and dedication has helped to make the California State Parks system outstanding in the nation," Mott spoke for a spirited 15 minutes about the need to preserve and protect open space in California, leaving an audience normally tough to impress warmly applauding . Behind the scenes, trustee member Robert Power performed equally heroically. Because no kitchen facilities were available at San Simeon, the staff of the Nut Tree, the famed restaurant Power owned, had catered the affair. In order to do so, they had transported food for 130 guests and the equipment necessary to prepare it more than 200 miles from Vacaville to San Simeon. The evening made the society pages of the Southern California newspapers, adding immensely to the foundation's cachet. (Indeed, the event was so popular that, despite the difficult logistics, the dinner was held at Hearst Castle several more times during the 1970s and 1980s and, in honor of the 25th anniversary of the foundation, once more in 1995.)

By the end of 1974, four major new sites had been purchased and turned over to the State Parks Department, adding 10,000 acres and $11 million worth of land and facilities to the system. They were Los Osos Oaks State Reserve, a 95-acre grove of magnificent and ancient oak trees (some up to 800 years old) near San Luis Obispo, purchased by the foundation with help from Dart Industries; Pine Ridge Visitors' Center, a $100,000 museum building commemorating early California cattle ranching and constructed in the mountainous Henry Coe State Park east of San Jose; Annadel State Park, 4,100 acres of near Santa Rosa, and a rebuilt chapel at Fort Ross, the state historic park that preserved an outpost built by Russian fur traders and Aleut Indians in 1812.

Not a bad record for "an unknown, untried voluntary group without funds or experience," as Long said, that by the mid-1970's was "nationally recognized as a dynamic conservation organization."

THE POPPY PARK

Looking ahead to 1975, the most important project was to nail down the "poppy park." Five years earlier, the state, with Mott as Parks and Recreation director, and the foundation, headed by Howard, had agreed on a 2,400-acre site in Antelope Valley near Lancaster in Southern California. There, according to Frederick A. Meyer, supervisor of the Environmental Resources Section of the state parks department, the annual flower displays were "so brilliant that they were almost fluorescent in their intensity." The valley was on the edge of the Mojave Desert east of Los Angeles and it was vulnerable to encroaching urbanization. The urgency of saving a prime stand of California poppies — Muir's "lake of pure sunshine" — "cannot be overemphasized," said Long.

The "poppy park" was Howard's baby, and Mott helped deliver it. Skillfully marketed by the foundation through posters, press releases, public service announcements and other media, the campaign captured peoples' imaginations. All who made contributions, no matter how small, were said to have "bought" units of the land and, thus, received a "deed" to their "property." A $2 contribution "bought" 100 square feet of wildflowers, for example, a $100 contribution, 7,000 square feet, and a $625 contribution one whole acre.

People sent in their donations and were delighted to receive their "deeds" (a certificate suitable for framing) by return mail. The campaign did much to expand participation in the foundation from the group of business and social leaders who had founded it to the wider ranks of ordinary citizens. Under the spirited leadership of Evalyn Bell of Walnut Creek, who was president of the statewide California Garden Clubs, her organization, along with the California Women's Clubs, California PTA, Native Sons and Native Daughters of the Golden West and Wildflower Preservation Committee signed on. Dedicated individuals like artist and noted wildflower authority Jane S. Pinheiro also worked toward the realization of the park.

Through Wilson Riles, the state superintendent of public instruction, the public school children of California eagerly adopted the crusade. Teachers organized fund-raising projects in their classrooms. Children chipped in their milk money and other small change, proudly sending in $25 or $30 to "save the poppies." They accompanied their donations with colorful drawings of the bright, orange flowers. The fact that the project was a lesson in conservation did not escape teachers' or pupils' attention.

CHANGING OF THE GUARD

With Jerry Brown's capture of the governor's office, 1975 was also the year that Mott returned to the Bay Area. With little discussion and even less fanfare, the board of trustees asked him to join the foundation in the newly created position of president and chief executive officer. As Robert Howard graciously indicated he looked forward to the new arrangement, there was little doubt that Mott would take over the reins. Shortly thereafter, Mott received rent-free office space, arranged by one of the members of the advisory board, in a bank building in downtown Oakland. The California State Parks Foundation moved across the bay so that on any given day Mott could more easily circulate between Orinda, Moraga and Oakland, all in a day's work.

It was from that office that the foundation coordinated the dedication on April 24, 1976, of the first portion of the State Wildflower Preserve in Antelope Valley, where ultimately nearly 2,000 acres of wild-growing California poppies were brought under protection. While enjoying that triumph, the foundation immediately took on the challenge of raising funds for construction of a Nature Center where the ecology of the wildflowers would be interpreted and an honor roll of donors put up. Paintings by Jane Pinheiro were planned for the center to help visitors identify the hundreds of types of wildflowers that, along with the poppies, blanketed Antelope Valley each spring.

When rumors circulated that the phenomenal work of the foundation was creating some jealousy within the Brown administration, Mott reacted quickly and forcefully. "There has come to my attention that there is some resistance on the part of the department towards the work of the Foundation primarily because I as the former director may be pushing projects that I was interested in rather than those the present administrator is anxious to develop," Mott wrote Rhodes in January of 1976. "Herb, I want to make it clear that the Foundation's only objective is to help the Department, and we will only move forward on those projects that you authorize and ask us to help develop..."

"If at any time you are concerned, please don't hesitate to

get in touch with me," he continued. "I mention the above only because I told you I would always keep you informed. My only objective is to be helpful."

Having cleared up any misunderstandings as far as he was concerned, Mott then hit Rhodes with a long list of projects local groups had brought to the foundation's attention, projects that could eventually become part of the state parks system. They included a potential natural history museum at Anza-Borrego Desert State Park, a new China Camp State Park in Marin County, a stretch of Central California beach contiguous to Ano Nuevo State Park, an interpretive center at Pescadero Marsh on the central coast, mobile interpretive trailers which the foundation would buy for the state to staff and restoration of an historical theater at San Diego Old Town.

Mott added another reassurance at the end of the letter. "On all of these projects, Herb, you should keep in mind that they will have local committees working on the financing and it probably will take, when and if you approve, a minimum of one year to raise the money; maybe two years. In conclusion, Herb, we can be working on several projects throughout the State, and such a scheme would be desirable, but I only wish to do those jobs that you as the director approve and the Foundation only wants *you* (his emphasis) and the Department to receive the credit for a culmination of a successful endeavor."

As it turned out, Rhodes most often agreed with Mott's judgment on what projects the foundation should pursue, nixing only those he felt the state did not have the budget to absorb. So did Russell W. Cahill, Peter Dangermond, Jr., and William S. Briner, the directors who succeeded Rhodes over the next 10 years. All seemed happy to have a nonprofit partner working so assiduously toward expansion and improvement of the system.

"When I was director I had one person on my staff who spent half his time just keeping up with Bill," recalled Dangermond, whose term of office extended from 1980 to 1983. "During that time the department and the foundation created an interesting partnership. We built major interpretive centers at Anza-Borrego and Fort Ross. The foundation would raise the money privately and get creative architectural plans drawn up. We would provide the funds to do the actual construction. The partnership really worked well."

Mott's ability to plumb both the public and private sectors, raise funds, work out complicated land-exchange deals and encourage the business and industrial barons on his boards to give so freely of their time and resources reflected his personal integrity and the rightness of the cause. "People responded because they knew Mott would do something with their money," said Howard Bell, an Oakland attorney who provided pro bono legal services to the foundation from its inception. "He'd get results. He was a very charismatic guy — he really was."

Mott's pace was cheerfully relentless and his ambitions for the foundation unlimited. "He never saw a project he didn't like," chuckled Bell. Although his "to-do" list sometimes appeared to go off in all directions — in pursuit of everything from vast tracts of land to individual items like an old boat or railroad car— "the truth is, that kind of job required that kind of enthusiasm and vision," Dangermond reflected. "You're constantly putting bread on the water and some things work while others don't." Mott's open-armed attitude, he said, "was a lot better than people who are too cautious or too deliberate."

The real problem was not that the foundation would confuse or contradict state park department work but that it operated so far out in front of the department most of the time. Hemmed in by shrinking budgets and bureaucratic red tape, Sacramento simply could not keep up. Not only that, Mott had such an encyclopedic knowledge of parks and recreation theory and practice that state parks directors often found themselves turning to him for advice and action rather than the other way around.

Having resigned the Moraga position in 1977, Mott now devoted mornings to the zoo and afternoons to the foundation. In the latter position, he simply transferred the visionary goals he had pursued as state Parks and Recreation director to the private sector, a nearly seamless exchange that seemed natural to all who observed it. One of those goals was to make interpretation of natural and historic resources equal to land acquisition. "The foundation is not only charged with the responsibility of helping the California State Parks Department enlarge the State Park system," he stressed, "but also with aiding in the interpretation of this million and one-half acre treasure."

He continued to support the environmental trailers that he, as director of state parks and recreation, had developed in 1972. The trailers roamed the state, taking "parks to the people" as one answer to the need to educate California's increasingly urbanized population. Similarly, the foundation produced teachers' guides aimed at getting city children, particularly from poor neighborhoods, out to the parks. The idea was to "help youngsters understand the environment and their relationships to it," a tactic that " in the long run" would "result in the improvement of urban life," he said.

Mott had a special place in his heart for children.

Along with the anecdote about researching Children's Fairyland in the Oakland Library children's room, he liked to tell of the city child who, upon taking his first walk along a path in the woods, exclaimed disapprovingly, "Look at all the dirt on these sidewalks!" Or the youngster who, upon first seeing a banana slug in the park, wanted to kill the defenseless creature, only to treat it more respectfully once he learned of its important role in the interconnected, interrelated world of nature. . "It is only through education that our Golden State can be preserved and its heritage passed on to future generations," Mott said

Adult education was given equal billing. Mott used different parables to get his point across.

As director of state parks, he'd tell about walking with an entourage on a path through a meadow, woods or other outdoor venue. "I kept noticing a can here and a can there," he'd relate, "But I didn't say anything. Then I picked up one can — just one — and walked along with the group. Then I picked up another can. Pretty soon they got embarrassed and started picking up, too. Before we got back to our starting point we had over 100 cans (or bottles or candy wrappers). One person explained that I came a day earlier than they had originally expected, just before a group of boys was due to pick up any fresh trash. But some of those cans — the non-aluminum ones — were a bit rusty. They'd been there quite awhile."

At that point, Mott picked up a large bag the audience hadn't previously noticed, dumped its contents on the floor and explained that this was the refuse the group had collected. "Just to pick up the litter from our state campgrounds costs us $500,000 a year," he'd say. "Give me that $500,000 and I will buy more lands for the system. But instead, I must spend this money for getting rid of all the things that should never have been dropped in the first place."

Then there was the cricket story, which he used to make a point about American values. It seems that he and a friend were walking down Fifth Avenue when he said to the friend, "I hear a cricket." The friend scoffed, saying, "How can you hear a cricket with all the noise these cars and pedestrians are making in the middle of New York?"

"I'll show you how," said Mott and took a dime out of his pocket. He dropped the dime on the sidewalk and several heads turned. "If they can hear the dime, I can hear the cricket," he said. And walking over to the gutter, he lifted a stick, and, sure enough, there was a cricket underneath it.

"We all hear what we want to hear," he said.

A PEOPLE PERSON

Mott worked virtually nonstop and expected almost as much devotion from his staff and from the most active members of his trustee and advisory boards. As with his other positions, Mott also professionalized foundation personnel policies and committed them to writing so that staff members knew what their employee rights and responsibilities were and what to expect as far as working conditions were concerned.

Jan Pynch, who became administrative assistant to Howard a year before Mott came on board, soon found herself caught up in an exciting round of activity. Once in a while, she got to ride to a meeting in a trustee board member's private plane or stay on location overnight in preparation for an annual dinner. On the other hand, she also worked long hours in the office, writing newsletters, doing the payroll, keeping the books and taking care of other foundation responsibilities.

"Whenever we were the main force in a fund-raising project we were successful," she recalled. "When we were a secondary fundraiser or just lent our name to a cause, the projects didn't always go so well. If things were not working out, Mr. Mott would say, 'Let's stay in the background.' There were too many other areas that needed help. He didn't have time to get into politics — when it got political, he backed away."

In 1980, Beverly Clark became the fourth person (along with Mott, Howard and Pynch) to join the staff. Not only did the four handle large volumes of telephone calls, correspondence, meetings and planning sessions for the quarterly and annual meetings of the trustees and advisors, Mott had also made the office one of many statewide Ticketron outlets through which people could make reservations for future camping trips on a first come-first served basis.

In her first real job, Clark didn't know much about office procedures or parks. At first, she was intimidated by the pace of activity and by the callers who became disgruntled when they couldn't get their first choices for campsite reservations. Yet Mott approached his work with such joy that his zeal proved virtually irresistible. When neophyte Clark was still learning how to placate angry callers, "Mr. Mott would get on the phone and smooth it out," she recalled. And despite his status as a former state official and his relaxed familiarity with other highly placed people, "he was always very easy to talk to."

"No matter how minor my problem at the moment might be, he always had time to hear it out," said Clark, now the foundation staff person with the most seniority. "I loved the man dearly. He was very, very fair. He and Mrs. Mott (who often attended foundation events and occasionally visited the office) were lovely, sweet people."

"He had an aura about him," agreed Pynch. "When he walked in he made you feel that you were very important at that moment. He traveled a lot and was only half time with the foundation when he was in town. When he was cross, which, of course, he was occasionally, he didn't show it. He radiated warmth. Even if he was working like heck, he very seldom said anything negative about anyone."

Mott would often come into the office "carrying little plant specimens from his garden," she said. "Sometimes, totally un- expectedly, he'd bring me a big bunch of fresh-picked flow- ers. 'Hello, Jan!' he'd say with that great big smile. The man delighted in seeing people enjoy their environment and he loved the outdoors himself." His fondness for and faith in people dovetailed with his ability and willingness to delegate. "He told us we could do it— and we could," Pynch said. But while handing off the details to his staff, Mott stayed fully engaged. "You could go to him for guidance and ask, 'Is this OK?' 'Am I going in the right direction?' And you'd get an immediate answer," Pynch said, "because he was up on every- thing that was going on."

A PERSONAL LOSS

That faith in people — and in God — was severely tested on November 24, 1980, when his daughter Nancy, who by that time had moved to La Mesa, California, where she was teaching art, died after a two year battle with cancer. This made the third close female relative Mott had lost to death at an early age. His mother, Mathilda, had died young, as had his sister, Lucretia. Now, his beloved daughter was gone, leaving her father, mother and brothers to mourn her premature departure. Memorial services were held both in Southern California and at Orinda Community Church. In their annual Christmas letter, Bill, Ruth, Bill III and John said the "kind words of caring, sympathy and support" they had received at the services had made it "easier to handle the grief we felt. We also realized how many lives have been touched by Nancy's personality and her art. She was a wonderful daughter. We close, thanking you all for your presence, your messages and your prayers. God bless you abundantly."

For all Mott's frequent travel and endless workdays, there was time for family togetherness. One of their favorite activities was to drive up with a few friends to Lake Pillsbury in the Mendocino National Forest in Northern California to spend a few days in a primitive cabin. Mott did much of the cooking, delighting in serving up hearty, *al fresco* meals.

Mott once described why getting out to the wilderness meant so much. "I sat on the bank overlooking Lake Pillsbury," he said. "The sun was setting behind the mountains across the lake. The hills were turning from dark green to purple. The few clouds in the blue sky reflecting the rays of the setting sun were tinged pink. It was the end of a perfect day. It was quiet and still and the lake was glassy, reflecting the purple mountains and the setting sun. The sky gradually changed from pink to greenish blue to slate gray and the hills became darker and darker shades of purple. The sun had set and in the afterglow evening had arrived and the first bat flew into view."

"Almost as if by magic," he continued, "more and more bats appeared and as if by some preconceived signal a chorus of insects played to the frantic, erratic but beautiful flight of the bats. The first star appeared and soon the whole sky was perforated by thousands of twinkling stars, providing a glorious background for the dance of the bats, which had now increased in action, reaching a crescendo with the music of the insects in the background signaling the end of the evening and the commencement of night. The performance was over."

Money could never buy such a performance, Mott knew. It occurred to him that the intrinsic value of what he had witnessed fully justified having state parks in the first place. The purpose of parks was not only to create open space for recreation but also to create "a place for one to find inspiration in the beauty and wonders of the universe."

Mott was not only kind to family, friends and staff members, but also to people who contributed to the advancement of parks and recreation. Whenever he and Ruth had occasion to drive to Southern California on Interstate Highway 5, for example, they stopped off at Fort Tejon State Historic Park, located 70 miles northwest of Los Angeles near the top of the desolate Grapevine Canyon. The park preserved buildings dating back to 1854 when the U.S. Army's First Dragoons were sent there to protect Native Americans quartered on the Sebastian Indian Reservation. A $5,000 donation from Paulina Harris, a widow who lived near the park, had enabled the foundation to buy new uniforms for the Dragoon exhibit. A visit to Mrs. Harris was the reason the Motts stopped off at the park.

Yet, despite his attention to the little things, Mott never lost sight of the big picture. "He had that wonderful quality that 99 percent of us don't have," reflected Pynch, "a vision for the future."

THE LEGACY

By no means was that vision perfect. Many of the projects the foundation started, it was unable to finish. Despite his determined efforts, Mott was never able to establish an historic state parks farm where urban children could see how their ancestors had lived off the land. Not enough other people shared that vision. Similarly, a scheme to produce a World's Agri Fair at Cal Expo, the state fairground site in Sacramento, fell through after its planners, including Mott and the foundation, were unable to work out funding with the state. Nor did plans materialize to turn a donated apricot orchard near Saratoga into an environmental center that would demonstrate what the Santa Clara Valley looked like before it became present-day Silicon Valley. And Mott's desire to add recreational facilities to Angel Island State Park was soundly rejected by environmental groups and other citizens.

Under a "Parks of the Future" proposal, the State Parks and Recreation Department would have designed two parks to be established in "ugly, scarred, eroded areas made derelict by the actions of man or of nature." Volunteers, working under expert guidance, would plant trees and shrubs, build check dams, and carry out other soil-conservation work. Fifty years later, the plan envisioned, the parks would flourish on what had once been wasteland. This concept proved to be too far ahead of its time. And occasionally, an idea simply veered off the charts. One proposal for an antenna-equipped van that would drive along the coast picking up sounds of migrating gray whales was terminated as unworkable.

But as 1985 dawned and his move to Washington appeared more and more likely, Mott could look back on his years as president of the foundation with pride. Land and historic artifacts worth over $50 million had been acquired and deeded over to the state parks. Many of these successful projects had been envisioned during his 15-year association with the foundation — five years as its founder and mentor from 1969 to 1974, and 10 years as its president and CEO from 1975 to 1985. And over the next four years, he returned to California to see other projects he had helped initiate come to fruition.

A major one was the visitors' center at the Poppy Preserve, which eventually did get built. Another was China Camp State Park, a 1,512-acre property in Marin County that preserves the site of San Francisco Bay's last 19th Century Chinese shrimp-fishing village. A third was the Bale Grist Mill in the park by the same name in Napa Valley. The rebuilt mill's meticulously-restored waterwheel still operates to show modern-day visitors how wheat was ground into flour for gold prospectors and the citizens of the burgeoning Bay Area.

A fourth was the addition of more than 5,000 acres to the rugged Santa Monica Mountains state park near Los Angeles (which later, in 1979, was designated by Congress a national recreation area). A fifth was the donation by Angel Kerley of nearly 1,600 acres of family ranch land to the westerly slopes of Mt. Diablo State Park in Contra Costa County, expanding the park toward the mountain's lower flanks which were threatened by creeping suburbanization.

"I was with Mott when he went to talk to Ms. Kerley," remembered John W. Blodger, a senior land surveyor for the State Department of Parks and Recreation. "She'd been pretty much calling the shots on the negotiations for the land, but had suffered a stroke not too long before our visit and was ill. Mott gently took her hand and held it while he patiently went over the proposal again in great detail. Eventually, the deal was closed." As he had been with the Meyers sisters back in his East Bay Regional Park days, Mott "was a real gentleman," Blodger said. "He treated Ms. Kerley with great courtesy and respect. The guy was a class act."

As for historic sites, the foundation bought, preserved and authentically furnished the City Hotel, a 19th Century lodging in the Gold Rush town of Columbia, whose old business district is preserved as Columbia State Historic Park. And in the category of historic artifacts, two rare watercraft became part of the state park system when an original steam tug, the *Hercules*, and a replica of a felucca, a type of sailboat brought over from Italy by immigrant fishermen, were given to the San Francisco Maritime Historic Park which later became a unit of the National Park Service.

After Mott departed from the foundation in 1985, Olompali State Historic Park and Marconi Conference Center State Historic Park, both in Marin County, were completed. Olompali is on land that once supported a large village of the Coast Miwok Indians. Marconi, on a 62-acre wooded hillside, was built in 1914 as a wireless receiving station and named after Guglielmo Marconi, the inventor of the wireless telegraph. It was acquired and renovated by the foundation, then turned over to the state parks as a conference center.

Also among projects begun during Mott's tenure and completed a few years later was Azalea State Reserve, located north of Arcata, a 60-acre stand of native azaleas. Evalyn Bell, who had worked so hard for the Poppy Preserve, once again chaired the fund raising campaign to acquire this property, rallying the California Garden Clubs, the California State Society-Daughters of the American Revolution and other civic groups to the cause

Both as state parks director and president of the foundation, "Mott was always looking for ideas on how to expand the state park system and make it better," recalled former state parks director Pete Dangermond. "During the 60s and 70s, the state park system played a prominent role in the state conservation movement, and Bill had a great deal to do with that. He worked with the Legislature and with the counties, helped get funding and pass bond issues that moved the state park system ahead in a very dramatic way."

MEANWHILE, BACK AT THE ZOO

As Mott waited to hear from Washington, he continued working for the zoo while grooming Parrott to take the lead. In
1985, it was Parrott who asked for and received emergency
funding from the Oakland City Council to keep the zoo open.
Along with the bailout, however, came criticism that Mott and
the zoological society had been overconfident of their ability
to run the facility on a strictly private basis. The city could
provide an annual subsidy, but it would not be enough. An
additional source of money was needed if the zoo were to
survive.

Finally, in 1988 and after intense negotiations with local
officials, state Assembly members Elihu Harris and William
"Bill" Baker, representing Alameda and Contra Costa counties, pushed a bill through the state legislature. The measure
mandated that a portion of the East Bay Regional Park District's
annual tax-based budget be earmarked for the zoo. On firm
financial footing at last, but maintaining its independence from
other jurisdictions, including the regional park district, the
zoo began the long climb back toward respectability.

In 1991, six years after the original condemnation, *Parade*
published an article that praised the Oakland Zoo as one of
four of "the 10 worst" zoos that had turned themselves around.
The article cited the $1 million raised from private sources,
the establishment of the tax-based support, and the new, more
naturalistic enclosures that had been built for the chimps,
elephants and baboons. It also quoted the American Association of Zoological Parks and Aquariums, the group that had
refused to accredit Oakland several years earlier. "Knowing
what you started with," the AAZPA wrote Parrott, including "
poor funding, old exhibits, limited personnel, etc. — I can
appreciate more than most people can, the absolutely tremendous job you have done there."

"We hold ourselves to high standards," Parrott said. "Through the keeping and care of our precious animals — and through daily research and observation — important learning is conducted. It is our responsibility, as caretakers of the wild, to share this information with the scientific and zoological community. By collectively putting all we know and learn together, we can work jointly to protect and save our environment and its animals."

As Parrott carried the torch that Mott had lit, Mott himself was moving on to a challenge even greater than all he had taken on before.

1985
National Park Service
Director Mott with
Actor-Envionmentalist
Robert Redford
at dedication of
Mt. Ansel Adams
at Yosemite National Park.
Modesto Bee photo

1984
Ruth and William celebrate their
Golden Wedding Anniversary
Mott family photo

Chapter 6

Mr. Mott Goes to Washington

*The very essence of leadership is that you have to have a vision.
You can't blow an uncertain trumpet.*

THEODORE HESBURGH

The rumor that Bill Mott would be the next National
Park Service director circulated quickly in late 1984 when
Russell Dickenson, appointed to the job after Ronald Reagan
was elected President in 1980, announced his retirement. But
even as they gossiped about it, many environmentalists wondered why Reagan hadn't chosen Mott the first time around.
His record in California was, of course, well known to the
President. And there were at least four additional reasons why
he would have made a logical choice.

First, Mott's love of parks and recreation spurred him to
accept professional leadership posts at the national level. Over
the years, he served as member of the board and president of
the American Institute of Park Executives; director, Pacific
Southwest Region, National Association of State Outdoor Liai-
son Officers; trustee, National Parks and Conservation Association; professional fellow, American Association of Zoological Parks and Aquariums and distinguished fellow, American
Park and Recreation Society. He was especially active in the

National Recreation and Park Association (NRPA), a fitting connection since his career embraced both disciplines.

When the NRPA was founded in 1965 it represented a powerful convergence of the American park and recreation movements that up to then evolved as two distinct professions. The New England Association of Park Superintendents organized in 1898, changed its name to the American Institute of Park Executives in 1921. That same year, the National Conference on State Parks got started. Concurrently, the Playground Association of America formed in 1906, with President Theodore Roosevelt as honorary president, changing its name to the National Recreation Association (NRA) in 1930. In 1938, the NRA spun off the Society of Recreation Workers of America which, in 1946, changed its name to the American Recreation Society. By the early 1960s, recreation and park people began to realize there was greater strength in combining forces than in continuing to operate separately. Two guiding lights, Mott in parks and Bob Crawford in recreation, had been among those to pioneer that concept when they had worked cooperatively in Oakland after World War II. In 1965, the American Institute of Park Executives, the American Recreation Society and the National Conference on State Parks joined together to become the NRPA. Mott was among the founders who hammered out the merger. He remained active with NRPA for many years, serving on the board of trustees, administrative board and executive committee.

Secondly, Mott's name was a household word in the parks and recreation movement. Colleagues sought out his knowledge, opinions and advice on a wide range of issues. They knew that no matter how busy he was he would give their requests his full attention. When Chris Therral Delaporte, director of the Heritage Conservation and Recreation Service of the U.S. Department of the Interior, sent Mott a review copy of the 1978 Nationwide Outdoor Recreation Plan, Mott's three-page reply included specific comments on particular aspects of the plan, all based on his personal experience in a wide variety of venues. Where the report spoke of the need for more recreation programs, for example, Mott reminded Delaporte to include those already being provided by the YMCA, YWCA, Boys' Clubs, Scouts, Campfire Girls, and other private groups. "All are engaged in recreation activities," he said, that "instill in youngsters many of America's social, recreation, and conservation values." As for how to finance parks in an age of diminishing tax support, Mott had three unorthodox suggestions: nonprofit foundations, volunteer citizen participation committees, and private, nonprofit management corporations set up to run a particular public facility. All provided "a permanent solution to the lack of funds," he noted, whereas "many of the ideas expressed" in the updated plan were "only temporary measures." Mott had used all in California.

When Crawford, Mott's old friend from the recreation side of the aisle, chaired the "Local Promotion of Parks and Recreation" committee of the American Academy for Parks and Recreation Administration, he asked colleagues around the country for ideas on how the Champaign, Illinois, park district, could rekindle waning public support in the wake of diminishing budgets. Since 1946, Mott had been urging parks and recreation people to market their "product." Among his suggestions for Champaign:

- Provide a well written, attractive annual report, including an audited fiscal breakdown. "This not only indicates how money was spent but creates an image of integrity which government today sorely needs."
- Launch an "adoption" project, inviting members of the public to adopt a tree, an animal, a park, or some other commodity the park district was trying to acquire or maintain.
- Encourage district personnel to become more visible in the community by taking part in service clubs, youth groups, local charities and other civic activities.

- Involve the community in the district's planning and budget preparation.
- Develop an interpretive division equal to all other divisions.

Mott's suggestions reflected his belief that "no longer can we allow the public to take parks for granted, assuming that the system will be enlarged to meet present and future needs without active citizen support." His willingness to share the wisdom he'd accumulated spoke volumes about his unparalleled devotion to the profession.

Thirdly, Mott traveled at every opportunity to conferences and meetings where he used his various professional positions as bully pulpits to share his unique set of operating principles, ethical gospels and visionary ideas. He could speak on almost anything related to management. No matter how many times he approached the microphone, colleagues never seemed to tire of Mott's message. "We always looked forward to hearing him speak," said John Davis of the Georgia Recreation Commission. "He had strength of character," said Herbert Brantley, chairman of the Department of Recreation and Park Administration at Clemson and Indiana universities. "If he couldn't sell you on an idea it wasn't worth selling." John L. Crompton, professor of recreation at Texas A&M University, considered Mott "way ahead of his time." Crompton used the story of how Mott persuaded "Trader Vic" Bergeron to donate to Children's Fairyland in a textbook entitled *Doing More with Less in the Delivery of Recreation and Park Services.* The written version of the anecdote, which Crompton transcribed from a tape recording of a Mott speech, "did not do justice to the humor which emerged in the oral version," he said, "but it was nonetheless an effective classroom tool."

Fourthly, the Californian was asked to fill leadership positions and speaking engagements not only because of his unmatched professional credentials but because he was, while occasionally irascible, almost always lovable. Like many great figures, Mott carried himself with such a lack of pomposity that people were sometimes surprised to actually meet, shake hands, and chat with the man they'd heard so much about. "When I found out he was coming, I'd never met him and I was quaking in my boots," said Paula Peterson about the day Mott visited Big Basin State Park where she had been hired, with his backing, as California's first woman state park ranger. "But he was so unassuming that I immediately felt completely comfortable. He just related to everyone at every level — no pretenses at all. It was as if I'd always known him, and from that moment on, I always did. He was in a suit and tie, not even the state park director uniform. I'm not sure," she added, thoughtfully, "that I *ever* saw him in uniform."

Mott's demeanor was so guileless — even at times childlike in its sense of wonder about the world — that it often brought out the maternal instinct in the women who worked for him. They fussed over him when he didn't take the time to eat lunch or when he wore the same couple of blue suits and white shirts — cleaned and pressed, of course — to the office all the time. On the other hand, Mott's straightforwardness, encyclopedic expertise, high spirits, toothy grin, cackling laugh, and love of a good tale endeared him to men. And children took to him when they discovered that he liked *them*. On an inspection tour of a park or playground, he often stopped to talk to kids and to delight them with his favorite (and per-haps, only) sleight-of-hand trick — the one that made a quar-ter magically appear from behind their ear.

STOP THE CAR!

Mott was spontaneous, and curious about everything. One year, when he was California state parks director, he rode with two other state park directors, Charles Odegaard of Washing-ton and David Talbot of Oregon, to a meeting in Oregon. Suddenly, Mott said sharply, "Stop the car!" He grabbed two empty bags, opened the car door and ran up the hill. "He came back with a couple of bags of berries, grinning from ear to ear, and said we'd hear more about them later," said Odegaard. Sure enough, that Christmas, the Talbot and Odegaard families both received a jar of berry preserves, put up personally by their friend Mott.

Another time, he was driving down a Georgia highway with longtime friend and parks colleague Robert "Bob" Baker at the wheel. The two had met in the late 1960s when Baker worked as a landscape and park designer for the California State Parks and Recreation Department. Later, Baker went to the National Park Service and was superintendent of the Southeast Region when Mott visited him in Georgia. At some point, as they sped along, Mott noticed a bright, green vine with large leaves that resembled very big ivy growing in profusion in the woods that ran for miles alongside the road.

"What in the world is that?" he asked Baker.

"That's kudzu," Baker replied. A plant brought over from China during the 1930s to control erosion, kudzu has flourished to the point of dominating some sections of Southern forests.

Upon hearing that explanation, Mott said, "Stop right here!"

"Right here?" asked Baker, eyeing the cars flying by on the busy highway.

"Yes," Mott replied eagerly. "I've got to go take a look at that stuff."

"So I pulled over to the shoulder, he got out and went over and looked at the kudzu," said Baker. This time, Mott didn't take samples, but did make the discovery of a strange plant part of his introduction to the flora and fauna of the South.

After meeting Mott, people often found themselves taken aback by this blunt honesty, droll wit, inquiring mind and love of life. They were delighted when he bucked conventional wisdom, suggested alternative methods of doing business, and challenged listeners to consider new ways of thinking. These same traits proved popular with journalists, with whom Mott had a cordial relationship. With his colorful expressions, frankness and customized licensed plate reading "4 Parks," Mott was a genuine character, "a good quote," a person who, if you could get catch him on the phone or at his desk, would be good for usable information, controversial ideas, and funny stories.

True, he sometimes "shot from the hip," as his public relations people cringed in the background. But he usually had a rationale for what he said. The fact that he was "great copy" as well as highly photogenic with his crinkly eyes, engaging grin, and — in later years — snow-white hair, was evidenced by the generally positive tone of news articles featuring him on conservation, parks, and recreation issues. He personalized a topic that might otherwise seem too broad and amorphous to capture the media's attention. He was a living example of how to market the parks.

TOO OUTSPOKEN

So, with all these attributes, why hadn't the Reagan administration appointed him to a high national post in 1980? After all, another California Republican, Richard Nixon, had offered Mott the plum in 1969. But then-California State Parks Director Mott demurred. "Bill not only declined the offer," said an obviously grateful George Hartzog, who was then National Park Service director, "but endorsed my continuing in the job."

Ike Livermore, Mott's boss in the Reagan gubernatorial administration, had one answer. There were too few environmentalists in Reagan's inner circle in Washington to push Mott's name, he said. That was different from Sacramento, where Livermore and Mott had come on board to represent the natural resources point of view. Harold Gilliam, the respected environmental writer, had another opinion. "Probably he had a reputation for being too outspoken, too dedicated to parks, too much of an individualist to merge into the federal bureaucracy," he wrote.

Instead, an anti-environmentalist crowd had swept into Washington, headed by the abrasive Interior Secretary James Watt, who quickly created a storm of controversy. When public outrage over Watt's efforts to curtail parkland acquisition, slash budgets, allow mining, logging, hunting, and other activities inside the parks and privatize aspects of parks operations forced him out of office in 1983, Reagan replaced him with William Clark, a California rancher.

But as the end of 1984 approached, both Clark and National Park Service Director Dickenson announced their imminent departures. Donald Hodel, who had been an undersecretary to Watt, was appointed Interior Secretary, and the names of Jack Fish, superintendent of national parks in the National Capital District, and Mott, out in California, surfaced as likely candidates for National Park Service director. People at Park Service headquarters favored Fish, a career man with whom they were familiar. Reagan insiders, including First Lady Nancy Reagan and Ed Meese, now Attorney General, liked Mott.

During his interview with Hodel, Mott was asked whether he was concerned about pending cuts to the Park Service budget. "No," Mott replied in his usual jaunty fashion, "That's an opportunity. If you have all kinds of money you don't have to be creative. If you don't have enough money you have to be creative in order to accomplish the same objective." Land, he explained, could be acquired for use as national parklands through easements, protective covenants, donations, and other means besides outright purchase, and emphasis needed to be placed on resource management as well as natural and cultural interpretation so that people could understand why parks were important to the health and productivity of the nation. Hodel nominated the feisty Californian.

Mott did not instantly accept the nomination. In a replay of the approach he'd taken toward the state parks, he put forth two conditions of his own. They were (1) approval of a draft broad-based mission statement, divided into twelve objectives he'd work for as director, and (2) remembering Governor Reagan's pledge that if "You take care of the parks, I'll take care of the politics," a promise of freedom from political interference. While the Interior Secretary mulled things over, the press gleefully jumped on the pending appointment, playing up the irony of a "tree hugger" like Mott working for a President who had once said, "A tree is a tree — how many do you need to look at?" The age factor was another delicious bone the press could chew on. When one reporter asked him whether he was too old to take on the job, Mott had a ready answer. "If President Reagan can lead the country at 74 years old, I sure as hell can lead the National Park Service at 75," he barked. The story and the quote were reprinted all over the country. Finally, Hodel approved the 12-point draft in principle and Mott was officially appointed National Park Service director on May 1, 1985. No public pledge was forthcoming, however, on shielding Mott from political interference.

FROM WATT TO MOTT

Environmentalists wary of the administration's sincerity voiced cautious approval. While Mott had a "real track record as a conservationist," Sierra Club executive director J. Michael McCloskey told the *Washington Post*, "he had [as California parks chief] a penchant for development of the parks that went further than we were always happy with." While the administration had "virtually forfeited its environmental credibility" when it appointed Watt Interior Secretary, commented Martin Rosen, president of the Trust for Public Land, Mott's selection as National Park Service director gave Reagan "a chance to get it restored."

The temptation to compare Mott to Watt was irresistible. The two had actually met in 1981 when Watt personally presented Mott with the Interior Department's Public Service Award for fifty years of parks and open space advocacy. Now, three years later, Mott was "the biggest breath of fresh air to come along in a very long time," McCloskey told *Newsweek*. Said Destry Jarvis of the National Parks and Conservation Association, "For the first time in this administration, the Park Service will have the clout within...and outside to compete for its own priorities." Added Clay Peters, a staff member of the Wilderness Society, "He exudes leadership. We think he is the man to lift the Park Service out of a terrible morale problem. After the years of...James Watt and his cohorts, the service is turned off and scared."

Despite these doubts, all three men hoped that Mott could stop the Watt legacy from riding roughshod over the parks. Yet, Mott was third down on the totem pole. Hodel resided at the top, followed by William P. Horn, another former Watt aide, who was now Hodel's Assistant Secretary of the Interior for Fish, Wildlife, and Parks and Mott's immediate boss. As Watt's point man in Alaska, Horn had favored more development and fewer parks.

Although less caustic than Watt, neither Hodel nor Horn was considered by the environmental community to be particularly close friends of the national parks. The fear among environmentalists was that unless Mott went directly to Meese or Reagan for help when he got in trouble with his bosses, the deck might be stacked against him.

Mott faced the challenge with the kind of resolution Ernest Hemingway called "grace under pressure." He called on his deep reserves of faith. While he never referred publicly to his religious beliefs, he did talk privately about his "call" with his minister, James Kitchens, at First Presbyterian Church in Oakland.

"In my understanding of the Bible," Mott mused, "it says we should manage the land; and I think that means managing it not just for ourselves, but for future generations. God didn't bring us onto the earth to destroy the very values he had developed in connection with the land and the animals that exist on those lands. From the beginning of my interest in the environment, I became aware of the desirability of developing people's attitudes toward the land to be stewards rather than to dominate the land. As you begin to become involved with nature — the interrelationship of plants and animals and people, and how delicate that interrelationship is, and how it all fits together — one has to believe there is a supreme person who put it all together. We are a part of that design. It seems to me we need to understand that. The creativity it took to do that — the imagination, the conceptualization — the more you study it, the more you begin to realize how significant that creativity is. We are called to exercise a similar creativity in providing for the stewardship of the creation."

Mott believed that the ministries of both Jesus and Paul urged upon humankind the need to make decisions for the good of all creation. "That's what Jesus was saying all the time: make decisions, don't procrastinate. As a public servant, I see that those decisions have to be made in the public's interest and not in an individual's interest. Jesus, in all of his teachings, was not making decisions for his selfish interest. He was making them in the interest of the general public that he served."

William Penn, Mott's namesake, said, "right is right, even if everyone is against it, and wrong is wrong even if everyone is for it." Armed with the courage of his convictions, Mott began making preparations to move to Washington.

EARLY CONFIRMATION

Swearing-in ceremonies for the new National Park Service director were set for May 29, 1985 in the nation's capital, but Mott didn't want to wait nearly a month to get started. Right after his appointment was announced, he asked his friend Laurence W. "Bill" Lane, Jr., to host a group of Park Service officials at a meeting in the Bay Area on May 17. The purpose of the meeting of this informal "transition team" was to discuss and refine what was now being called the 12-Point Plan. Lane and his brother, Mel Lane, published *Sunset*, the popular magazine of Western living. Both had worked with Mott on California park bond elections, the California State Parks Foundation and various other environmental issues. In 1972, Bill Lane had served as chairman of President Nixon's National Parks Centennial Commission and at the time of the meeting was serving as U.S. Ambassador to Australia.

Mott got permission from Washington to be sworn in at the meeting. A federal judge came to an office of the U.S. Geological Survey, Department of the Interior, located in Menlo Park, south of San Francisco, and administered Mott's oath of office. Among witnesses were Lane, Bob Baker, and Robert Stanton, one of the few high ranking African-American officials in the Park Service. After the swearing in, Lane threw a reception for Mott and the other officials at the offices of *Sunset*, also located in Menlo Park.

Baker's secretary, Gloria Ballard, was present to help with the paperwork. Baker overheard an unusual exchange between Mott and Ballard. "I was doing some other things but was within earshot of the conversation, and he was asking some really basic kinds of things," Baker said, "like 'Do you know what kind of insurance comes with the job?' and 'What is the pay?' Here he was asking my secretary these questions and she was sort of dumbfounded: [The look on her face said] 'You mean you accepted this job and never asked that?' Well," he chuckled, "you had to know Bill Mott."

Ruth Mott was present in Washington when her husband was formally sworn in three weeks later. As do the finest of career spouses, she supported his vision unwaveringly. She accompanied Mott to many professional and social activities and was photographed by his side innumerable times. While he had a tendency to forget names, she always remembered them. She handled the family finances from the homestead in Orinda. She took care of the household correspondence, send-

ing notes, letters, and a typed Christmas greeting with an update of the family's yearly activities to a wide circle of friends
and colleagues. But Bill would be traveling much of the time
in his new position. There was little point in Ruth, also now in
her seventies, going to the trouble of moving to Washington
to live in a small, rented apartment. Her sons — John had
grown up to become a California State Park ranger and was
engaged to be married in 1986 — and growing cadre of grandchildren were in California. And she had her own set of interests, including her memberships in Orinda Community Church
and First Presbyterian Church of Oakland and local chapters
of various gardening and women's clubs, the Republican Party
and the Daughters of the American Revolution.

Ruth enabled Bill to remain grounded, both as a person
and as a public servant. She tended the home fires while he
preached the environmental good news like an old-fashioned
circuit rider. And no matter how far away he went, he circled
back around for a weekend or several vacation days at home
as often as possible. He could take a turn in the garden, whip
up a meal for friends, put up some jams and jellies, touch
bases with the local civic, cultural, social and community organizations that had spawned him and generally remember who
he was and where he came from. To be sure, Mott enjoyed the
basic creature comforts and the security that a good income
provided. He soon discovered that his new salary was $72,000
— 10 times the $7,200 his job as superintendent of Oakland
parks paid back in 1947. But, with Ruth's blessings and loving
support, his mind was not so much on the salary as on the
intrinsic value of the job and what he could try to accomplish
as the top parks person in the nation

UNPRECEDENTED: A PLAN

In the memory of National Park Service veterans, no director had ever brought to the office a written proposal, much
less a 12-Point Plan. By the time the draft was finalized in the

summer of 1985 and printed up as a brochure entitled *12-Point Plan: The Challenge,* it had already taken on mythic proportions in the minds of many Park Service employees. The ideas themselves were unusual enough. But it took columnist Harold Gilliam to point out just *how* daring they were. In a column in the July 7, 1985 *San Francisco Chronicle,* Gilliam interviewed Mott summarizing the twelve points and included his own sardonic but affectionate comments in parentheses.

Here are some of the excerpts from Mott's "Twelve Commandments" and some comments on each:

- Develop a long-range planner's strategy to better protect our natural, cultural and recreational resources over the next 50 to 100 years...I expect to involve the best minds, both within the service and outside." *(In a bureaucratic atmosphere where the horizon is usually bounded by next year's budget, to think in terms of 50 to 100 years shatters all precedent.)*
- Pursue a creative, land protection initiative." *(There are two of Mott's favorite words, "creative" and "initiative," both anti-bureaucratic.)*
- Additional lands must be made available to meet public demands for increased use and for the protection of this country's natural and cultural heritage." *(These words sound like heresy in an administration that has previously opposed adding parkland.)*
- Some of this need must be met through fee acquisition, but I do not feel we have adequately used other innovative acquisition strategies involving states and other federal agencies and the private sector." *("Fee acquisition"? That's buying land, and that costs money. "Private sector"? Problems there, for certain.)*
- Effectively share understanding of critical resource issues with the public...We must better communicate with the public on a frequent basis...Expand the role and involvement of citizens groups. In my experience some of the

best ideas and most stimulating thoughts for improving
management...have come from an interested public... " *(More
heresy. Typical bureaucrats cannot work with busybodies from
the environmental organizations or from the public looking over
their shoulders and kibitzing.)*

Mott went on to say he would "expand career opportunities
for employees and encourage creative management...The freedom to take calculated risks must be one of our guiding principles. We must evaluate all ideas both old and new." *(He has
not learned, apparently, that taking risks is a violation of the very
nature of bureaucracy, and that new ideas are automatically classified as crackpot or harebrained.)*

Gilliam's misgivings notwithstanding, Mott forged ahead,
surprising Park Service regulars by calling a plenary session
for early June in Yellowstone Park. All regional directors (and
their families) were invited, along with representatives of thirty-
two environmental groups, concessionaires and other constituent
organizations. In his talk to the group, Mott drew a line in the
sand on the issue of protection of resources versus human use
of the parks:

"When in doubt, we must err on the side of preservation,"
he declared, even if that meant limiting access to popular
parks when crowded beyond their carrying capacity during
peak seasons of the year. "Of course, should we find ourselves
wrong," he added judiciously, "we can always provide for more
public use." He also astonished Park Service employees by
urging them to "think creatively" and admonished them not
to worry about getting in trouble — at least, not with him —
for making honest mistakes.

Leading environmentalists in attendance were pleased and
surprised. "He not only knows how to talk eloquently, he knows
how to listen and respond thoughtfully," David Brower of Friends
of the Earth told Gilliam. "He just didn't sound like a government official. They always hedge. He came right out and said
what he meant very plainly." The meeting was "an historic

event," Martin Rosen of the Trust for Public Land told the *Washington Post.* "It was so open and unpretentious and mission-oriented" very much, he could have said, like Mott himself.

Once back in Washington, Mott continued to take quick action and throw out new ideas. He:

- Told all who would listen about his dreams for two new national parks, one to preserve a remaining section of tallgrass prairie, the other to protect an entire wild river system.
- Ordered a $700,000 cash infusion to pick up the pace of a Yosemite refurbishment plan that had been lagging.
- Opposed the nearly 100,000 helicopter and airplane tourist flights per year below the rim of Grand Canyon. The flights, he said, were "taking away from the beauty and quiet we are preserving."
- Agreed with a report from the nonprofit Conservation Foundation that too many visitors, increased development both within and outside park borders, commercialization, pollution, and other problems threatened to overwhelm the park system. The foundation urged increased spending and land acquisition to restore the natural and cultural resources of the parks, something Mott deeply believed in, at a time when the Reagan administration proposed a thirty- percent budget cut for the system.
- Advocated an increase in national parks entrance fees from $2 to $5 per car to help make up for anticipated budget cuts.
- Came down on the side of protecting grizzly bears in Yellowstone National Park by removing a popular campground that intruded into the habitat of the magnificent creatures.

At headquarters in Washington, D.C., Mott appointed Denis Galvin, a career Park Service man, his deputy director. Relying on Galvin's analytical mind, administrative experience, and capacity for a punishing schedule to take care of many of the day-to-day details, Mott traveled much of the time, visiting as many Park Service units as possible. He wanted to touch bases with employees and communicate to them and to all Americans the importance of supporting their parks — all their parks. When a Sierra Club interviewer asked what his favorite national park was, he replied: "We can no longer talk about the 12 crown jewels — Yosemite, Yellowstone, Grand Canyon, Mount Rainier, and so forth. We have 337 jewels in the crown and each one of them is important."

"I went down to Maggie Walker's home [Maggie L. Walker National Historic Site] in Richmond [Virginia]," he continued, by way of illustration. "What's important about Maggie Walker? She was the daughter of a slave living in Richmond right after the Civil War. Developed a penny bank that went right through the Depression without failing, developed an emporium, developed a school. What a tremendous personality she was. What does that mean? It means that people can go there and hear that story and be inspired: 'By golly, I can do if it she can do it!' That's as important as going to Yosemite."

On another early trip, Mott found himself at Hot Springs National Park in Hot Springs, Arkansas. Comprising forty-seven springs of hot water emerging from a fault at the base of a mountain, Hot Springs had been declared a federal reservation by Congress in 1832. After the Civil War, according to National Park Service Historian Barry Mackintosh in his book, *The National Parks: Shaping the System,* the Interior Department permitted private entrepreneurs to build bathhouses to which the spring waters were piped. Hot Springs became a popular resort and then a national park in 1921. But in later years, it deteriorated. Now, in 1985, Mott heard young Arkansas governor Bill Clinton, who was born in Hope but grew up in Hot Springs, explain that a Central Business Improvement District had been formed in the area surrounding the park and a pool of low-interest loans created to spark private sector renovation. Mott vigorously supported the public-private partnership. "You can't win by just piddling along with the minor stuff," he told the local business and government officials in a resounding voice. "You've got to think big!"

A DIFFERENT KIND OF PERSON

Mott was bemused by Washington's sometimes pompous federal government culture. He lived in the little apartment at 2301 E. St., N.W., just a few blocks from the massive Interior Building and walked to the office every day. It bothered him to see homeless men sleeping on the ground or on heating grates during cold weather, and to have to shrug them off when they begged for money. One day, he decided the least he could do was to buy a paper cup of coffee and offer it to one of the regulars. He did so, and did so again the following day. Pretty soon, the word got around about the white-haired little old man who gave coffee to the street people. When Mott discovered he'd set up an expectation, he had to stop. "Geez, I can't feed them *all*!" he complained to his secretary. Another day, when a snowstorm shut down the city, Mott repaired to the office as usual. He discovered, much to his amazement, that, other than the faithful security guards, he was the only person in the building.

For their part, staff people were surprised at Mott's lack of pretense. When he traveled, he insisted on carrying his own luggage. When he walked down the wide, dimly lit, high-ceilinged halls of the Interior Building, he initiated pleasant verbal exchanges with employees no matter what their rank. Earl Henderson, Mott's Park Service driver, grew to love the man. "He was my buddy," Henderson said. "He was really down to earth, one of the most beautiful persons that you would want to know. He wasn't the kind that pushed his authority. He was a very generous person, a very people-oriented person."

When Mott occasionally was given free tickets to events, such as a performance at the historic Ford's Theater in downtown Washington, he frequently invited Henderson to go with him. When Henderson drove Mott to his official appearances, the director would often ask the driver to go inside with him. "When he was introduced to a group of people, he would turn around and introduce me, too," Henderson said. "In other words, he wanted people to know that I was with him." It meant a great deal to Henderson to be recognized by a boss who could just as easily have taken him for granted.

Mott was terrible on names, his handwriting was indecipherable, and he kept unbelievable hours. He arrived at the office at 7:30 in the morning, and "the minute he walked in I walked in right behind him," recalled his secretary, Mary Lou Phillips. "His first appointment usually was at 8 o'clock," although it was "not unusual" for him to have "a breakfast appointment before that." Phillips booked appointments for Mott every thirty minutes and blocked out time for lunch. "Often, of course, he had luncheon engagements, but still I didn't care what he did with his lunchtime...he had the time blocked. I was not going to put appointments in for that hour." When Phillips left at around 5:30 in the afternoon, "he'd still be there. He worked probably until 7 or 8 o'clock, if he didn't have an evening function to go to, which was very frequent."

But Mott found time for relaxation. One time, Phillips and her husband, also named Bill, invited the director to a fish fry dinner at their home in Northern Virginia. "What's his favorite dessert?" she asked Ruth by telephone. "Blueberry pie," Ruth replied, reflecting the tastes her husband had forged during his New England childhood.

Since Phillips was not a good baker, she laid in the best store-bought pie available. Despite prepping her other guests on Mott's work so they could engage him in stimulating conversation, she noticed that he seemed shy that evening. "He ate a humongous dinner and enjoyed the trout tremendously," Phillips said, but remained "very, very quiet." At the end of the meal, her other guests complimented her on the fish.

Mott finally broke his silence. "The pie wasn't too shabby, either," he said. Only later did Phillips find out that among his many talents, Mott had been a pastry chef during those long-ago summers on the Great Lakes. He spent a lot of time in social situations listening, observing and learning from others — as he believed his Quaker background had taught him to do — rather than dominating the conversation just because he was perceived as a VIP.

With the Reagan administration in town, California cuisine was all the rage. Mott decided to teach the chef at the Kennedy Center how to fix a special dish. On his day off, the chef met Mott at the center's restaurant whereupon the director cooked up a concoction of scrambled eggs and oysters called Hangtown Fry. The chef evidently liked the dish because it was rotated into the Center restaurant menu for awhile.

Once, when he'd returned to Washington after a weekend at home in Orinda, he brought Phillips a bouquet of fresh flowers from his garden. He'd carried them three thousand miles back on the plane. (When Bill went home to visit Ruth and the family, he'd leave on the last flight out of Washington National Airport on Friday night and return on the Sunday night "red eye" from San Francisco. Arriving early Monday morning in Washington, he'd hail a cab at the airport, go directly to his apartment, shower, shave, change clothes and walk to the office, showing up in time to put in a full day.)

On another occasion, when he was going to Maine for a speaking engagement, Phillips kiddingly asked him to bring her a lobster. A couple of mornings later, she looked up, "and here he came, chugging up the hall, carrying this little white Styrofoam container. He plopped it down on my desk and said, 'Here it is.' " It was a live crustacean which Phillips hastily stashed in a department refrigerator until she could take it home that night and cook it.

On weekends when he stayed in town, Mott often went hiking, or backpacking, often along the Potomac River in the

Chesapeake and Ohio Canal National Historic Park. Whether on duty or off, Mott "was more passionately involved with parks, wilderness and open space than anybody I'd ever been around," said deputy director Galvin. "He was committed to the very fiber of his being." That commitment meant lively stepping for those around him. Working with the idea-a-minute man was "like working with a juggler who threw plates up in the air," Galvin said. "He didn't care if you caught them or they crashed on the floor and broke. He had his agenda items, and he knew if he kept pushing them he'd eventually find someone to get some of them done."

In general, Mott challenged the massive, self-protective and slow-moving federal government machinery. "When people talk about bureaucracies, it's because no one is willing to take action," he said. "People who reject the new or the novel solely because it is different will need to change their style," he alerted staff members in one of his first messages in the employee newsletter. "Change is to be our agenda, though not for its own sake alone, because we are in the business of protecting resources of changeless value." He continued: "On the flip side, inertia is unwelcome. Foot dragging will gain no reward. Biting the backs of fellow workers is unappreciated. Trust must be our hallmark. Those with gripes will always have my ear and I will not shirk a decision that can free up the effects of a wet blanket."

This outspoken attitude set jaded employees on their ear. "He's zany and outrageous," said National Park Service spokesman George Berklacy with unmasked delight. "He's a great guy. We see a tremendous opportunity for the Park Service — a renaissance."

Mott found members of Congress to be generally supportive. He discovered that Congress recognized how much Americans loved their parks and often put back into the Park Service budget many of the cuts the administration tried to make.

He developed his own way of communicating with individual members of the House and Senate. Whenever he returned to Washington from a visit to a "unit" of the park system, (along with parks, National Park Service sites also include monuments, preserves, reserves, lakeshores, seashores, battlefields and others), he personally visited the Capitol Hill office of the representative or senator from the district or state the unit was in. He would report the problems or progress he had observed in that unit. Since members of Congress did not always have time to keep up with this information, they appreciated this first-hand briefing from the chief himself and remembered it when budget time came around. During congressional hearings, they would ask his personal opinion on the issue at hand, even if it differed from official policy. In that way, his reputation as a man of integrity survived his sojourn in an administration with which he differed in fundamental ways but served faithfully.

TROUBLE ON THE HORIZON

By the time Mott's first year anniversary rolled around, however, the honeymoon, as Harold Gilliam had feared, was fading. Granted, two new Park Service units had already been dedicated. They were Tao House, the home of Nobel Prize winning playwright Eugene O'Neill in Danville, California, and the Maggie L. Walker House in Richmond, Virginia, commemorating the banker and civic leader Mott had expressed such admiration for.

Despite these and other early accomplishments, a series of clashes made it clear that Mott was caught between the tremendous expectations of the environmental lobby and the contrasting political viewpoints of the Interior Department. When air pollution reduced visibility by thirty percent at Great Smoky Mountains National Park and obscured views of Grand Canyon, environmentalists suggested that a list of the nation's grandest views, its "integral vistas," be put together, including those within and around national parks. The list would guide states in their enforcement of the Clean Air Act. In 1985, the Environmental Protection Agency and Mott, as director of the National Park Service, supported the proposal but Hodel thought otherwise. He ruled that recognition and protection of integral vistas should be left to the states. When the Greater Yellowstone Coalition and other ecologists argued for a wider zone of territorial protection around Yellowstone to be administered by the Park Service, and Mott agreed, they got no support from Interior.

Where Mott advocated early action on developing tallgrass prairie and wild river national parks, Hodel said he favored expanding the system, but only "when we can." At the moment, he said, the administration had a "different priority" for the parks budget. When Mott's comments opposing a suggestion by top Interior officials that some smaller Park Service units be turned over to private management were left out of a departmental report favoring the policy, Park Service spokesman Duncan Morrow told the McClatchy News Service that Mott was so appalled he summarily ended a meeting with officials reviewing the report. "The things he said you can't put in a family newspaper," Morrow said.

After Mott agreed to speak to a "Save the Everglades" conference in Florida, Assistant Secretary Horn asked him to cancel because he reportedly feared that Florida Governor Bob Graham, a Democrat, would use the occasion to announce his candidacy for the U.S. Senate against Republican incumbent Paula Hawkins. Conferees and Florida officials were angered by the no-show. Asked why he backed out, Mott said bluntly, "I was told not to go." It looked as though Reagan's promise when he was governor of California to "take care of the politics" and let Mott run the state parks would not hold up in Washington. On a rare trip home in August, 1986, the still-loyal Mott joked, "Reagan's a great conservationist, but he expects *me* to do the job."

The natural resources community noticed these strained relations. "Mott has been opposed at every turn" by top officials of the Interior Department, said Paul Pritchard, president of the National Parks and Conservation Association. He had "been trying hard and doing a terrific job," Pritchard said. "The problem is he just isn't getting any support."

Characteristically, Mott fought back. He turned to his long-time ally, the press, granting interviews in national publications in order to get his views on the record. Within 21 days in 1986, he and the national parks were prominently featured in *U.S. News & World Report* (July 7); *Time* (July 14) and *Newsweek* (July 28). When automatic federal budget cuts loomed under the newly-passed Gramm-Rudman deficit reduction act, Mott warned some parks might have to be closed in fiscal year 1988 unless higher entrance fees closed the gap. When Interior officials said there was no money for new acquisitions, Mott continued to advocate vocally for new parks or preserves as though he could make them happen by sheer willpower.

UNUSED PIPELINE

From the moment Mott arrived in Washington, there was a strong perception the Californian had a direct pipeline to the White House. As the disagreements between Mott, Hodel and Horn grew more frequent and public, Mott's friends and colleagues urged him to go directly to the president for help. But while the presumption of a close relationship with Reagan made some federal officials think he was politically untouchable, Mott was loath to act on it. He chose to conduct his own battles — which sometimes ended up being lonely struggles.

One skirmish involved an outstanding job performance rating, known in Civil Service parlance as a "4," that Mott gave National Park Service Western Regional Director Howard Chapman. Horn, as was his prerogative as Mott's supervisor, changed the rating, downgrading it to a much lower "2." Chapman accused Horn of trying to ease him out of the Park

Service as part of an Interior Department plan to rotate senior managers between the Park Service, Bureau of Land Management, and Fish and Wildlife agencies. Mott challenged Horn's action concerning Chapman. "I am best qualified to make that decision because I am working with [personnel] every day," he told Horn. "I know what they are doing and how they are operating." After that, Mott recalled, Horn "never changed a personnel evaluation without talking to me about it and giving his reasons why he felt that it should be changed. Frequently, I would point out to him that he had the wrong information and that he ought to stay with my recommendations." In the Chapman case, Hodel, Horn's supervisor, stepped in to mediate, and compromised by giving Chapman a rating of "3."

A running debate within the Interior Department centered around how to balance protection of the National Parks' delicate natural resources with demands for use of the resources. Mott leaned toward erring on the side of preservation, while Hodel and Horn thought preservation, if taken too far, meant going to extremes to keep people out of the parks. "These people [his bosses] don't understand that use and recreation values of national parks are not on the same plane as preservation among National Park Service priorities and never have been," he told syndicated columnist Thomas Elias in February, 1986. "There are some who feel that use and recreation should be equal to preservation." Horn readily acknowledged he was one of them. "We have to engage in a balancing act between the use and conservation mandates," he responded. "But I didn't think we had a dispute with Mott. The fact that Hodel hired Mott indicates we see eye to eye." Mott disagreed again. "We [the National Park Service] are under pressure constantly from above," he said. But he insisted the squeeze was not coming from Reagan. "When I was state parks director, the president was very supportive of parks acquisition and I know he has a real interest in the national parks," Mott said

Mott tried to convert Horn to his way of thinking. "I finally got to Bill," Mott recalled, "by saying, 'Bill, you spend a lot of money buying fishing tackle and flies and licenses, and you're an outstanding fly fisherman, but when you go to a stream, it's beautiful, it's clear, it's attractive.' He said, 'That's right, I don't like to go to these places that are not very attractive.' I said, 'That's what we're talking about —that's the values that we hold dear — those intrinsic values of beauty, of the silence, of the quality of the water, et cetera, et cetera.' and he said, 'Yeah, I think I understand.' I said, 'Isn't that really more important than the dollars you spent or the size of the fish you caught?' He said, 'Yeah, that's right.' I said, 'Well, that's what we're talking about.' "

SKIP THE EIS

But conflict arose again. In January 1987, Shell Western Exploration and Petroleum, a subsidiary of Shell Oil, asked the Park Service for permission to explore for oil and gas reserves under the surface of Big Cypress National Preserve in Ochopee, Florida. When the preserve was set aside in 1974, it encompassed 570,000 acres. It had historic and environmental significance and assured a supply of fresh, clean water to Everglades National Park immediately to the south. It provided habitat for the highly endangered Florida panther, among other species, and protection for at least four hundred significant Native American cultural and archeological sites identified within its boundaries.

As with some other parks and preserves, the National Park Service had bought from private owners the surface property to create the preserve. But the private owners had retained the parks' subsurface rights. Thus, the oil company had every right to seek permission from the owner to poke around. The exploration, reported Tom Turner of *Mother Earth News*, would involve detonating ten-thousand charges of dynamite in holes between six and twenty-seven feet deep along eighty-five miles of survey lines. It would require the cutting of sixty-eight miles of new off-road-vehicle trails through what were then roadless areas of the preserve. Park Service scientists and Mott, their boss, strongly recommended that an environmental impact study (EIS) be done before any decisions were made. Horn disagreed, ordering Mott and Southeast Regional Superintendent Baker to sign off on a far less rigorous "environmental assessment" statement instead. The two men "made a very strong case that this was not only inappropriate and not in the best interests of the park but that in fact it was illegal," Baker said. They warned that on those grounds the Sierra Club would likely sue — and sue successfully — to prevent the drilling. And if the Sierra Club did act, Baker told Horn, "It was going to be terribly embarrassing to the Park Service. It wasn't going to be [Horn] saying it was okay for Shell Oil [to drill], it was going to be Bill Mott and myself, " he said. "We were all going to look like fools, [as if] we were giving away the National Park Service."

After the fourth meeting on the matter, Mott and Baker realized they had failed to change Horn's mind. Full of foreboding, they both signed the documents. But Baker took another step. He wrote and signed a confidential memo to Mott and mailed it to his home in Orinda. In the document, dated December 23, 1987, Baker told Mott:

I want you to know that [Big Cypress] Superintendent [Fred] Fargergren and I appreciate your efforts to convince the Assistant Secretary that the National Park Service [should] undertake an environmental impact statement (EIS) on Shell Oil Company's proposal for seismic exploration in the [preserve].

   As we all agreed during our meeting on Thursday, December 3, it was the prudent professional judgment to undertake the EIS, to explore all implications of the 85 miles of seismic exploration. It is unfortunate that the Assistant Secretary's office did not concur with our position and instructed us to issue the environmental assessment.

   What is troublesome is not only that the Park Service did not have the opportunity to explore all alternatives, i.e., hand-held drilling, feasibility of wider spacing of the holes, etc., but that the decision to go with an environmental assessment, which was a political decision, appears to be the National Park Service's proposal. Certainly the political leadership has the right to override our professional judgments, but I believe there should be a clear record of that decision.

Later, Baker said he wrote the memo to thank Mott "for the strong, principled stand he had taken in an effort to protect the interests of the park. I went into details about what happened, really to make it a matter of record, because we knew that the Sierra Club was going to file suit immediately and that we were both going to be on the stand." That way, Baker figured, when he and Mott had to testify they had been verbally directed to bypass an EIS, the letter would provide a written record of what had transpired. Since there were only two copies of the letter, one, an unsigned, carbon copy in a personal, locked file in Baker's office, the original in Mott's personal possession, Baker was in for another shock. When the Sierra Club Legal Defense Fund did, indeed, file suit, and its action was reported in several magazines, so was the content of the private memo. Syndicated newspaper columnist Jack Anderson quickly picked up the story and the public reacted strongly. Shell backed out and the controversy abated.

When Baker asked Mott how the memo got out, Mott professed ignorance. Later, Baker obtained a copy of the suit and saw that the copy of the letter attached to the suit had his signature on it. He concluded that Mott leaked it but provided him deniability by not telling him. Baker admired Mott's determination to protect Big Cypress National Preserve knowing he'd likely suffer "some real [political] consequences" as a result.

THE INVESTIGATION

In April, 1988, Hodel called Mott and his special assistant, Loran Fraser, into his office. The two men were told they were the subjects of an investigation by the U.S. Inspector General concerning "violations of code of conduct and conflict of interest" charges. The charges apparently had something to do with the fact that three years earlier, Mott had asked Fraser, a career Park Service employee, to take a temporary assignment as deputy executive director of the President's Commission on Americans Outdoors.

The commission, chaired by Tennessee governor Lamar Alexander, had been appointed by Reagan to assess America's outdoor recreational needs and report them to Congress. When the commission's report was issued in early 1987, it called for a trust fund of $1 billion a year to acquire and protect open space, a network of "greenways" connecting urban areas, and ignition of a "prairie fire" of community interest in outdoor recreation. This was more proposed action than the administration had anticipated, and the report never got the national attention it deserved. In an effort to overcome that, some of the disbanded commission members organized a private, follow-up group to "ignite the prairie fire" by planning a National Celebration of the Outdoors for May, 1989. Mott wanted the Park Service to participate so, under regulations that allow federal employees to temporarily work in the private sector, he assigned Fraser as a liaison and signed himself up as a member of the organizing committee. Other committee members included National Geographic Society President Gilbert M. Grosvenor, retired CBS anchorman Walter Cronkite, and Garden Clubs of America President Jane Ward; "Hardly," columnist Jack Anderson later noted, "a group of subversives." But the committee couldn't raise sufficient funds. The celebration never got off the ground. In March, 1988, the White House Domestic Policy Council's Task Force on Outdoor Recreation proposed a different course of action. It advocated expanding an already-existing Take Pride in America program. This was an advertising and public relations campaign to urge Americans to do their part as individuals to take good care of public lands.

In April, when Mott and Fraser were called on the carpet, "we were accused, at minimum, of inappropriate conduct, and, at maximum, of possible criminal behavior," Fraser recalled. Both were ordered to withdraw from the National Celebration of the Outdoors. "Bill and I were badly shaken," Fraser said. The *New York Times* reported that while Mott and Fraser were under investigation, nobody knew what for. The investigation dragged on for months, but no action was ever taken against either man. Though Mott's reputation was "secure from the worst that Hodel can do," as the *Sacramento Bee* put it, "this is shabby treatment nonetheless for a man who has served Reagan and the environment with distinction. Mott certainly isn't the only official of this administration to come under investigation. But he may be the first who's being investigated for doing something right."

For his part, Fraser felt badly burned. He and other Park Service veterans already believed that Mott made a major mistake in not bringing a special assistant with him from California, someone who knew him well enough to serve as advisor and protector. In this instance, Fraser also thought Mott could have done more to insulate them both by trading on his political capital with the White House. "Good, God — all he had to do was pick up the phone," Fraser said years later, "and none of this would ever have happened!"

So, against the better judgment of his subordinates, Mott tried to take care of his own problems at Interior, knowing full well that his mentors, Reagan and Meese, were heavily involved in national and international issues over at the White House. As far as he was concerned, it was enough that people *thought* he had a pipeline to the top. But when he climbed into the unmarked sedan in which Park Service driver Earl Henderson got him from one appointment to the next, he would joke with Henderson about that assumption. "I don't know why people think I'm going to the President," he would tell Henderson. "Hell, I'm not going to the President." The only time Mott would see Reagan, Henderson said, was when he was called to the White House to attend some social function like the reception. "I never went to Ed Meese about anything," Mott later told Park Service historian Macintosh. "I never went to the governor [as he called Reagan] about anything. People assumed that I could do that, but I never did."

THE VIEWS OF HODEL AND HORN

Despite reported clashes between Mott and himself, and frequent criticism from environmental activists, former Secretary of the Interior Hodel saw the period differently. In nearly four years' time (he left office in January, 1989, Mott in March, 1989), those disputes — over the integral vistas issue, territorial protection, privatization, job performance ratings, oil exploration at Big Cypress, and the investigation (which Hodel said he did not recall) — "strike me as being relatively minor," he said in a 1998 interview. Hodel's beef was more with what he called "environmental extremists" than with Mott. "In fact, what impressed me about [Mott] was that I thought the values he was espousing and the approach to the parks was precisely what this administration was all about," he said. "In my view, the environmental community was highly partisan," he continued. "The leaders had endorsed Jimmy Carter [in his 1980 bid for a second term], were upset by the election of Ronald Reagan, and were determined throughout [Reagan's] administration to paint him in an anti-environmental light, regardless of the facts. And since they liked Bill Mott and they had this stereotypical view of what we [the members of the Reagan administration] were like, they assumed there had to be this conflict between Mott and me. That was not true."

On the integral vistas issue, for example, "it would not surprise me that Mott leaned toward a federal policy and we didn't. Every bureau director faces this. He's got a constituency out there. When he meets with them it's sometimes convenient to indicate that he fought on an issue but lost. I think we're all inclined to do that in the political area." Besides, the "extremist" position on the integral vistas "would require shutting down every activity that might generate particles which would obscure the view from the highest point of any park in America." On new national parks, "I supported Mott on the Tallgrass Prairie effort," Hodel said. "The thing that impressed me about him was that on the one hand he could wish for the day that you could acquire a block of land, but, practically, he knew it wasn't possible. None of the leaders in the environmental movement would acknowledge that I had been favorable toward Mott's proposal in that regard." The idea that the Interior Department favored exploitation of natural resources within or under the National Parks "was a lie perpetrated by people who knew better but made such statements to raise money," Hodel said. "The real issues related to whether people would be allowed in the parks. The environmental extremists consistently sought to shut down overnight lodging, make it harder for concessionaires to provide services, close roads, and impose mass transit solutions." On those "battle lines," Hodel said, "Mott was an ally of ours although maybe at the risk of cutting off his constituency." When it came to rating job performances, "management was not Mott's strong suit," Hodel said. "He didn't go to the National Park Service to process paper and deal with personnel. He went there as a visionary and to try to have a long-term beneficial impact. That's why I brought him in, not as a manager."

Overall, said Hodel, "my recollection of Bill Mott was that he was a very vigorous man, and certainly very vigorous for his age. He would spin off more ideas than it was ever possible to implement. He was dedicated to the Park Service, but also did not appear — at least in our internal discussions — to suffer from the same blind biases that the more extreme among his constituency seemed constantly to be espousing. In that regard, he was a very important buffer for us, and it was a tough job for him. He had a constituency out there for whom nothing was enough. Our administration intended to balance everything we did in this area with everything else we were doing. They [the "extreme" environmentalists] used that rhetoric because it gave them a partisan advantage."

William "Bill" Horn, Assistant Secretary for Fish, Wildlife, and Parks, had similar opinions of Mott. "I found Bill to be a delightful, enjoyable, energetic guy," he said in a 1998 interview. "He was a real visionary, a preacher, with a deep, abiding commitment to the parks and the out-of-doors. But Bill was no nuts-and-bolts administrator, at least not at that stage of his life. He was very apolitical. There are times when being apolitical is refreshing, but at other times it caused great frustration and difficulty."

One of those times came for Horn when Shell Oil asked for permission to explore for oil and gas reserves under Big Cypress National Preserve. Split ownership, incidentally, not only of surface and subsurface rights at Big Cypress but at some other national parks as well, lay behind the frequent, but unfounded charges — according to Horn — that the Reagan administration was interested in allowing private exploitation of natural resources. "Privatization was pure speculation, pure rumor," Horn said. Rather, because some private owners had been promised retention of subsurface rights, either verbally or in writing, when they sold their lands to the Park Service, the government was obligated to honor those rights in a timely fashion, Horn argued. In the case of Big Cypress, Horn said, completion of an EIS would take about 24 months, versus a probable two or three months for an environmental assessment. Horn favored the latter in order not to "string these people out for two years." But when the Sierra Club sued, a Florida judge ordered the EIS, and the exploratory request was withdrawn. In Horn's opinion, "It was a classic example of how procedural requirements had the effect of reneging on the promise that had been made years earlier to these people."

When Horn asked Mott not to speak at the Everglades conference it was because Governor Graham wanted the Park Service to buy another 100,000 acres of Big Cypress land from a private owner for $50 million, Horn said. He was stalling on the proposal while working quietly on a better deal. "I didn't want Bill to go to the conference and wind up in the middle of the controversy," Horn said. Some years later, the private owner agreed to swap his land for a similarly valued plot of government-owned land in Phoenix, Arizona. As for rating Howard Chapman's job performance, Horn said Chapman "wasn't doing a good job of running his region" and was asked by Mott either to take what was called a 'directed reassignment' or resign. Chapman appealed and Mott changed his mind. Horn then countermanded Mott, issued the unsatisfactory rating and was called before the congressional committee to explain. "Shortly thereafter we issued a satisfactory rating and, not long after that, Chapman resigned," Horn said. In other, less public personnel disputes, he and Mott were able to "sit down and work things out."

SURPRISING GROWTH

Few others saw Mott's role quite the way Hodel and Horn did. But despite the distractions he faced, Mott's single-minded devotion to the national parks brought results expected by neither the administration nor the environmentalists closely watching the administration. By the end of 1987, four more units had been added to the system: Great Basin National Park in Nevada, El Malpais National Monument in New Mexico, Steamtown National Historic Site in Scranton, Pennsylvania, and portions of Plains, Georgia, home of former President Jimmy Carter.

The creation of Great Basin National Park was particularly gratifying for Mott. In 1933, as a young landscape architect for the National Park Service, he had been sent to Nevada by the regional office in San Francisco to study the desolate area surrounding the Lehman Caves. The caves, a series of eerie limestone caverns, had been declared a national monument in 1922. With excitement, he reported back the area's stunning attributes: the rugged South Snake mountain range with the southernmost glacier in the United States; the caves themselves; Lexington Arch, a six-story natural rock formation; a surprising variety of alpine flora and fauna, and stands of bristlecone pine, some of the world's oldest trees. Ranchers and miners successfully blocked Mott's recommendation for a national park. But he never forgot it, and brought it up again when he became director. When Congress and Reagan approved enabling legislation in 1986 to make Great Basin the nation's forty-ninth national park, Mott expressed joy. The fifty-four-year-old dream had become a reality. The new, 77,000-acre-park illustrated not only Mott's vision but also his improvisational skills. He put together the caves with an adjacent portion of the Humboldt National Forest and designated the combined entity a national park. Since no private land had been acquired, the park was created at virtually no cost to the government. However, National Park Service management gave the area the highest possible level of resource protection.

El Malpais is a spectacular volcanic area, featuring spatter cones, a 17-mile-long lava tube system, and ice caves near Grants, New Mexico. The area is also rich in ancient Pueblo Indian history and features diverse ecosystems. The Jimmy Carter National Historic Site includes former President Carter's residence, boyhood home, and the high school he attended. The railroad depot, which served as campaign headquarters during the 1976 election, is now the park visitor center. The Jimmy Carter National Preservation District, separate from the park, includes part of the town of Plains and its environs. As a place where people live and work, it is a highly unusual national site.

Deep skepticism greeted establishment of Steamtown National Historic Site, a collection of old railroad equipment housed at the former Delaware, Lackawanna & Western Railroad Yard in downtown Scranton. The site was established in 1986 in legislation sponsored by Congressman Joseph McDade but without the usual public hearing process. The train yards were ugly and a new pedestrian mall was to be constructed adjacent to the park site. To many Park Service people, the project smacked of rank commercialism, unbecoming the dignity of one of the nation's most revered government agencies. Undeterred by the criticism, Mott thought Steamtown would be similar in significance to the California State Railroad Museum, another important example of the role of the Iron Horse in America's heritage. But hardly anyone else did. Ed Bearss, National Park Service Chief Historian, did not think the Steamtown collection was "historically significant." But Mott stuck by Steamtown. "The opportunity to tell that whole story down there of railroading with the yards and everything else is going to be fascinating — you wait and see," he told National Park Service historian Barry Macintosh in an interview.

TELL THE REAL STORY

Mott felt about Steamtown the same way he felt about the need to preserve the story of slavery, and the story of Native Americans before European colonization. On the controversial subject of chattel bondage, his was a simple and direct statement. "I think personally we need to do a better job of telling the story of slavery. [It] was a part of our culture. It shaped this country. We ought to tell that — not to camouflage, but to tell the story. Obviously we don't feel good about slavery today, but I think we ought to tell that story, and tell what it did for this country. Thomas Jefferson, Washington, and the whole enchilada couldn't have done what they did for this country if they hadn't had slaves."

"I think we ought to tell the Indian story," he continued, "and we ought to be frank about it and honest about it and tell the public what this was all about. I think we did some shameful things at Yosemite with those Yosemite Indians.

I think we ought to admit that it was wrong, but at that time and under the circumstances and under the conditions of that particular moment in time, it wasn't looked upon as wrong."

When Mott got rolling, his passion for his topic sometimes overrode the precision of his expression. Victoria Clarke, then a secretary in the Park Service director's office, saw what happened when Mott was misinterpreted. "One day, I was the only person in the director's suite — it must have been lunchtime — when Mr. Mott came in from a trip down South [probably to visit Melrose in Natchez, Mississippi, a pre-Civil War mansion he and others were proposing as a national historic site]. While there, a radio news broadcast had apparently carried a sound bite from something he'd said that was construed by some listeners as being a comment favorable to slavery. He was livid and deeply hurt to be accused of 'glorifying' slavery rather than simply acknowledging that its story needed to be told," Clarke said. "He was beside himself. He ranted and raved for fifteen minutes." When he recovered his composure, he gave Clarke a rare peek into his innermost self. "My father, grandfather, and great-grandfather were all Quakers," he said. "People of that persuasion hated the idea of indentured servitude."

EMPATHY FOR THE UNDERDOG

Throughout his life, in fact, Mott empathized with the underprivileged, whether the Civilian Conservation Corps teenagers he supervised during the 1930s or the low-income teenagers in "Workreation" programs in Oakland. Mott also backed members of minority groups taking on new responsibilities. One of those was William "Bill" Patterson. As an example of the kind of quiet diplomacy Mott practiced outside the limelight, Patterson's experience is worth recounting.

A college student in the early 1950s, Patterson became one of the first African-Americans to be hired by the Oakland Recreation Department after World War II. "At my level, you didn't get a lot of interaction with the superintendents [Mott for Parks and Jay M. Ver Lee for Recreation], but I knew who Mott was and what he represented in the City of Oakland," Patterson recalled. During those years, Oakland's African-American citizens, including Patterson, were still fighting for full access to public facilities. "Mott recognized what was going on and said something positive to me. As a part-time college student from the playground, support from the superintendent of parks meant a lot." The two men's paths crossed again during the 1960s when Patterson supervised Oakland parks and Mott managed the nearby East Bay Regional Park District. "Mott heard about the programs we were developing and complimented us." By 1974, Patterson was in charge of many of the Oakland Park facilities and work forces that Mott had established years earlier. To get more background on those programs and personnel, Patterson renewed his acquaintance with Mott, who was by then director of California State Parks. "I began to seek him out and continued to do so for a number of years," Patterson said.

In Washington, when Jack Fish retired as regional director of the National Capital Parks region of the National Park Service, Mott appointed Robert Stanton as Fish's successor. This move made Stanton one of the highest level African-American officials in the agency and a member of the top management team. Stanton later became the first African American to head the National Park Service when he was appointed director by President Clinton in 1997. Upon that occasion, Stanton looked back. "Director Mott strengthened the interpretive and educational programs of the Park Service, provided expanded training opportunities for employees, and improved the overall protection and preservation of natural resources. He will always have a warm spot in my heart. He was one of my heroes."

Mott also made it his business to highlight Park Service sites that commemorated African-Americans who had achieved against great odds. "So much has been gained from Mary

McLeod Bethune, George Washington Carver, Frederick Douglass, Booker T. Washington, Maggie Walker, and, of course, Martin Luther King, that it is impossible to estimate the good they have inspired because of their legendary accomplishments and achievements," he wrote during Black History Month one year in the *Courier*, the monthly magazine of the National Park Service. "While I believe it is good to laud the contributions of Harriet Tubman and other individuals," he continued, "I also believe the National Park Service has the responsibility to interpret and tell the whole story of slavery and its influences on the economic growth and cultural heritage of this country. We must not be afraid to discuss this subject, no matter how painful, or we may find that we cannot learn from this chapter in our history."

NATCHEZ AND MELROSE

An opportunity to do that came up in the instance of the Melrose Plantation in Mississippi. In the decades before the Civil War, Natchez had become a commercial, cultural, and social center of the South's "cotton belt," with power and wealth unmatched by other southern towns of comparable size. The power and wealth was based, of course, on slave labor. Now, 120 years later, Mott joined those who were interested in preserving Melrose, an excellent example of an antebellum plantation. The proposal was a controversial one. Some people, like Mott, argued that the story needed to be told, while others didn't want to dignify the cruel practice of slavery with the seal of the National Park Service. Mott's point of view eventually prevailed. The park was authorized in October, 1988. It consists of three separate sites: the 78-acre Melrose; the home of William Johnson, a prominent free black businessman; and a stretch of land on a bluff overlooking the Mississippi River where a French fort once stood.

Yet, learning could not be confined to looking only at the past, Mott said. "History is a continuum and, as part of that continuum, we make tomorrow's history today. At this moment, although we may not yet recognize them, we have in our midst the Harriet Tubmans, the George Washington Carvers, even the Martin Luther Kings, those who will guide not only black Americans, but all Americans, to a better future."

Mott wanted neither to ignore history nor to sugarcoat it. He simply wanted the National Park Service to honor it as truthfully as possible. That was why he had also been supporting a completely different kind of campaign. Several natural resources groups were working to reintroduce the gray wolf to its primeval home in Yellowstone National Park. Now, Mott unleashed even more of his considerable energies toward that crusade.

1987 - William Penn Mott made honorary chief.
Glacier National Park
NPS photo

Chapter 7

The Year of the Wolf — and the Fire

The ultimate measure of a man is not where he stands in moments of comfort and convenience, but where he stands at times of challenge and controversy.

MARTIN LUTHER KING, JR.

For many years, a group of naturalists and scientists had been advocating the return of the wolf to its ancestral homeland in Yellowstone National Park. One of the leading proponents of this campaign was Hank Fischer of the Defenders of Wildlife, whose 1995 book, *Wolf Wars* (Falcon Press, Helena, Montana) tells the story.

Once prolific in North America, wolves had held their own against exploration, hunting and trapping. But by the late 1800s, when ranchers settled on the land, wolves were perceived as threats to domesticated cattle and sheep. Systematic eradication of the wolf was allowed—in fact, coordinated—by the U.S. Biological Survey and the National Park Service. Hunters were paid bounties to shoot as many wolves as possible.

Wolves had been eliminated from Yellowstone by 1923. Over the next thirty years, herds of elk, the wolf's natural prey, increased geometrically in the park, where they soon threatened to outstrip available forage. Gradually, scientists and naturalists began to realize that predators were necessary to restore the balance of nature. In the 1960s and 1970s, as the resultant studies moved from scientific journals into popular culture, the wolf went from pariah to hero. A few individual wolves were spotted migrating from Canada to Glacier National Park on the Canadian-Montana border. But it was too much to expect male and female pairs to make their way from Canada to Yellowstone, hundreds of miles to the south. There were calls from both within and without the Park Service to capture several wolves in Canada and transport them to Yellowstone. And, as required by the Endangered Species law, the U.S. Fish and Wildlife Service began work on a wolf recovery plan.

But how to overcome the fierce opposition of some Western ranchers and their elected representatives? Interpretation and compensation emerged as two possible answers to the problem. At about that time, "Wolves and Humans," an interpretive exhibit created by the Science Museum of Minnesota, was traveling around the country. Seeing it converted thousands of people to reintroduction. Wolf advocates asked Mott to view the display when it stopped off at Yellowstone. The scene, as recalled by Fischer, went like this:

They brought Mott to a small log cabin on the shore of Yellowstone Lake and launched into a presentation on elk, wolves, and grizzly bears and the controversy that managing these species generated. The discussion had scarcely begun when Mott became animated. He jumped out of his seat, brimming with enthusiasm. Forget the charts and graphs. Mott grasped the merits of the park's bear and elk policies and wolf restoration instantly, and he quickly offered his solution to the controversy. The problem wasn't biology, he said, but people. The Park Service simply wasn't getting its message across to the public. He proposed a massive public education campaign to make people understand, for example, why wolves belong in Yellowstone Park.

Even more amazing than Mott's zeal was his quick follow-up. Within a week, he had dispatched a team of public education specialists to Yellowstone from the Park Service's Harpers

Ferry Center in West Virginia. And within months, several surveys of the public were taken by various pro-wolf organizations, turning up majorities of those questioned in favor of restoration. Mott also suggested another strategy which Fischer later successfully implemented. "It seemed to come off the top of his head, but it was the most foresighted piece of wolf wisdom anyone's ever given me," Fischer recounted. "He said, 'The single most important action conservation groups could take...would be to develop a fund to compensate ranchers for any livestock losses caused by wolves.' It was simple economics that caused ranchers to fear wolves, Mott explained. Pay them for their livestock, and the controversy would subside."

By the summer of 1987, the Fish and Wildlife Service had approved a restoration plan. Now the ball was in the Park Service's court. Mott advocated an environmental impact statement as the next step. But the Wyoming congressional delegation wanted no part of the plan. Mott argued it was his responsibility as Park Service director to support restoration of native species. He got nowhere. Finally, he reluctantly agreed with Assistant Interior Secretary Bill Horn and Fish and Wildlife Service Director Frank Dunkle to take no action without the congressional delegation's consent.

Yet, while "Mott could be brought to heel," as Hank Fischer wrote, "he couldn't be muzzled." Turning to his old friend, the press, Mott gave an extensive interview to the *Star-Tribune* in Casper, Wyoming. "I think many people have been sold on the idea that the wolf is a bad animal...that it's going to kill all the livestock," he said. "In my mind, [wolves] would add a great deal to the natural values of Yellowstone and balance the ecosystem. The wolf...is not only a marvelous animal, but it is a symbol of the West. For people to be able to hear a wolf howl is going to be a very exciting experience."

The people weren't hearing a wolf call yet, but they did hear a howl of outrage from a more familiar source. In an angry letter to Interior Secretary Hodel, Wyoming Representative Richard "Dick" Cheney said he was as committed to preventing wolf reintroduction as Mott was to fostering it. "If he wants to fight, I'm ready," he huffed. The next day, an obviously chastised Mott reiterated that wolf restoration was "on hold" until — and unless — the Wyoming delegation approved it. He apologized if he'd given any other impression.

Chances of restoration looked bleak that summer until Representative Wayne Owens of Utah, a congressional newcomer and a member of the House Interior Committee, decided to buck his more senior colleagues and introduce legislation directing Interior to reintroduce wolves to the park within the next three years. "Yellowstone Park does not belong to Wyoming," he said by way of explanation. "It belongs to all of us."

Several years of intense skirmishing followed with ranchers, the Wyoming and Montana congressional delegations, and top-ranking Interior officials ranged against the National Wildlife Federation, the Wolf Fund, Fischer's Defenders of Wildlife, Mott and rising public opinion. Now that people were interested, Mott used those avenues open to him to further the public's education. In one instance, he made wolf restoration the subject of his monthly Director's Report as printed in the April, 1988 issue of the *Courier*. And he pulled no punches in doing so.

"As some of you may have heard," he wrote in "Bringing Back the Wolf," "I have been rather aggressively advocating the restoration of the gray wolf into Yellowstone National Park. My position has not only generated a bit of coverage in the press, it also has provoked strong reactions from farmers and ranchers who believe wolves will prey on livestock outside park boundaries as well as from others who see wolves as potentially dangerous threats to park visitors. While I do not want to minimize these concerns, I believe my decision to recommend that the National Park Service sponsor a wolf restoration program in Yellowstone is the right one to make. I am committed to working with the local communities, the congressional delegation, and other interested parties to develop a viable program that is acceptable." He went on to explain how wolves had been eradicated earlier in the century, leaving an empty niche that had not been refilled. He continued:

"There are those that recommend we fill the void left by the wolf with hunters. True, hunters could serve the role of predator, and help achieve an ecological balance of sorts by reducing the ungulate [hoofed animals like elk and bison] population, but I don't believe introducing hunters...is an acceptable or natural replacement for the wolf. Too often, people forget that the National Park Service's mission is to maintain the integrity of natural ecosystems, or those parts of ecosystems that are within the parks...I see restoring the wolf in Yellowstone as helping to set things right there — in effect giving the park back some ecological balance."

The statement suggested that a payment plan could compensate for any sheep or cattle losses, that judicious use of radio collars could enable scientists to monitor the wolves' movements, that carcasses left behind by wolves could provide welcomed sources of meat for endangered grizzlies and that as a last resort, he would "be willing to consider supporting departmental regulations under the Endangered Species Act that would allow [farmers and ranchers] to shoot wolves on their property that are posing a threat to their livestock."

In the next three paragraphs Mott spoke out not for political expediency or personal gain but for what he thought was right. His words revealed an unimpeachable integrity and a grasp of the big picture:

"Ultimately, the question that keeps coming to my mind is: why not bring the wolf back to Yellowstone? I realize that my aggressive stance on this issue has created some controversy, but I don't take a stand on any issue, based on the kind of reactions I expect to receive. Actually, when considering my position on wolf restoration, I find myself faced, time and again, with no other possible alternative. What other position could I take as director of the National Park Service?

"I ask this not in defense of my decision, but as an acknowledgment of my role — our role — as stewards of the national park system. If we don't accept this responsibility as stewards of the Yellowstone ecosystem, who else will? Furthermore, if we fail to accept the challenge at Yellowstone, what does this say about our ability to be stewards of this system into the next century? It's a big responsibility, one too important to abdicate and one that we must continue to carry out, not only with flexibility — when flexibility is needed — but also with strong commitment and determination in keeping with the mission of the Service.

"I feel that wolf restoration is just such an issue. It is one that I am approaching with personal commitment — to the wolf, to the Yellowstone ecosystem, and, ultimately, to the protection of resource values inherent in the national parks throughout the system."

THE GRAND CONCLAVE

In the midst of these side battles, Mott tried to keep his eye on the main purpose of his being in Washington: to improve the functioning of the National Park Service. To that end, he called a conference for all 341 park unit superintendents and their families for June 1-4, 1988, at Grand Teton National Park, Wyoming.

At Mott's direction, Yellowstone Superintendent Robert Barbee organized the conference with a $600,000 budget and the theme, "Planning for the 21st Century." The purpose of the gathering was "To share and discuss ideas face to face," Mott said in the June, 1988 issue of the *Courier*. "Such opportunities come along all too seldom: there is no excuse for not taking full advantage of them." Other, if undeclared, purposes were to boost morale among the superintendents and to counteract critics on both the right and the left.

The rare gathering attracted heavy coverage from the media. At his first opportunity, therefore, the Director told the superintendents to speak out in defense of park values. "We cannot expect someone else to do that for us," he said. "We must aggressively, with facts, present our case and defend our mission. We must take the leadership unhesitatingly and with vigor." Accordingly, superintendents of some of the major parks told the press how resource management had improved during the twelve years since the last general superintendents' conference: Upgrades such as demolition of two dams in Rocky Mountain National Park, removal of wild burros at Grand Canyon to allow bighorn sheep to rebound, and signs of increasing numbers of grizzlies at Yellowstone. "Biologically, we're in better shape than seventy-five years ago," said Barbee of Yellowstone. And Mott praised the service for its realization that "we can no longer manage the national parks as islands without concern for what happens outside their boundaries," its professionalization of interpretive programs, and its increased emphasis on research. Still, major threats to "the resource" continued, including overcrowding at the most popular sites and continuing pressure from interest groups to allow commercial development and exploitation of natural resources within and around park boundaries.

Some Park Service personnel and invited environmentalists believed threats from within the administration were just as serious. With a bevy of reporters on hand, here was their chance to say it. The National Parks and Conservation Association charged, for example, that Interior Secretary Hodel had proposed fundamental changes in park policy "over the strenuous objections of park professionals." Rep. Bruce Vento, Democrat from Minnesota and chairman of the House Parks and Public Lands Subcommittee, was even more blunt. "There have been repeated instances where the director has had the rug pulled out from under him in presenting issues before Congress," he said. Mott and other high-ranking park managers, Vento said, had "all too often been limited and disciplined by those in the Interior Department who share different political views with respect to the use of the resources and what the purpose of the parks should be. The national parks are the crown jewels of this nation," he declared. "We can't stand by as others would turn them into rhinestones." But the words of retired National Park Service Director George Hartzog Jr., an honored guest at the conference, cut closest to the quick.

Revered by many Park Service veterans, Hartzog had served under Presidents Johnson and Nixon from 1964 until 1973. When
he weighed in, the gravity of his viewpoint escaped no one.

"I believe Mott has been countermanded, overruled, and
politically frustrated by the administration," he said. "Mott is a
legend in his own time among park people around the country. Everybody acknowledges his prowess. On balance, I think
the Reagan administration is going to be faulted as having the
most obscene environmental record in history."

THE CALL OF THE REALLY WILD

Mott kept his mischievous sense of humor through those
trying times. It bubbled to the surface far more often than, for
example, any frustration he may have felt or even his deeply-
held articles of faith. One of those moments came as he approached the podium to address the convention's closing ban-
quet. Among those in the audience was Assistant Interior
Secretary Horn.

Suddenly, the lights went out. Then, from little, battery-
powered wolf-head buttons pinned to almost every lapel in
the audience, tiny, red, wolves' eyes began to blink on and off
in the darkness. As if on cue out came a long, drawn-out
"OOOOOOOOO!" —500 voices raised in their best imitation
of a primeval howl. When the lights went back on, everybody
looked at the legends on each other's pins which read: "Bring
Back the Wolf. The 'Eyes' Have it!" and laughed and applauded
uproariously.

Even Horn, who along with Hodel, had doubts about the
timing and validity of the wolf restoration proposal, got a good
laugh out of the stunt. Then Mott owned up to authoring the
prank. Some months earlier, the idea had occurred to him to
have the button designed and produced as part of the public
education campaign about the wolf. In fact, he'd mentioned
the pin in the Director's Column in the June issue of the
Courier distributed at this very conference. "Though some may

see the pin as a gimmick," he had written in the column, "I think it will be useful in building public support. As a highly condensed, eye-catching form of communication, it conveys to the viewer exactly what we are trying to do — encourage people to learn the facts about the wolf." The column was titled, "Thinking Creatively, Acting Boldly." Mott was never one to advocate a course of action he wouldn't take himself.

Eventually, when Fish and Wildlife called public hearings in Cheyenne, Wyoming; Helena, Montana; Boise, Idaho; Salt Lake City, Utah; Seattle, Washington, and Washington, D.C., public opinion in favor of wolf reintroduction greatly outweighed public opinion against. In 1993, when the Fish and Wildlife Service completed the environmental impact statement Mott had advocated back in 1987, environmentalists saw the light at the end of the tunnel. The EIS suggested introducing wolves to Yellowstone as an experimental population and then seeing what happened. Wyoming Senators Malcolm Wallop and Alan Simpson grudgingly accepted the EIS. "If we're going to have it shoved down our throats," Simpson said, "it should be done as an experimental population so we have the proper management flexibility."

The range war now entered its last battle. Some of the more hard-line environmental groups attacked the plan as too weak while the Montana Farm Bureau said it was too strong. With the help of the Mountain States Legal Foundation — a law firm founded by former Interior Secretary James Watt — the bureau took the plan to court. In the federal courtroom of U.S. District Court Judge William Downes in Cheyenne, the Fish and Wildlife Service — now in favor of reintroduction — argued that little livestock was being lost to predation and that which *was* being lost was being paid for by the Wolf Compensation Fund. On January 4, 1995, Judge Downes denied the Farm Bureau's request for an injunction to postpone reintroduction. Ten days later, the Fish and Wildlife Service released four wolves into the edge of the Frank Church-River of No Return Wilderness. Restoration was under way at last.

Many true believers, both inside and outside the government, had worked together to make reintroduction happen. All deserved a place in the hall of heroes. But Hank Fischer of the Defenders of Wildlife thought Mott had done the most of any government official to educate the public to the wisdom behind the dream. He "ultimately did more to advance Yellowstone Park wolf restoration," Fischer wrote, "than any other agency leader before or since."

THE YELLOWSTONE FIRES

On June 4, 1988, as the Grand Teton convocation wrapped up, most attendees felt spiritually renewed. "This week has been almost like a religious retreat," said Bob Heyder, superintendent at Mesa Verde National Park in Colorado. "I'm going away refreshed and inspired." Mott returned to Washington, D.C., mission accomplished. The peaceful feeling lay like a blissful blanket over park employees at nearby Yellowstone, too. Little did they know that Mother Nature was concocting a devilish convergence of climatic conditions. A terrible natural disaster was brewing in the clear, "big sky" air. One of the most destructive firestorms of the 20th century was about to explode into being.

The 11.7 million-acre Greater Yellowstone Area is composed of parts of Beaverhead, Gallatin, Custer, Shoshone, Bridger-Teton, and Targhee National Forests; all of Grand Teton and Yellowstone national parks; and some state and privately owned land. The area, located where sections of the boundaries of Montana, Idaho and Wyoming meet, holds a special place in America's heart. In 1872, Yellowstone, a square-shaped reservation occupying the northwest corner of Wyoming, was designated the nation's and the world's first national park. Yellowstone's spouting geysers and bubbling hot sulfur springs vent titanic volcanic forces lurking underground. Its crystalline lakes, roaring cascades, high mountain meadows, and Yellowstone River-hewn canyons attest to the power of water and ice to shape the landscape. Millions of visitors from all over the world go there every year to experience these natural phenomena. Just as spectacular is a nearby section of the Grand Teton Mountain range. Linked to Yellowstone to the north by the eighty two-mile John D. Rockefeller, Jr., Memorial Parkway, the Grand Tetons heave a mile straight up from the flat plains below. This area, too, was preserved when the national park of the same name was created in 1929. Within the two national parks, well over ninety percent of the land is classified as "Natural Zone," meaning that "conservation of natural resources and processes is emphasized." Less attention is paid to the national forests surrounding the two parks, parts of which are classified for "multiple use," including commercial logging. Nearly all of the Greater Yellowstone Area lies at elevations of 6,000 feet above sea level or more. Although famous for its rugged mountains, including the Grand Teton, Absaroka and Gallatin ranges, the flatter terrain of the Yellowstone Plateau comprises the majority of the area and nearly all of Yellowstone National Park. Most of the 1988 fires burned across that plateau.

It had been at least three hundred years since a truly major forest fire had swept through the area, so that by 1988 the vast majority of the douglas fir and lodgepole pine forests dominating the area consisted of trees from one-hundred to three-hundred years old sheltering thick stands of underbrush below. Other dominant plant life in the park included sagebrush, grasslands, alpine tundra, spruce, and whitebark pine. Fire had been a naturally occurring player in the regional ecosystem since the retreat of the glaciers at the end of the last ice age twelve thousand years earlier. Before the advent of humans on this landscape, lightning provided the primary source of ignition. Flames crept across Greater Yellowstone Area grassland, shrub and savanna areas every twenty to one hundred years. But major conflagrations raked through the forests less frequently, every two hundred to four hundred years. The last one as large as the 1988 disaster had occurred, as near as scientists could tell, in the early 1700s. The arrival of European Americans increased the frequency of human-caused blazes, so suppression of flames, whatever their origin, became from 1886 to 1972 a central feature of military, Forest Service and National Park Service policy. After 1972, however, and in recognition of the natural role that fire played in the ecosystem, Park Service policy changed to give Park Service personnel discretion over naturally caused fires. They could take their course as long as they posed no threat to human lives or private property or until Park Service personnel decided to intervene.

What was not under control, however, was the weather. Rainfall in late June of 1988 and throughout July and August, normally about two inches per month, abruptly stopped. No rain fell from June 15 to the middle of September. The summer was the driest in the park's recorded history. Humidity fell to record lows of six percent, an extraordinarily low moisture content (kiln-dried lumber has twelve to fourteen percent). A series of six unusually dry cold fronts crossed the Greater Yellowstone Area, bringing with them winds gusting from forty to sixty miles per hour. This combination — no rainfall, extremely low humidity and unusually high winds — spelled danger.

Early in June, some twenty lightning-caused fires had inaugurated the 1988 fire season in Yellowstone. By the end of June, eleven had died out without human intervention. The other nine persisted and were allowed to burn, according to Park Service policy. Meanwhile, four blazes were burning in Forest Service land adjacent to the park. Under Forest Service policy, firefighters were brought in to put the flames out. But the high winds foiled those efforts and pushed the fires across Forest Service boundaries where, with plenty of tinder-dry fuel to kindle, they converged with those already burning in the park. In the twelve-day period between July 5 and July 17, fifteen more fires started in the Greater Yellowstone Area, thirteen by lightning strikes unaccompanied by rain. Eating into the dry forests, the fires began to combine into tremendous conflagrations. As they were empowered to do, Yellowstone Superintendent Robert "Bob" Barbee and his staff made decisions. After July 15, any new lightning-caused fires were fought unless adjacent to existing fires. After July 21, all existing fires were fought. On July 24, three thousand people were evacuated from Grant's Village, a camping facility on the shores of Yellowstone Lake. Interior Secretary Hodel flew out to Yellowstone on July 27 to reaffirm the decision to fight all current and new fires. No more "let it burn" policy, he assured the public through the assembled media.

But the expanded attempt to fight all the fires proved ineffective. Despite the suppression efforts, five of the largest eight blazes spread into Yellowstone from forest service land and eventually accounted for over half the total burn in the Greater Yellowstone Area. During that period, Barbee briefly closed most of the park to tourists. Residents of Silver Gate and Cooke City, two towns in Montana just outside the park's northern border, were temporarily evacuated. Altogether, more than fifty fires, most caused by lightning strikes, burned some 1.3 million acres in a patchwork across the Greater Yellowstone Area. Rain and snow beginning late in September finally put out the last smoldering embers by the end of November.

Nine thousand-five hundred men and women had battled the fires. One man had been killed in October by a flaming snag falling from a tree in Forest Service land. Twenty-four buildings had been lost, but Yellowstone's most famous tourist facilities had survived. Carcasses of a few large mammals were found, but the vast majority of the big animals threatened by the flames had simply walked away to areas that were not ablaze. And new growth was already inching up from the scorched forest floor.

COVERAGE LACKED DEPTH

Had the fires been in territories more remote than the Greater Yellowstone Area they would have merited only cursory mentions in the mass media. After all, during that same summer, a total of 30,000 firefighters fought a total of 70,000 that burned more than five million acres in seventeen states. But Yellowstone's accessibility, its fame, and perhaps even the recent coverage of the Director's fabulously successful conclave at nearby Grand Teton made the park a familiar place to media outlets nationwide. As Ohio State journalism professor Conrad Smith later wrote in one of several evaluations of media coverage, the fires at Yellowstone got coverage almost from the beginning and became a top national news story after the July 24 evacuation. Then, on August 20, quickly dubbed "Black Saturday," the flames, which had appeared to be slowly subsiding, suddenly flared completely out of control. They burned two hundred-fifty square miles of national park and national forest lands in one day. News crews, some of whom had left the park, returned in force. Some outlets did a thorough and objective job of putting the disaster in a wider scientific context. But others simply sought out the most dramatically burning sites. They got reaction shots from frightened tourists or angry merchants but gave less time and space to the more complicated responses available from park officials and scientists. On August 29, more than a month after Hodel visited, Mott flew out to Yellowstone. Until then, he had backed staff management of the fires from his Washington office. Once he got there, his sanguine explanation of the intrinsic ecological value of intense heat for ridgepole pines and other flora and fauna infuriated area business people who thought their tourist dollars were going up in smoke.

Coverage reached a crescendo on September 5, when *Time's* headline quoted a frustrated firefighter saying, "We Could Have Stopped This," while *Newsweek* announced: "Yellowstone: Up in Smoke." Even though the stories under both headlines were reasonably balanced, the initial impression was one, as Ohio State's Smith said later, of "brave firefighters, endangered national icons and bumbling land managers." On September 11, the *Billings Gazette* in Billings, Montana, demanded that Hodel, Mott and Barbee all be dismissed. Wyoming senators Alan Simpson and Malcolm Wallop, ever mindful of their unhappy constituents and long since tired of sparring with the stubborn Mott over wolves and other issues, called for the Director's resignation in particular.

Speaking for President Reagan, Press Secretary Marlin Fitzwater flatly rejected those calls. "The problem here," said Fitzwater, "was that this fire was simply bigger and more difficult to deal with than anyone had ever experienced before and therefore [they] were not prepared for it." Further, Fitzwater noted, "We have some of those fires where the fireball is jumping 200-foot firebreaks. And there just doesn't seem to be any way to stop it under those conditions, no matter how many people you can put on the line." Also appearing unruffled by the attacks, Mott forthrightly declared his intention not to resign. Then he seized the opportunity to turn the news coverage to his advantage: "If we had more sympathetic feelings toward the parks," he told the *New York Times*, "a lot more could be done. The public supports a lot more vigorous land acquisition than we have had."

The issue, he proceeded to enlighten *Times* reporter Philip Shabecoff, was one of values. "We think in long term objectives that have to do with intrinsic values while others think in terms of dollars. For example, if you are trout fishing and you have to buy a rod and reel and lures, you know [how] much it will cost you. But how do you demonstrate the beauty and quality of the environment in which you do your fishing?"

Interior Secretary Hodel went on record as fully supporting Park Service fire-fighting policies. He claimed that previous reports of conflict between Mott and the Interior Department, revisited by the media in connection with their coverage of the fires, had been exaggerated. In keeping with his theory that the environmentalist community assumed that a *bona fide* ecologist like Mott could not possibly get along in the Reagan camp, he took a poke at his rivals. "There are people who rightly respect Bill Mott, as I do, as one of the most knowledge-able and expert park persons in this country," he said. "But it galls some people that he has done so well and been able to survive in this Administration."

THE SECOND WAVE

After awhile, the alarmed coverage cooled down. Wrote the *Los Angeles Times* in a September 13 editorial: "The unwar-ranted criticism of the Park Service, the U.S. Forest Service and environmental experts has reached a level of misinformed hysteria that is racing out of control as the fires have done." And on September 14, the *Christian Science Monitor* noted that "costly forest fires can still carry benefits." As the weeks went by, the discussion became even more balanced. Myriad re-ports appeared in scientific journals, dissecting the effects of the blazes on the flora, fauna, water, and soil of the park. Most concluded that those effects, while fearsome to humans, were in fact neither permanent nor particularly damaging to Nature. In more general-interest publications, commentators asked how Americans wanted to define their national parks, as wild places where Nature should be allowed to take its course, as parks wholly managed by humans, or as something in be-tween?

While environmentalists, public policy makers, elected offi-cials and the public debated that question, Mott chipped in with his usual directness. "Although the media generated a great deal of public sympathy and interest toward Yellowstone," he wrote in the November, 1988 *Courier*, "it also has provided a great deal of misinformation, or maybe I should character-ize it more correctly as a lack of information, about what took place there. Yellowstone is *not* a charred wasteland; the fire did burn through areas totaling more than one million acres. But fire doesn't burn evenly, so much of the vegetation within those areas was not touched. We need to make sure the public knows that. We want to encourage people to visit the park, for it now offers the opportunity to see nature at work, to see first-hand the regeneration process." However, to allow that process to occur, he wrote, would "take a lot of commitment and resources and patience to let Yellowstone do what it needs to do *at its own pace* and as it is naturally best."

The people took Mott at his word. By the summer of 1989, they were flocking to Yellowstone in greater numbers than ever. Most were surprised that while there was ample evidence of the fires, the park didn't look as bad as they had expected. The merchants, some of whom had demanded Mott's head a year before, were now ecstatic. "I have a pretty sophisticated clientele from an ecological point of view," said Richard Parks, owner of Parks' Fly Shop in Gardiner, Montana. "They know there's more to this [fire] story than what they saw on the television news, so they'll be back." And at Grant Village, where the evacuation of the three-thousand visitors had kicked off the intensive media coverage the previous summer, Superintendent Barbee's irrepressible staff had put up a $120,000 exhibit explaining fire ecology — complete with video footage of the 1988 blazes. The process of interpretation and education continued.

When George Bush won the November, 1988 presidential election, Mott was asked by San Francisco columnist Harold Gilliam if he were game for another four years. "If I'm asked," he replied, "I'd like to stay a while." Gilliam tried to help make that happen by summing up in a few broad strokes his old friend's achievements. Mott, he said, had reversed the demoralization of the National Park Service that had set in under James Watt, had started research programs, had updated management policies and had focused attention on the impact of development adjacent to the parks. But Mott wasn't asked. Bush replaced Interior Secretary Hodel with former New Mexico Representative Manuel Lujan and Lujan named James Ridenour as National Park Service director. On March 27, 1989, Mott announced his resignation, effective April 15. After nearly four years in Washington, it was time to take stock of what he had accomplished.

As the conflicts over Park Service philosophy, policy, and purpose, raged, Mott had been quietly signing off on new National Park system sites. Besides the six units added from late 1985 through 1987, eleven more units were added by the end of 1988. This brought to seventeen the total number of new sites added to the system during Mott's tenure. Some were conceived and acquired during that four-year period while others had been designated in previous years but not authorized until then. Still, it was an amazing feat, given the circumstances. In an era of reduced park budgets, the variety of public-public and public-private partnerships the Park Service utilized to preserve and protect important natural and historic sites spoke once again to Mott's role in fostering creative management models. Examples included The City of Rocks National Reserve, administered cooperatively by the Park Service and the Idaho Department of Parks and Recreation, and Poverty Point National Monument, cooperatively administered with the state of Louisiana.

OTHER ACCOMPLISHMENTS

Albright Fund. The most unusual program started by Mott during his years as National Park Service director was the Horace M. Albright Employee Development Fund (now the Horace M. Albright-Conrad L. Wirth Employee Development Fund). Interest from the fund's endowment was earmarked for a paid sabbatical-leave program. The program would allow Park Service employees to apply for time off to renew individual commitments, advance their education, acquire additional skills, develop new ideas useful to the service, or undertake related studies. Nothing like it had ever been proposed for a federal government agency. At first, the notion was ridiculed by those within the service as an impossible innovation and just another one of Mott's strange ideas. But after he personally raised the initial $1 million to endow the fund from private donors Laurance Rockefeller and the *Reader's Digest*, employees soon warmed to the imaginative concept.

The Albright Fund's fiscal affairs are managed by the National Park Foundation, the private, nonprofit support organization that operates similarly to park foundations in individual states. Its program is administered by the Park Service. Since its inception, thousands of Park Service employees have taken sabbaticals, returning renewed and refreshed to serve the Park Service even better than before.

Reconstruction of Andersonville Stockade. Andersonville National Historic Site in southwest Georgia preserves the largest of several military prison camps established during the Civil War. During its 14-month existence, more than forty-five thousand Union captives were confined behind its tall pine log stockade under adverse conditions. More than twelve thousand-nine hundred died of disease, malnutrition, or exposure. By the time Mott visited Andersonville in 1985, accompanied by Baker, now National Park Service southeast regional director, the stockade — originally built by slaves — had long since rotted away. Mott told Baker he had trouble picturing the scale and appearance of the barrier that kept prisoners from escaping. "Why not reconstruct part of the stockade wall?" he suggested.

Baker and Andersonville superintendent John Tucker favored the idea. Archeological research and planning were authorized. The authentically reconstructed stockade added "a new, somber reality to the tragic story" of Andersonville, wrote Paul Winegar in the October 1989 *Courier*. Coupled with the park's other programs and features, Winegar said, the eerie stockade wall "has turned what used to be a mildly interesting park into a visitor experience that's well worth the 30-mile detour off Interstate 75."

Protecting Chickamauga. The National Park Service had waffled for years over a proposal by the State of Georgia to widen a road through Chickamauga and Chattanooga National Military Park from two to four lanes. When Mott became National Park Service Director, he vetoed the proposal on the spot in favor of the park superintendent's counterproposal to reroute the four-lane section around the park entirely. "It was a courageous decision," said Park Service Historian Ed Bearss. "Bill realized that the national significance of the park overrode local interests." Bearss feared Congress would overrule a solution that cost three times as much ($36 million to reroute versus $12 million to widen the existing road). But Congress agreed with Mott and the section of the road was rerouted. Mott had made a decision, Bearss said, "that nobody else in the historical program had ever had the nerve to make."

Shielding Manassas. Mott helped protect from visual degradation the Manassas National Battlefield Park in Virginia, site of two major Civil War battles (also known as the Battles of Bull Run), by enabling the Park Service to acquire private land to head off a large-scale housing and commercial development next to the battlefield.

Statue of Liberty and Ellis Island. When no federal funds were made available, Mott contributed inspired leadership to a campaign run by the private, nonprofit Statue of Liberty/Ellis Island Foundation, to raise the first $200 million to $300 million dollars in private donations toward restoration of the Statue of Liberty in honor of its one-hundredth anniversary in 1986. Additional donations went toward restoration of nearby Ellis Island, the facility where fifteen million immigrants were processed on their way into the United States.

"Director Mott brought in the sense that it was OK to do major fundraising for the park system," recalled Edie Shean-

Hammond, assistant regional director of communications for the northeast region of the National Park Service. "The word 'partnership' became part of the everyday language of the Park Service during his tenure." Before Mott, "many Park Service people thought the service was 'above' the need to market," she said. "Now, our mission statement stresses going beyond the boundaries, outside the box, as it were, to get out, make friends and create partnerships. Mott's leadership was very important in getting us to think that way."

National Park Foundation. Just before he left Washington, Mott encouraged the appointment of Alan A. Rubin, former president of the foundation that ran the National Park Service's Wolf Trap Farm Park for the Performing Arts in Northern Virginia, as director of the Washington, D.C.-based National Park Foundation. Created in the 1930s essentially as a nonprofit holding company for donations of land, historical and cultural artifacts, buildings and money to the Park Service, the foundation, unlike its counterparts on the state level, had fallen on hard times. "When I got there in 1989 there was one employee," Rubin remembered. Over the next eight years, he increased the foundation's assets by five times their previous worth and spearheaded the campaign to raise $1 million to match the Rockefeller endowment of the Albright Fund. "During the next several years, I got to know Bill pretty well," Rubin said. "He had twelve ideas a day for what we should do at the foundation. If eleven of them didn't work, the twelfth one did. He was one of the most knowledgeable people in our lifetime about how to build park systems."

FAREWELL TO WASHINGTON

Environmentalists, some of whom hadn't been so sure of Mott when he was appointed nearly four years earlier, were now sorry to see him go. He was, said Robert Cahn, former member of the White House Council on Environmental Quality, "the hardest working park director I've ever seen." He "stood up for the values of the National Park System, and he was open and accessible" to the concerns of the public, said Sally Kabisch, Sierra Club Western regional spokeswoman. He "worked well with the relevant congressional committees to accomplish things the administration opposed but he favored," added Dr. Edgar Wayburn, Sierra Club Vice President for National Parks and Protected Areas.

Park Service employees also made it clear they would miss him, perhaps none more eloquently than John Reynolds, manager of the system's Denver Service Center. "You were a great director," wrote Reynolds on April 25, 1989 on the front page of a copy of the 1988 annual report. "You had vision, caring and guts. You were able to see what the National Park System can be to Americans, and to the world. You woke us up, challenged us, made us 'Mott's army'...and you left us with renewed vigor to dedicate ourselves to the protection of the parks, to helping people enjoy them, to using them as places of education, and to doing all of that with quality and excitement. It has been an honor to work with you. Also, all of the people at the Denver Service Center are similarly honored to have worked for you, and are deeply appreciative of the support you have given us. I hope our paths continue to cross. You were a great Director...you are a great human being."

Some aspects of Mott's 12-Point Plan had moved toward realization, particularly those points having to do with expansion of the interpretive side of the Park Service, better communication of Park Service values to the public and greater participation by the public in protecting those values. The goals of creating tallgrass prairie and wild river national parks had not. Still, "The fact that the Park Service didn't deteriorate more than it did and that [Mott] stayed in office for four years," Wayburn said, was "a tribute to his ability." It was also a tribute to Mott's determination first to stop and then to reverse the anti-parks direction that had begun during previous years. All the wisdom he had gathered over a nearly sixty-year career went into that valiant campaign. And as he packed up his belongings and mementos, Mott knew that he had served his country as steadfastly and selflessly as possible.

Though he was returning home, however, once again it was not to retire. He had accepted an appointment as special assistant to the regional director, western region, National Park Service. His assignment was to help plan the conversion of the San Francisco Presidio, the historic Army base overlooking the Golden Gate Bridge, into one of the nation's newest national parks. At age seventy-nine, he looked forward to yet more challenges.

1955 - William Penn Mott, Jr., Superintendent, Oakland Park Dept.
Oakland Park Department photo

Chapter 8
The Six Mott Leadership Principle

*"In matters of style, swim with the current.
In matters of principle, stand like a rock."*

THOMAS JEFFERSON

Throughout his long and productive career, William Penn Mott Jr. lived by an enduring set of leadership principles. What were they? How did they guide his mind and heart as he, in turn, guided large organizations? If one in a position of organizational leadership today is looking for new ways of thinking about leadership, how can one adapt Mott's principles to one's own life and work?

What constitutes successful leadership is the topic of scores of books and hundreds of talks each year. The ability to lead the way toward constructive goals is, after all, an important characteristic in a democratic society where people work together of their own free will.

William Penn Mott, Jr. never wrote a book, although a draft he started in the 1970s survives today as a series of annotated talks. But as a nationally and internationally renowned parks and recreation pioneer, he did function as an informal consultant, speaking on the topic of leadership to a wide variety of audiences. His subject matter ranged from the practical — how to get the most out of oneself, one's employees, and one's organization — to the visionary — the need to plan far ahead into the 21st century to save the environment. From those teachings, we have synthesized six basic principles. These principles are as important for today and tomorrow as when he first formulated them.

THE SIX MOTT LEADERSHIP PRINCIPLES

Principle No. 1. Be Visionary. Guide Today's Decisions by Tomorrow's Reality.

As his colleagues noted with amazement, Mott was always thinking ahead. "We not only must live with our day-to-day decisions," he said, "but we must be responsible for long-range decisions, the results of which may not show up for several hundred years."

Mott envisioned conditions that will prevail in the new millennium. "As we move from the 20th century — a century that may be known as the 'Century of Wars,' into the 21st century that may be known as the 'Century of the Environment,' we face a new kind of war — preserving Planet Earth," he said. "That war will be a war we must win if humans are to be living on this earth to celebrate the beginning of the 22nd century." There were at least six fields of battle raging in this war, he continued: acid rain, the piercing of the ozone layer, the greenhouse effect, habitat destruction, loss of biological diversity and the international illegal trade in plants, animals, and their products. To the question of how to bring these environmental dangers under control by the year 2020 when "it is predicted that 90 percent of the population of the United States will be living in twelve major metropolitan centers," Mott answered:

- Urban populations must be educated to appreciate and take responsibility for the natural and cultural assets of the nation.
- Research must be enhanced in order to find solutions to environmental problems.

- Laws protecting wildlife must be strengthened and strictly enforced.
- Human-created ingredients must be substituted for endangered plant and animal species traditionally used in folk medicines.

"Aldo Leopold put it very well," Mott added, "when he said, 'We abuse the land because we regard it as a commodity that belongs to us. When we see the land as a community to which we belong, we may begin to use it with love and respect.'"

Principle No. 2. Think Creatively: Dare to Try New and Controversial Ideas.

Not only did Mott think ahead, he thought creatively about the present and the future. Mott believed not only in his own aptitude for musing "outside the box," but in his employees' abilities as well. "When you start asking questions instead of stopping questions," he told one group of managers, "and when thinking, reading, and communicating take the place of regimentation, directions and 'that's the way we've always done it' attitudes, your department will be energized into action, and positive, creative thinking will take place, ideas will flow, things will happen and the community's consciousness will rally to your support in a most rewarding way."

Mott laid out 12 steps for both managers and employees to follow toward that goal:

- Permit free and open discussion of all problems.
- Give department heads equal opportunity to review all plans.
- Encourage the flow of periodicals and books through all departments. READ.
- Provide incentives and opportunities for employees to receive continuing education. THINK.
- Hold regular staff meetings and general meetings of all employees. COMMUNICATE.
- Give due credit for ideas, or if rejected, give reasons why.
- Encourage inquisitiveness.

- Create an atmosphere of Urgency and Action.
- Allow employees freedom of judgment and permit "calculated risk" decisions.
- Make the public's interest your interest.
- Do not base your decisions on private, special, or political interests.
- Review your operations and make sure they're up to date.

Principle No. 3. Be Aggressive: Market and Sell a Quality Product.

As far back as the early 1940s, Mott found that parks and recreation careerists were loath to talk about marketing. "The idea of borrowing the disciplines of marketing from the business world and applying [them] to park management is risky in the minds of many parks people," he noted. "Others resist the idea of selling parks because they associate this concept with the mass marketing of products like soap and cigarettes."

But Mott had a different explanation of marketing. "Properly applied, marketing a park system should relate to the community or the users and their aspirations for a higher quality of life and a better environment" rather than putting emphasis on "the internal needs of the system such as more equipment, higher salaries and so forth. The successful [marketing] approach is one that springs from the needs, desires and aspirations of the people themselves, rather than from the needs and desires of the organization itself." "Why should park people be timid about adopting the proven techniques of big business?" he asked in 1981. The truth was, parks and recreation *were* big business. Some $5 billion had been spent on outdoor recreation in 1976 alone.

Parks and recreation departments, like other big businesses, could no longer operate as they had in the past. Since World War II, dramatic social changes had altered personal values, individual expectations, institutional structures, and the national economy. Among the forces bringing about those changes, Mott noted, were the civil rights movement, the war in Vietnam, the women's movement, increased mobility, technological advances, greater interest in physical fitness, regional population shifts, more single-parent families, higher rates of inflation, altered attitudes toward work, and changes in how people spent their discretionary time and income. The latter two factors, especially, were leading the public to become "smart shoppers," Mott said, "looking for quality at the best price." With that understanding, parks and recreation would have to aggressively market a quality product, as their competitors in the leisure industry were doing, or continue losing taxpayer support and market share.

Marketing didn't have to mean huckstering. Rather, Mott said, marketing was "the total impression your department makes on the community through the acts and attitudes of every individual in the organization as well as the organization's pronouncements and actions." Such marketing could be enhanced by several techniques, including the following:

A distinctive logo on all stationery, equipment, uniforms and other items

A trademark color scheme that allows employees to take pride in their equipment and care in their work habits. Identifying an organization gives the community a chance to recognize it. "Being at a party or a meeting and having a perfect stranger compliment your organization or you personally for the outstanding job your organization is doing is the strongest kind of stimulation," Mott said.

Turning an identifiable image into a favorable one by:

Setting up volunteer citizens committees, non-profit fund-raising foundations, and other participatory vehicles. These points of contact also help to establish an organization's reputation as being relevant to the times and needs of the community.

Keeping the public informed through regular news releases, frequent appearances on media outlets, speaking in person to local groups, and publishing annual reports that include financial statements.

Establishing credibility by being honest with yourself, your employees, the media and the community.

Encouraging patronage of your product. This seems obvious, but isn't always. Mott liked to tell the story of being at Grand Canyon one day when he spotted a road-weary car pulling into the parking lot. Out tumbled a family group who went over to the railing at the edge of the vast natural wonder. Arranging the mother and three children in front of the yawning precipice, the father snapped a couple of photos. Then he said, "Okay, kids, let's get back in the car. We've got four more national parks to see this week." Other campers arrive in sophisticated recreational vehicles equipped with all the conveniences of home. Isolated in their RVs, they watch television, play cards or read, causing rangers to wonder why they bothered to come outdoors in the first place.

Should park personnel stand by in despair? Not at all, said Mott. He urged staff members to approach campsites and engage families in friendly conversation. When the employee took the initiative — not unlike a salesperson in an appliance store pleasantly asking, "May I help you?" —it broke the ice, Mott noticed. Soon the families were fishing, hiking, and attending campfires. They tended to stay in the park longer and enjoy its offerings more. This is marketing and its importance made Mott realize that park rangers needed to be trained in people management as well as natural resources husbandry.

Principle No. 4. Share the Credit: Hire Good People and Let Them Do Their Jobs.

Regardless of which level he was operating from, whether local, regional, state, or national, Mott always made clear the importance of the people who worked for him. "I am impressed with the quality of our employees," he would say, and the need to encourage the greatest productivity out of each. In order to do that, he said, "The questions which return over and over again to my mind are these:"

1. Are we making effective use of our field personnel?
2. Do we use their intimate knowledge of the park in which they work in the planning, development, and management of that park?
3. Do we encourage initiative?
4. Do we motivate and praise innovators?
5. Do we provide our field personnel without restrictions the authority they need to carry out their daily work?
6. Do we listen to their problems and take action promptly to solve them?

By way of illustration, he often told a story. "Recently," he said, "I visited a park and was talking to one of the employees. During the conversation, I asked if he had any ideas about developing the park. His immediate response was, 'Since you asked the question, I can tell you. I have been waiting for someone to ask me what I thought.' He then explained with enthusiasm an idea that was based on his day-to-day knowledge: an idea that was practical and worthy of serious consideration. I suspect there are many such ideas germinating in the minds of our employees— ideas that should bubble forth like an artesian well if we provide the proper atmosphere and give the originator recognition for his contribution."

This story, like many of Mott's favorite anecdotes, was probably a composite. But no matter. The important part was the point it made: That "manpower resources are as important in the development of an outstanding park system as are natural resources" — or, in a different setting, as are industrial or commercial resources. "Both must be managed wisely to achieve the best results."

Principle No. 5. Educate Your Constituency then Trust It to Make an Informed Choice.

One of the finest illustrations of this principle in action was the way in which Mott, in his position as National Park Service director, joined others in turning into reality the controversial proposal to reintroduce wolves to their ancestral home in

Yellowstone Park. When they started their campaign, proponents of restoration knew four things for sure:

- That the forces ranged against restoration included such
  powerful figures as the Wyoming and Montana congressional delegations and the top brass at the Interior Department.
- That as dominant as those figures were, the one thing
  that would put pressure on them to change their minds
  was organized public opinion.
- That an uninformed public would probably cling to the
  longstanding and negative myths about the animals and
  come down against reintroduction
- That an informed public, on the other hand, would at
  least make an educated decision.

What pro-wolf proponents didn't know was whether an educated decision would be favorable or not. But they took what
Mott called "a calculated risk:" There was a better chance of
the decision being favorable if the public had the facts. So,
they set about educating their constituency — the American
public — through traveling exhibits, public opinion polls, and
wide-ranging public dialogue. The U.S. Fish and Wildlife Service, the agency that would be ultimately responsible for reintroducing the wolves, distributed 750,000 information documents, held more than 130 public hearings, and collected
160,000 comments and letters; the most, according to *National
Geographic Magazine,* ever received on an endangered species
issue.

**Principle No. 6. Never Give Up: Hold On to Your Dreams Until They
Come True.**

Mott held onto his visions with great faith, but he was no
daydreamer. Instead, he worked tenaciously and persuasively
toward their fruition at every opportunity. Bureaucracies are
slow, "but there are ways to get around that situation," he
said, "and if you have the right combination it works." For

Mott, that combination included planting the seeds among the right people, generating public opinion, and making use of good timing, among other strategies. While waiting for all those factors to gel "it sometimes looks like you're losing," he said. "But in the long run you're actually winning." Among four of his long-held dreams that came true were:

Great Basin National Park. Mott first proposed creating Great Basin in the 1930s when he was a rookie National Park Service landscape architect. Fifty years later, in 1986, Congress signed Great Basin into reality with the personal support of National Park Service Director Mott.

Steamtown National Historic Site. A decade after Mott agreed with Congressman Joseph McDade on refurbishing the historic railroad yard, it looked as though his gamble was paying off. After some 10 years of intensive planning and construction — much of it under the leadership of Steamtown Superintendent John Latcher — early critics, such as Bill Withuhn, curator of Transportation History at the Smithsonian Institution, now think more highly of the site. By 1998, Steamtown was rapidly becoming "one of the best educational centers of industrial history in the United States," said Withuhn. "The Park Service brings to the site its strong suit — interpretation."

Tallgrass Prairie National Preserve. This vision came into reality after Mott returned to Orinda, but not in Oklahoma where he had envisioned it. Instead, the nonprofit National Park Trust, in partnership with the National Park Service, bought the 11,000-acre Z Bar Ranch in the Flint Hills region of Kansas during the early 1990s. There, on November 12, 1996, Congress created the Tallgrass Prairie National Preserve. You can almost hear Mott talking when you read the preserve's Statement of Purpose: "To preserve, protect, and interpret for the public, an example of a tallgrass prairie ecosystem; to preserve and protect the cultural resources found within the preserve; and to interpret for the public, the cultural resources and the social and cultural values represented within the preserve."

Bay Area Hiking Trails. In the 1980s, San Francisco environmental columnist Harold Gilliam recalled a vision Mott had shared with him in the early 1960s. Mott wanted to make it possible, Gilliam wrote, to "walk through natural areas entirely around the Bay, along shorelines, up streams, through canyons, through forests, along ridges with panoramic views. There were then existing trails in several parks, but they stopped at park boundaries; Mott envisioned one linked network joining the parks and greenbelt land throughout the entire region." He "fired the imaginations of conservationists with his dream of a continuous greenbelt in the hills around the bay," Gilliam said.

That was no small vision. Nine counties circle the Bay. But today, two separately located trails are more than halfway finished toward closing the 300 to 400-mile circle around the immense estuary. One, the Bay Area Ridge Trail, follows as closely as possible the lofty ridgelines of the hills that jut up from the basin. The other, the San Francisco Bay Trail, runs closer to the actual shoreline below. As general manager of the East Bay Regional Park District, Mott was able to create the beginnings of a trail system. Since then the regional park district along with hundreds of other government jurisdictions and private landowners as well as voter-approved bond measures have brought the trails closer to fruition.

Mott's sense of public duty toward the preservation and protection of the nation's natural, cultural, and historical resources guided his life's work. His legacy allows present and future citizens of the world to appreciate and enjoy those irreplaceable assets. The principles he forged while carrying out a sacred mandate can be utilized by succeeding generations of leaders in pursuit of their own individual visions. For even as Mott neared the end of his long and productive life, he continued to lead the way, always looking over the next horizon.

Mott Memorial Fund photo

Chapter 9

The Vision Persists,
The Passion Continues

*"Ah, but a man's reach should exceed his grasp,
Or what's a heaven for?"*

ROBERT BROWNING

In late April, 1989, Mott came home to a hero's welcome and prepared to start his new job helping to plan the conversion of the Presidio of San Francisco from a U.S. Army Base to a national park. President Bush sent a telegram saying, "Every American owes you a debt of gratitude for all you have done. Barbara and I send our warm best wishes for every happiness in the years ahead." The Bay Area media also lauded his return. "At a time when most people are happy to retire, Mott is taking on new challenges," said one newspaper. "Every American who cares about his country's national heritage should be glad he's still on the job."

Without skipping a beat, Mott resumed his passionate involvement in parks, open space preservation, and programs for youth. It was as if he had never been away. The Orinda Community Church hosted a dinner in his honor. He delivered a guest sermon at First Presbyterian Church in Oakland. The City of Oakland proclaimed May 10 William Penn Mott,

Jr. Day. He embarked on a challenging fund-raising campaign to finance new construction at the Oakland YMCA's Camp Loma Mar, located in the Santa Cruz Mountains. So successful was the campaign that the new assembly hall built at the camp was named after him. In Sacramento, he spoke at a statewide conference on the Economic Impact of Parks and Recreation, sponsored by the California Park and Recreation Society. The conference was a response to the recommendations coming out of the President's Commission on Americans Outdoors that parks people educate the public on the economic value of open space.

Although Ruth was happy to have Bill's whirlwind of activity focused in California once again, her smile in a photo taken on William Penn Mott, Jr. Day belied her worsening heart trouble. In the snapshot, she gripped her husband's hand as if for support. When she accompanied him to an event, she walked slowly or sat down to wait while he bustled off to take part in the program. Though he had said back in Washington a few months before that he would like to have remained on as National Park Service director under Bush, colleagues knew — and so did he — that he was needed now more than ever at home.

THE RESOLUTE WARRIOR

Within close range of Orinda, however, Mott continued to advocate vigorously for his lifelong causes. One warm September, he lauded one of his own personal heroes at the dedication of Newton B. Drury Peak in Mount San Jacinto State Park and State Wilderness in Southern California. Drury, a pivotal figure in the parks field, had been director of the National Park Service for eleven years, and the California State Division of Beaches and Parks for eight. After mandatory retirement at age 70, he had served as executive secretary, president and chairman of the Save the Redwoods League until his death in December, 1978 at the age of 89. "It is important that [Drury

Peak] is a granite peak because it will be there forever," Mott said, as his audience gazed upward at the towering pinnacle several miles away. Drury was "the right person at the right time," he continued, who through "diplomacy and coopera- tive efforts," was "instrumental in securing Mount San Jacinto as a wilderness area." Drury worked "to assure the wilderness area would be kept relatively free of intrusive cars while acces- sible for hiking and horseback riding," Mott said, and recog- nized that "The intrinsic values of beauty, clean air and clean water...were more valuable than their dollar values."

On other days, he went to meetings of the board of direc- tors of the East Bay Conservation Corps. The Corps, based in Oakland, was a youth work and training organization founded in 1983 that operated in cooperation with, but independently of, the statewide California Conservation Corps. Ever since he had supervised federal Civilian Conservation Corps crews in the 1930s, Mott had believed deeply in the value of such orga- nizations. He had been on the East Bay group's board of di- rectors since its inception, showing up for meetings whenever he was in town. Now that he was home for good, he was able to attend regularly.

Although a "big man in his own right," he was the only member of the board who had ever run his own nonprofit group, remembered Joanne Lennon, founder and executive director of the organization. "He was my biggest supporter and the one I could go to for any kind of advice." Yet, on a board full of important people, he was always a steady, humble person, Lennon said. "He was the best in the world," she con- cluded. "I adored him." So did Executive Assistant Rita Bregman. "He brought a great deal of sage advice," she said. "He was vociferous about the work we were doing and was a great de- fender of that work." Like Lennon, Bregman was struck by Mott's lack of arrogance. "There were not many people with his background and experience who didn't walk around with a giant ego," she said. "He didn't have that. When I called to remind board members of upcoming meetings, he would call back and make me feel as though my job were important, too. He cared about peoples' feelings. He was an extremely fair person, a very good soul. I remember him with great fondness."

The only thing that interrupted Mott's busy schedule that Fall was the Loma Prieta Earthquake of October 17, 1989. At a powerful 7.1 on the Richter Scale, the quake knocked the Bay Area to its knees for several weeks. Along with game three of the "Bay Bridge" World Series between the Oakland Athletics and San Francisco Giants and thousands of other events, an eightieth birthday party the California State Parks Foundation had planned for Mott on October 19 in San Francisco had to be postponed.

On November 17, Mott shared with a Presidio Challenge Conference in San Francisco one of his long time dreams. Back in the 1960s, he had envisioned a "Pacific Basin Center" somewhere on the headlands of the Golden Gate. The center would feature the natural history and cultures of the nations around the ocean, heralding the coming era of the Pacific Rim. "He never had a chance to follow up on the idea," columnist Harold Gilliam had written earlier in 1989, "but if the National Park Service takes over the Presidio, that vision may well be revived." Now, Mott said, the new national park was a perfect place for an international research center. The center "could be a think tank, a second United Nations, focusing on some of the challenges of the environment and in the medical field. We've got people working on global issues around the world and I'd like to get them together." The idea went into the hopper along with all the other proposals for what to include in the new Presidio National Park.

THE UNPRECEDENTED CONVERSION

On a high bluff overlooking the Pacific Ocean, the Presidio was founded in 1776 by Spanish explorer Juan Bautista de Anza. Its purpose was to guard the narrow strait, later named the Golden Gate, leading from the ocean into a large and navigable bay. Later, a little town called Yerba Buena grew up around the fort. By the time California was grabbed away from Mexico by the Americans who made it a state in 1850, the hamlet of Yerba Buena had transformed into the Gold Rush city of San Francisco, on the Bay by the same name.

Three years later, the U.S. Army assumed command of the Presidio. The Army ran the military base until 1988 when it was declared obsolete by the government. In anticipation of that day, San Francisco Congressman Phillip Burton had sponsored important legislation to fold the Presidio's 1,480 acres into the surrounding Golden Gate National Recreation Area. However, the Park Service was put on notice that the Presidio had to become financially self-sustaining by 2013 or face possible sale of the land. The Park Service asked Mott to contribute to the planning part of this conversion.

Mott usually rode the Bay Area Rapid Transit (BART) train from the East Bay to San Francisco and his 14th floor office in the federal building on Golden Gate Avenue. He was, as always, brimming with one-of-a-kind ideas. He pushed his notion of a world-class think tank just as years earlier he had imagined the Dunsmuir House in Oakland fulfilling that role. While the Dunsmuir House had eventually evolved into a popular center for East Bay community events, it had never become an international conference center. The Presidio possessed major assets that gave it greater potential for doing so.

"Bill believed strongly that the Presidio should be a mecca for helping to resolve some of the world's greatest problems," said Don Neubacher, who headed the National Park Service team in charge of developing the master plan. "His thinking was critical in shaping the overall vision for the park and the concepts that help guide the management plan today." Much of that thinking found its way into the final plan's mission statement, eventually published in 1994. "The Presidio," the statement said, "will pioneer a new role for a national park by creating a global center dedicated to addressing the world's most critical environmental, social, and cultural challenges." The new role symbolized the "swords-into-plowshares concept." The transformation was inspired by a "newly emerging definition of protection — one that recognizes that security is no longer based solely on political and military strength, but on stewardship of the world's human and physical resources through global cooperation. Long the guardian of the Golden Gate," the statement continued, "the Presidio now stands ready to house a network of national and international organizations devoted to improving human and natural environments and addressing our common future. The site will be used as a working laboratory to create models of environmental sustainability that can be transferred to communities worldwide. Its inspirational setting," the mission statement concluded, "will provide a respite for reflection and personal renewal."

Neubacher and his wife, Patricia, also a Park Service employee, reached out to Mott, occasionally inviting him to lunch at Greens, a sophisticated vegetarian restaurant on the San Francisco Bay waterfront, or to their Marin County home for backyard cookouts. They discovered that no matter what social setting he was in, Mott was always his unaffected self. "At Greens, which has a very elegant menu, he'd order something like pizza," Neubacher smiled ruefully. "At our cookouts, there Bill would be in a chef's apron, happily barbecuing oysters on the grill. Here was this visionary who had worked at a very high government level, and yet he was totally down to earth. He was a bundle of energy. I just loved him."

1990: A BITTERSWEET YEAR

The new decade started out joyously when the quake-postponed birthday party finally took place in February. The gala affair included a resolution from the Alameda County Board of Supervisors, a prayer composed by The Rev. John E. Turpin, pastor of First Presbyterian Church, Oakland, and a poem written to Mott by his son, John. The resolution thanked Mott for his contributions to the preservation of parks and the environment. The prayer thanked God for His gift "of the human mind and spirit." But it was John's untitled poem that evoked in all its simplicity Mott's special relationship with his family and with the world:

Growing up with Dad was special, he taught me many things
Like love, strength and honesty and the joy nature brings.
We hiked the hills of Briones Park, the sky was clear and blue,
We climbed Mott's Peak, the highest point, which was named after you.
The cabin at Lake Pillsbury was always lots of fun,
We'd rake the leaves, chop the wood, and sometimes shoot a gun.
Cooking over an open fire and sleeping 'neath the stars,
Exploring nature everywhere by foot and boat and car.
You taught me to catch turtles by swimming up behind,
We'd lct them go and race them, a favorite sport of mine.
Gardening is your passion, a source of pride and fun,
Your yard blooms forth with many plants a'basking in the sun.
For some people gardening is a chore — it's one more thing to do,
But planting bulbs and pruning trees brings lots of joy to you.
Planes to catch, speeches to make would put most people in a spin,
But somehow the plants are cared for — you always fit them in.
Happy Birthday, Dad, and thank you for all the wonderful things you've done
We've certainly shared some special times and I'm proud to be your son.

Eighty years old or not, Mott continued to jump into local controversies. He spoke out against a plan to construct expensive housing and a private golf course in the Gateway Valley, a last remaining area of open space in Orinda. Remembering how the agricultural Santa Clara Valley became the high tech

Silicon Valley, he lamented the similar loss of rich farmland in eastern Contra Costa County to mile after mile of tract homes. And when he supported John Coleman, a water conservationist, for a seat on the board of directors of the East Bay Municipal Utility District, Coleman's opponent accused Mott of being a "radical environmentalist." In his usual spirited manner, Mott dashed off a letter to the editor of a local paper. "I can assure voters in Ward 2 that neither John Coleman nor I is a radical of any sort," he said.

In May, Mott was saddened by the death at age eighty-one of his friend, Paul Covel, the man he had hired to be the nation's first urban park naturalist at Lake Merritt in Oakland and who had gone on to have a nationally distinguished career. But Mott pushed on, traveling that same month to Aukland, New Zealand, where he gave the keynote speech and served as a facilitator at a seminar on public open space. The seminar was sponsored by the Auckland Regional Park Service, a sister agency of the East Bay Regional Park District, in conjunction with the University of Auckland. Mott's message included the familiar warning that rapidly increasing population would put the squeeze on existing land reserves. "You are going to have to have more space," he warned the New Zealanders. "You are going to have more pressure on the parks." His hosts were astounded by Mott's vigor. Philip J. Jew, general manager of the Auckland Regional Parks Service, noticed that the visiting American had "a vitality, enthusiasm and perception that would have done credit to a person half his age."

But Ruth grew steadily weaker. For her few remaining public appearances, she needed a wheelchair. In the last weeks, she rarely left home. Finally, after several days at Alta Bates Hospital in Berkeley, she died of heart disease on December 11, 1990. She was 78.

The Motts had been married for 56 years. Together, they had weathered some very sad times, including the premature loss of their daughter, Nancy. But they had celebrated far more happy moments, including anniversaries, holidays, trips, weddings and other important occasions, sustained by a large circle of family and friends. At services at Orinda Community and First Presbyterian churches, Ruth was remembered as the loving and supportive wife of a dynamo husband who, for all her quiet demeanor, was no shrinking violet. "There is a saying that behind every great man is a great woman," noted Jim Hupp, a longtime family friend. "That was true in [Ruth's] case." Added First Presbyterian Pastor John Turpin, "She was such an even-tempered person and was always empathetic with the situation of others."

If Ruth seemed to sacrifice being with her husband while he traveled much of the time pursuing his vision, the truth was she was enormously proud of his achievements. In 1985, the annual Christmas letter she sent to friends (written by her in the third person) had provided insight into her philosophy: "Since it is impossible for Ruth to criss-cross the country with Bill, she keeps the home and garden here in Orinda and Bill comes when business sends him westward; his visits vary in length from a few days to a short eleven hours. Their two trips to Yosemite in the early fall were brief but beautiful. He is privileged to have Thanksgiving and Christmas at home and he and Ruth recently enjoyed a three-day conference trip to Oregon. Due to careful planning he will be at 'home base' for 13 days for the holidays — too tremendous to believe! He is actually in his Washington office about 20% of the time, so his main diet is airplane food plus luncheons and dinners on the chicken, carrots and green peas circuit." Ruth never learned to drive. In that same Christmas letter, she and Bill (whose name, if he wasn't home when she wrote it, she signed to the letter) thanked family and friends "who have helped Ruth with painting, gardening, errands, shopping and going to social functions during the months that she has been alone. We can't tell you how grateful we are for your many loving deeds of kindness."

LIFE GOES ON - BUT DIFFERENTLY

Now, without Ruth to provide a smooth functioning 'home base,' the fiercely independent Mott would need help for the first time in his life from some of those same friends and relatives. After he composed the text for a thank-you note to be printed and mailed to the people who had sent cards and letters on Ruth's death, Jo Hemphill, the fellow First Presbyterian member whom Mott called his and Ruth's "church family surrogate daughter," helped him order 100 for National Park Service distribution and 400 for personal distribution. She rounded up a group of friends who stuffed and sealed the envelopes after Mott personally signed all 500 cards.

Next came the 1990-91 Christmas family letter. Ruth had always taken care of this tradition. Now, it was up to Bill. Its text, so different from Ruth's cheerful, chatty style, made abundantly clear the inextricable intertwining of Mott's personal and professional life; his total absorption in family and work, the relentless optimism with which he approached life and his stoic acceptance of pain and sorrow as an inevitable part of life:

"I want to thank each and every one of you for your Christmas cards and words of encouragement," he wrote. "Your concern and well wishes mean a great deal to me and they have helped me reorganize my life. One doesn't realize the support, help and personal sacrifice one's mate gives to build a loving and successful lifetime relationship. Ruth raised and developed three beautiful children into men and women who [have] respect for each other, their community and the people of the world and they care deeply for the natural and cultural environment of this country. The home environment which she created of love, order and respect was an inspiration for all of us. I, as well as Bill III, John and her many, many friends have and will continue to miss Ruth's warm and loving council and friendship.

"I have been kept busy with my responsibilities in the overall planning for the San Francisco Presidio, Yosemite and various other National and State Park matters. In addition, I was asked to serve as chairperson of a committee charged by the City of Orinda to look at the possibilities of conserving an open space, the last remaining large undeveloped parcel of land in

Orinda known as Gateway Valley. A development organization would like to develop the land. The short time objectives look good, but we must consider the future and the need for open space 50 years from now.

"I have done some traveling, but not as much as when I served as director of the National Park Service.

"Bill III and Zee Zee are healthy and busy. Bill III's Agri Business includes international as well as national clients. Zee Zee has been doing more painting in oils and exhibiting her art, and has done quite well.

"Bill III and Zee Zee's children are grown up. Brian has gone back to school. He is attending [the] University of California at Los Angeles getting his master's degree in Business Administration. He announced at Christmas his engagement to a wonderful girl. We are all so pleased. Larie has been advanced to Public Relations Director for KPIX, Channel 5 (CBS) in San Francisco.

"John and Marsie's two children are keeping them very busy. Adam, 1 1/2 and Stephanie, 3 1/2, are great fun to be with. John is Supervising Ranger for the California State Parks [and] Recreation Department, San Mateo area. Marsie received her State certificate as an approved certified Public Accountant.

"We all get together quite often.

"Between keeping up the garden and my National Park Service work, I don't have too much free time.

"I wish you a very healthy, constructive and wonderful New Year."

The letter seemed to sum up all that was important to Bill Mott. The next year and a half without Ruth would be difficult. He continued to live by the Oliver Wendell Holmes, Jr., motto, "To be 70 years young is sometimes far more cheerful and hopeful than to be 40 years old." But his eighty-one-year-old body finally began to catch up with his youthful spirit. More than the deaths of Paul Covel and other contemporaries, the departure of Ruth, his soulmate and best friend among best friends, marked the beginning of the earthly end for the Prophet of the Parks. As one of those best friends, Burton Weber, wrote in April, 1991: "He's an octogenarian now, still climbing the punishing switchbacks to that ultimately unattainable mountain-top. The magnificent physique falters a bit these days. More and more, the white flame consumes. But the vision persists. The passion continues. That is Bill Mott's greatest gift — his heritage — to us."

NEVER GIVE UP

The spring before Ruth died, Mott had suffered his own frightening episode of heart trouble. One day while at work in San Francisco, he collapsed on the steps of the Federal Building. Rushed to a nearby hospital, he was fitted with a pacemaker. After the procedure was completed, the doctors advised him to slow down as befit this new condition. But as soon as the orderly pushed him out to Hemphill's car in a wheelchair — and she, at Mott's insistence, gave the startled employee a tip — he asked her to take him directly to a speaking engagement he'd made weeks before the collapse. Although he did reduce his schedule for a few weeks, the pacemaker monitoring his heartbeat and the heart pills the doctors prescribed soon gave Mott renewed energy. The vision did, indeed, persist. The passion — and the prodding, always the prodding – continued.

In June, 1991, he was invited to make a return visit to Hot Springs, Arkansas, to survey the progress that had been made since 1985 when he had challenged the townspeople to "Think Big!" about revitalizing Hot Springs National Park. This time, while acknowledging the positive steps that had been taken toward that goal, he once again urged the city to enlarge its vision and expand its horizons toward renewing the greatness of earlier times. "William Penn Mott, Jr. recognizes what Hot Springs has and what it can be," an abashed local columnist wrote after he left. "Isn't it time we did, too?"

August found him at Lassen Volcanic National Park in rural northeastern California, where he applauded the remodeling of an abandoned ranger's residence into a new interpretive center. However, while "the future holds great promises for the environmental education center," he warned his audience, "its goals will not be achieved without your active, enthusiastic support." And shortly after October 20, 1991 the infamous day the Oakland Hills firestorm burned 1,900 heavily populated acres, consumed 3,354 dwellings and fatally trapped 25 people, he respectfully suggested that some of the devastated area not be rebuilt but be returned, instead, to open space as a memorial to those who had lost their lives. A "ludicrous" idea, fumed the manager of one of the destroyed housing developments. "People want to get things rolling [toward reconstruction]. I've heard this week from some older residents who feel their whole world has lost course," he said. "But most people say they wouldn't live anywhere else." Mott's idea went nowhere. But survivors did convert a plot of open space into a beautiful memorial garden to honor the dead.

The year ended on a happier note with the inauguration of the Bay Area Ridge Trail Council's first annual William Penn Mott Awards. Recognized were nine Bay Area citizens, one from each county, who had taken part in the campaign to build the trail. Mott was asked to speak at the event and hand out the awards. At eighty-two he remained in demand, fully capable of commanding the center of attention.

And he remained the foremost expert on parks. In addition to working on the Presidio conversion, Mott was called back into service for the state. In January, 1992, Pete Wilson, newly elected governor of California, appointed Mott chairman of a panel of current and former state park executives. The panel was asked to consider ways to cut $30.2 million from the 1992-93 budget of the Parks and Recreation Department. True to form, Mott didn't go along fully with the program. He accepted the chairmanship, all right. But when it turned out that such cuts would force almost a third of the state parks to either reduce hours or personnel or even close down seasonally or entirely, Mott immediately went public: "We're going to destroy the system if they cut the park budget as heavily as they're [considering] doing," he warned.

More recognition came Mott's way. In February, he was in-

ducted into the prestigious Berkeley Fellows, an honorary so-
ciety of distinguished friends of the University of California,
Berkeley. The society's roster boasted such illustrious mem-
bers as World War II hero James "Jimmy" Doolittle, former
Secretary of Defense Robert McNamara and actor Gregory Peck.
But perhaps more significant to Mott, he was joining such Bay
Area business titans as Kenneth and Stephen Bechtel, Henry
J. and Edgar F. Kaiser, Harold Zellerbach, and William F.
Knowland, all of whom had contributed over the years to his
park and open space campaigns, and such giants in the parks
and conservation movements as Horace M. Albright, Newton
B. Drury, Robert Gordon Sproul, and Clark and Kay Kerr.

In an interview in the March, 1992 issue of *Diablo*, a monthly
magazine that covered Contra Costa County, Mott advocated
development of in-fill housing in existing cities rather than
construction of new homes on open space lands. Not everyone could have the traditional cottage with a white picket
fence, he said. As for people who wanted to garden, community gardens might be one answer. Not only that, he said,
buildings can have gardens for visual enjoyment, like the roof
garden he'd designed years earlier at the Kaiser Center in
downtown Oakland. In a later issue, a letter writer angrily
responded, calling Mott the preeminent hypocrite of the entire environmental community. "Demolish your home, Mr. Mott,
and return your property to open space," the writer sarcasti-
cally suggested. "No fair selling it, of course. Move into a con-
dominium and do your gardening at the Kaiser Center. Do
this, Mr. Mott, and you will have credibility. Fail, and we will
know who you really are."

The attack was unusual. "Throughout your career," the
magazine's interviewer, Devin Odell, had noted in the earlier
issue, "you've certainly been known as someone who is not
afraid to be wrong and to put forward your ideas forcefully.
Yet you don't seem to be the target of the kind of criticism

and opposition that environmentalists often meet. Why do you think that is?"

"I think it's because we're talking about things that are right, and people understand that," Mott replied. "I talk about intrinsic values all the time as being more important than dollars. I think people recognize the parks as the only things that are stable. Cities are being torn down and rebuilt, people move back and forth across the country, but Yosemite is always going to be there. Mount Diablo [the dominant landmark in Contra Costa County that is also a state park] is always going to be there. Their kids can go back to Mount Diablo and their kids' kids can go back to Mount Diablo. Twenty-five years from now, what will be here? Who knows? But Mount Diablo will be there."

While surrounded by people during public appearances, Mott was very much alone at home. If he was lonely, he didn't admit it. He also refused to accept housekeeping help. "He felt he could take care of himself," said Jo Hemphill, and, of course, he was a good cook. Bill III and John stayed in close touch, as did their wives and children. They dropped by often to check on Mott and take care of anything he needed. Hemphill assumed the role of de facto personal assistant, taking him to doctors' appointments, typing some of his voluminous personal correspondence, and making daily phone calls to a list of people he dictated. He kept up with his projects, communicating with parks people and public officials by telephone and letter. He was deeply troubled, for instance, by the riots that occurred in Los Angeles early in May, 1992, after two police officers were acquitted of beating motorist Rodney King. Mott wrote not only to the Bay Area congressional delegation; but also to Congressman Bruce Vento of Minnesota, Senators David Bowen of Oklahoma and Dale Bumpers of Arkansas, and to 1992 presidential candidate Bill Clinton.

It was time, he told them all, to re-establish the Civilian Conservation Corps. "Today we need to get the young people out of the negative city environment into the out-of-doors and give them a productive work experience," he advised Clinton, whom he had met on his first trip to Hot Springs, Arkansas, in 1985. "Like the old CCC, it will give their lives direction, enhance their self-esteem, make it possible for them to complete their education and make them responsible men and women. I serve on the board of a local California Conservation Corps [actually, it was the independent East Bay Conservation Corps]. It is doing a good job, but we need a massive national program today. I would hope you might consider such a program and turn a very serious urban problem into an opportunity."

In a similar vein, he urged his old friend, Bill Patterson of the Oakland Office of Parks and Recreation, to run for a seat on the board of directors of the East Bay Regional Park District. "He felt there should be more ethnic diversity on the board," Patterson said. "He felt like the minority communities should have a stronger voice in regional affairs. He thought I had some unique qualities that could make a major contribution."

While Patterson campaigned for the seat, Mott flew off on August 22 to Theodore Roosevelt National Park in Medora, North Dakota, where he spoke at the dedication of the new North Unit Visitor Center. Five years earlier, on June 7, 1987, National Park Service Director Mott had met with Park Service and North Dakota state officials at Fort Union Trading Post National Historic Site on a typical Mott-style marketing campaign: mapping a strategy for promoting a tour of state and Park Service areas in remote western North Dakota. Included in the proposed American Legacy Tour were Fort Abraham Lincoln State Park, Knife River Indian Villages National Historic Site, Fort Union Trading Post National Historic Site and the two units of Theodore Roosevelt National Park. Mott also discussed with officials that day strategies for getting a new visitor center built at the North Unit of TR National Park. In his familiar pattern, he suggested that a private, nonprofit citizens group raise the funds for the architectural and engineering work for the new building followed by actual construction by the Park Service. He also said the North Dakota congressional delegation would have to help raise money since the project was low on the Park Service's priority list.

The Theodore Roosevelt North Unit Park Committee promptly raised nearly $50,000 to fund the design work. The congressional delegation secured funding for site preparation, building construction and exhibit planning and production. Construction began in July, 1991 and the facility opened in May, 1992. "Without this community support, it is doubtful the visitor center would have been built," Theodore Roosevelt National Park Superintendent Pete Hart told Mott. "It was your challenge that motivated us all to work to make this dream a reality."

THE VALIANT CRUSADE COMES TO AN END

Despite the pacemaker, Mott's heart was inexorably growing weaker. After returning from North Dakota, fluid began to accumulate in his lungs and he was diagnosed with pneumonia. While fighting to recover, he insisted on keeping a speaking engagement that Jo Hemphill had previously set up. It was at a reunion in Oakland of the veterans of the famed 442 Regiment of World War II, a group of Japanese-American soldiers who had fought heroically for their country while their families were interned in prison camps.

"Bill, I don't think you should come," Hemphill told him when she called his house that morning. "Besides, I can't pick you up because I'm busy with the reunion."

"No, no, I'm coming," he barked. "I'll drive myself. What these men did was outstanding. I want to be there."

Less than a month later, on Monday, September 21, Hemphill called to check on Mott.

"How are you?" she asked. "Not too good," he said. He hadn't slept well the night before. He'd had trouble breathing. For him to admit that much was an indication of real trouble.

"Do you want me to call the doctor?" she persisted.

"Well, yes, I guess so."

When the operator at the hospital in Oakland discovered Mott's regular physician was out of town, she suggested Hemphill take Mott to the emergency room. Hemphill's husband, Ben, drove behind her in his car the couple of miles from Lafayette, where they lived, to Orinda. He helped the older man get dressed and prepare to leave. As they walked out the door, Mott reached down and picked up the *San Francisco Chronicle* on the doorstep. "I want to read this on the way in," he calmly informed the Hemphills. While she drove, he scanned the paper, giving her tidbits of the morning news. Ben followed them in his car to make sure they got to the hospital before proceeding to his office in San Francisco.

They spent most of the day at the hospital, as Mott underwent tests and outpatient treatment. "He was so quiet," Hemphill remembered. "I knew he was very ill." Finally, the doctors said Mott had cardiomyopathy, or chronic congestive heart failure, which was causing the pneumonia as well as poor kidney function. They supplied him with the proper medications and even suggested one glass of red wine per day. But when Hemphill asked them to admit him, they said there was nothing more they could do. To keep him would entail enormous expenses not covered by insurance.

On the way back to Orinda, Hemphill asked Mott what he had in the house to eat. "Oh, nothing much," he responded.

"Let's stop at the store and get something really good!" she said, trying to put a cheerful note in her voice. He had told her many times before that her "can-do" disposition, much like his own, had always been a motivator for him. This time, he asked for ice cream and a package of catfish, the kind that came already spiced and wrapped in cellophane. He would cook the fish when he got home.

When they got to the house, Hemphill went up the long, steep back staircase, opened the door and put the groceries inside. The staircase consisted of about 30 steps. "Bill, I still don't like the idea of your being here by yourself," she said when she returned to the car. "Why don't you stay with Ben and me until you feel better?"

"No, I'll stay here," he said firmly, and she knew that when he spoke like that, the subject was closed. "Well, then, if you insist on walking up these stairs, I'll walk behind you," she said. "If you get tired, just stop and rest a bit."

Mott started climbing the stairs with Hemphill following a couple of feet below. "This is not the Bill Mott I know," she thought as he ascended each step very slowly. "He used to take these stairs like lightning," she remembered with increasing distress.

As if he had read her mind, Mott suddenly trotted up the last four steps. When he got to the door, he pitched forward. Hemphill ran up the rest of the staircase in a panic, turned him over and pulled him into the house. It was about 1:30 p.m. She ran to the phone, called 911, then rushed back to the limp form on the floor. He had gasped for air several times, but now lay unmoving. The emergency vehicles quickly arrived and the technicians put an oxygen mask over his face, but to no avail. They were confused when they felt his heart beating. "That's the pacemaker," Hemphill told them quietly. By now, she knew he was gone. After reaching family members by phone, she followed in her car as the ambulance took Mott to a hospital in Oakland where he was pronounced dead. He was a month shy of eighty-three years old.

In the days following, Hemphill couldn't help but think of the symbolism of those last moments. "He didn't get just halfway up those stairs, he got the whole way up," she mused. "He'd been climbing mountains all his life. To me, the way he died stood for the way he'd lived and all that he had accomplished."

In his chosen profession, William Penn Mott, Jr., did accomplish a great deal. One environmental writer estimated he had a personal hand in creating, planning and administering more acres of parkland and open space than any other American in history. In fact, Mott the husband, father, friend, co-worker, employee, manager and leader was an example of that rare individual whose physical, mental, emotional and spiritual selves were nearly perfectly united into a coherent and awe-inspiring whole. Like an oracle of ancient times, he seemed born with a sixth sense, an innate intuition. Recognizing that gift, he discovered early in life what his calling was and pursued it with all his heart.

That vocation — to create, build, preserve, protect, improve and make available millions of acres of parklands for the people — seemed to come from deep within his soul. He could barely articulate its origins. At a taping session with Jo Hemphill one day, he tried. "How do you put a seed in the ground and end up with tomatoes, beans or whatever," he ruminated. "Who put all this together to make it work? It's like a person. Look at the infinite parts to a person. We have trouble running an automobile, yet millions of parts make up a person. Somebody figured out how to make those parts work together and end up being a human being that works. The same thing is true of plants. Who figured this out? This is why I think God is real because somebody had to have the superior knowledge of how to do these kinds of things and make them work."

Though inchoate at times, the intensity and consistency of Mott's dedication to environmentalism had a lasting effect on others. He counseled, cajoled, commanded, and convinced "all who would listen" to share his vision. It was a dream that if America's wondrous natural resources could be protected now, our children and grandchildren would be able to enjoy them in the future. Today, that future has arrived.

Bill Mott, Jr., at the helm.
NPS photo

EPILOGUE

At 2 p.m. on Sunday, September 27, 1992, a service was held at First Presbyterian Church in Oakland in memory of William Penn Mott, Jr. Interment had taken place during the preceding week at Oakmont Cemetery near Orinda.

The church was beautifully decorated with real trees and masses of fresh greens and flowers. One side room was set aside to display the plaques, awards and other honors bestowed on the man over a lifetime of service. Tributes flowed in from those present and from throughout the country, as much for Mott's effervescent personality and the triumph of the human spirit he embodied as for his lifelong love of the land.

"We will miss his boundless energy, quick follow through, and his self-deprecating sense of humor," said Stanley T. Albright, western regional director for the National Park Service. He was "a man of unimpeachable integrity and character," said James Ridenour, Mott's successor as director of the National Park Service.

"He had a bigger-than-life presence in this department, more so than any other director" said Bob Hudson, spokesman for the California Department of Parks and Recreation. "He was a very distinguished conservationist," said John DeWitt, director of Save the Redwood League in San Francisco.

"I am proud to say that knowing Bill as Governor and later as President, it was a pleasure to work with a man whose dedication, optimism and cheerfulness was an inspiration to us all," wrote former President Reagan. "We can never thank him enough; and he will never be forgotten." Among the organizations naming awards of excellence after Mott were the Orinda Association, the Bay Area Ridge Trail Council, the Sierra Club, the National Society for Park Resources, the California Department of Parks and Recreation, and the National Parks and Conservation Association.

It took John Mott to bring a bit of levity to the otherwise-solemn proceedings. John got a chuckle out of the massed mourners when he launched into a Mott story with smiling understatement:

"My dad was not typical, as most of you know. Despite being a man of uncanny vision and capabilities, he lived rather simply. I remember in 1989 when he came back from Washington, D.C., he was complaining about not getting his compost sifted because of all the calls. I told him I'd handle the phone and give any visitors a shovel. The phone rang and a very persistent dean from San Diego State really wanted to talk to dad about being an instructor. He simply could not understand that Bill Mott was sifting compost and could not be disturbed!" Laughter lightened sad faces.

"He delighted in making jams, canning fresh fruits and vegetables, and making cinnamon rolls from scratch," John continued. "Although he spoke with legislators, Governors and Presidents, he always had time for students and garden clubs. His second home — a remote, rustic cabin at Lake Pillsbury — still has no phone or electricity and only recently did he replace the privy, 'La Casita,' with a septic tank." John's father "saw beauty and goodness not only in mountains and flowers but also in people and cities. He knew that recognizing the intrinsic non-economic values in our parks and wild lands, our communities, and our citizens is essential to human livability on a thriving earth." He was "frustrated," his son said, "by people who could not or refused to recognize intrinsic values. He was angered by bureaucrats who discounted intrinsic values and chose 'CYA' ['cover your ass'] safety over daring to stand up for what is right.

"His spirit and drive outlasted his merely mortal body," John said. "He was giving speeches, raking leaves, and daring to dream 'impossible dreams' until the very end. His spirit has not died, but lives on in the legacy he left behind. You can see his spirit in the shimmer of a grizzly bear's fur. You can hear his spirit in the howl of wolves running free and you can feel his spirit in the warmth of a natural fire burning through decades of underbrush in an over-protected forest."

Newspapers nationwide noted Mott's passing. "Sunny Californian" was what the *Washington Post* called the man who shook up federal complacency and "sought to bring adversaries together. He visited critics in their offices and invited them to conferences at scenic national parks," the *Post* remembered. "He told Interior Department workers that his name was 'Bill,' not 'Mr. Mott, Sir' ... And he drove a car with license plates that read '4-Parks.'"

"Like most dreamers, Bill Mott never lost his optimism or his determination, despite the many setbacks he endured at the hands of people with vision much more limited than his," wrote environmental reporter Andrew Melnykovych in *High Country News*, a newspaper that covers ecological and rural community issues in the 10-state West. "And he never lost his humor," Melnykovych added, contributing still another Mott story to the canon. "Once after I had interviewed him yet again about wolf reintroduction, Mott handed me a postcard picturing a trio of wolves," he wrote. "On the back, he had written, 'We would like to once again live in Yellowstone. With your support we can.' Wolves are once again living in Yellowstone. I'm glad that Bill Mott got to see it happen. And when packs of wolves again roam...I know that Bill Mott's spirit will be there, laughing and howling with them."

Mott ranked among history's top National Park Service directors, according to several environmentalists and Park Service veterans. One, Paul C. Pritchard of the National Parks and Conservation Association, said, Mott "was a true conserva-

tionist and one of the last half century's greatest defenders of
the national parks. His term as National Park Service director
came in a dark period for national parks and our environment, and [during that period] he was a ray of sunlight."
Added the East Bay Regional Park District's Ron Russo, "To
some of us outside the Park Service, he entered a nightmare
in Washington, stood his ground, and paid the price."

But Mott's influence went beyond his considerable accomplishments as National Park Service director to include the
conservation movement everywhere. "If you look at the whole
history of the parks movement, Bill would be among the top
half-dozen leading figures," said Joseph H. Engbeck, Jr., an
historian, director of publications for the California Department of Parks and Recreation and author of *State Parks of
California from 1864 to the Present.* "His influence on conservation has not been intellectual but rather hands-on. Wherever
he goes, programs just seem to spring to life."

Among his monuments is the William Penn Mott Visitor
Center in Presidio National Park, San Francisco. The visitor
center's name commemorates the integral role Mott played in
the conversion of the Presidio from a military base to a national park. It is the building from which visitors start their
journey through the park and the place where they learn more
about the unique site. The center is also the place where exhibits illustrate Mott's pivotal role in the national and international parks movement.

Mott's legacy goes still further, to embrace a way of thinking and believing that not only benefits the Earth but also sets
a standard for one's own individual intellectual and spiritual
growth. In that regard, "What he left for us all, goes well
beyond a simple collection of memories," wrote the eloquent
Russo. "Bill created a model for living and working; a clear
message exemplified by his own actions, that if you believe in
anything, you must pursue it vigorous, passionately. To make
things happen, you must give more than you initially think

you can. He left the world pushing us to stretch our thinking," Russo said. "He didn't always have all the facts or answers. But, then, that wasn't his task. He was a torchbearer. And, perhaps, that was his greatest legacy."

We, too, must take up the crusade. For if the Earth's natural resources — the beautiful blue oceans, green hills, brown deserts and white-capped mountains we see so clearly from outer space— are to survive into the next century and beyond, we must all make a commitment to their health and conservation. Simply put, that is what William Penn Mott, Jr. asked us to do.

Appendix A

The University and the Conservation Movement

By 1998, eighty-two years after the founding of the National Park Service in 1916, four — or more than one-fourth — of the Park Service's fifteen directors had been alumni of the University of California at Berkeley. They were Stephen T. Mather, Horace M. Albright, Newton B. Drury and William Penn Mott Jr. This is an extraordinary record for one institution of higher learning.

In the pantheon of National Park Service directors, the four Berkeley alumni are among the most renowned. Stephen T. Mather and Horace M. Albright, the first and second directors, conceived of and gave birth to the Park Service. Newton B. Drury kept the dream alive during and after the difficult years of World War II. William Penn Mott, Jr. stood firmly against suggestions by some federal officials during the 1980s that parts of the parks be exploited for their natural resources.

Mather, Albright and Drury were native Californians and Mott had migrated West as a young man. In addition to matriculating at UC Berkeley, they had all absorbed the raw sense of power and mystical might emanating from the state's geologically young and restless landscape. Out of the West, they had carried that sense to the rest of the nation through their devotion to the National Park Service and its role in protecting and preserving America's natural and cultural heritage.

Mather, who went East to become "a wealthy Chicago businessman, vigorous outdoorsman and born promoter," according to Park Service historian Barry Mackintosh, was one of the first Americans to recognize the need for a systematic national park service. The U.S. Geological Survey (established 1879), the Forest Service (1905) and the Reclamation Service (1907) studied, managed and transformed natural resources for human use. But though a few national parks existed by that time, no federal agency spoke for the overall protection of wilderness for its own sake.

"In 1914," Mackintosh writes in *The National Parks: Shaping the System*, "Mather complained to Secretary of the Interior Franklin K. Lane, [himself] a former classmate at the University of California at Berkeley, about the mismanagement of the parks. Lane invited Mather to come to Washington and do something about it. Mather accepted the challenge, arriving early in 1915 to become assistant to the secretary for park matters. Twenty-five-year-old Horace M. Albright, another Berkeley graduate who had recently joined the Interior Department, became Mather's top aide." Within a year, on August 25, 1916, President Woodrow Wilson signed legislation creating the National Park Service.

Named by Lane as National Park Service director, Mather served from 1917 to 1929, followed by Albright from 1929 to 1933. Both men did much to organize the parks as they are known today, Mackintosh explains, expanding what was primarily a series of vast national parks carved out of the Western wilderness to include a wide-ranging network of historic sites in the East. Albright was aided immensely by philanthropist John D. Rockefeller, Jr., who donated more than $8 million to buy land along the eastern seaboard for inclusion in the system, and by President Franklin D. Roosevelt, who signed executive orders to transfer to the Park Service natural and historic sites previously managed by the War Department and the Forest Service. Several of these sites were east of the Mississippi.

In 1940, Roosevelt's Interior Secretary, Harold Ickes, persuaded Newton B. Drury to head the National Park Service. Drury was well known in Washington. He had been president of the student body at UC Berkeley and, after graduation in 1912, an assistant to UC Berkeley President Benjamin Ide Wheeler. Later, he had started his own public relations and advertising firm and eventually had been hired to successfully drum up public support for creation of the Save-the-Redwoods League in 1919, passage of legislation to create the California State Park System in 1925 and approval of a $6 million California State Park Bond Issue in 1928. Now, Drury had the tough task of making National Park Service facilities available to the war effort while preventing cannibalization of the parks. "Drury successfully defended the parks against most such demands [for natural resources]," says Mackintosh, "yielding only in exceptional circumstances."

Out of California, then, and more specifically, the University of California at Berkeley, have come some of America's greatest park creators and open space protectors. With his ability to bring varied public and private interests together, to foster interpretation of the importance and uniqueness of natural resources, to move quickly to save endangered land and to take the message of preservation and protection to the general public, William Penn Mott, Jr. takes his place in that fraternity of champions.

Appendix B

How Mott Defined Leadership

The following Director's Report, published in the November 1986 issue of the *Courier*, the monthly magazine of the National Park Service, shows how William Penn Mott, Jr. saw the difference between good management and superior leadership. It is worth reproducing, with just a few trims made to slightly reduce its length.

SEEING THE FOREST *AND* THE TREES

In the course of my travels as Director, I have taken every opportunity to meet and talk with NPS employees because I greatly enjoy making the acquaintance of Park Service personnel and because I obtain special insights into the Service and its operations from them. There's no question that meeting and talking with you has helped me do my job better. As I have traveled around the parks, I have been much impressed by the number and variety of opportunities for action, and of the need for capable managers to carry these actions out. Recently I have been reflecting on the various management styles I have dealt with over the years and have come to realize that for me one style has repeatedly proven more successful than others. . .

During my career, I have known basically two types of managers. The first I view as passive. Such managers travel the road of least resistance. They unflaggingly follow the rules: rarely question decisions handed down; are careful to stay within the mainstream of opinion; and deliver assignments and handle responsibilities in a satisfactory manner. There is not necessarily anything wrong with such managers — they do their jobs. They help keep an organization "afloat," and on a steady course. They are, however, by no means the "movers and shakers" of an organization. They do little to provide the kind of support, leadership, and creative initiative necessary for an organization to continually grow and develop, and in today's world we must grow and develop!

Then there are managers that I consider to be assertive in nature. These use their own judgment, handle situations on a case-by-case basis, and make the best use of the rules by interpreting them sensitively and practically. By that, I do *not* mean that rules are bent or broken to fit the confines of a situation. On the contrary, all decisions made by a manager must address the possible ramifications of such decisions; be tempered by the objectives of the organization; and fall within all legal and policy parameters. It is important to remember to play by the rules, but it is also important to recognize that there are unusual circumstances when rules may unintentionally prohibit appropriate outcomes. It is in such special situations that good judgment becomes critical in finding reasonable ways to handle a problem.

Assertive managers know when to act effectively by knowing when to call the shots themselves; when to seek higher approval; and when to seek clarification or the interpretation of a rule relative to a special situation. The trick is knowing when and, obviously, much of knowing when is intuitive. However, I believe much may also be gained through experience and learned behavior. If a manager isn't lucky enough to be born with that kind of intuition, there's no reason not to learn it.

I want to encourage every manager in the Park Service to become an assertive manager. I don't think the Service, or any organization for that matter, can have too many. I want to see NPS managers doing as much as they can to interpret intelligently guidelines so as to promote the Service's goals. Sure, managers acting assertively may make mistakes; we all do. I'm willing to risk that, and I hope our managers are too. There's just one hitch—learn from mistakes and don't repeat them.

There are many types and styles of managers. In one way or another, they all get the job done. For me, though, assertive managers stand apart from the rest. They aren't interested in just getting by. They don't want second place. They look, instead, to the future. They are creative and optimistic. They make problems into opportunities!

I think we can all be assertive managers — giving our all to the Service. . . The Service is its people, and so the welfare of both are vitally important to me. I see the forest *and* the trees. I want you to know that as an assertive manager, I intend to take on as much as I can and expect you to do so too. More importantly, I want you to be aware that I will support you and back you when you act assertively in the ways I have described. I hope in turn you will do the same for those reporting to you. With that kind of commitment and backing, we will make the Service a more effective organization.

CHAPTER NOTES

Introductory Pages

On the pages titled "What They Say About William Penn Mott, Jr.", the comments of Clinton, Wayburn,Vento, Alexander, Rockefeller, Baker and Barbee were requested and verified by Mott family friend Jo Hemphill and her colleague Roxanne Foster during an initial but uncompleted effort in the early 1990s (when Clinton was governor of Arkansas) to write a book about Mott. Dianne Feinstein's comment was made in connection with the 1994 dedication of a lodge building at Camp Loma Mar, a Metropolitan Oakland YMCA summer camp in the Santa Cruz Mountains, in Mott's name.

Throughout the book, direct quotes from Mott not otherwise attributed to printed sources or personal interviews with colleagues and others are taken from the tapes Hemphill and Foster made with Mott between 1990 and his death in 1992 or from myriad speeches Mott gave at all stages of his career that have been preserved in the family files.

Chapter 1. A Visionary by Nature.
  Page 12. "A vision is a powerful thing..." Speech to the
    Sacramento Open Space Conference, February 23, 1991.
  Page 18. "This ability to squeeze water out of a rock..." was
    a comment carried in the Observer, a neighborhood news
    paper in Oakland, on March 3, 1962.

Chapter 2. A City Blooms.

Page 27. "The estate became..." Report in the San Francisco Call, March 30, 1914.

Page 30. "Among the noteworthy projects..." Your Parks, the newsletter of the Oakland Park Department. Date unknown.

Page 51. "By the mid-1950s..." Oakland Tribune, January 15, 1956.

Page 52. More evidence that "The Oakland Park Department enjoyed a national reputation for excellence" included Mott's appointment in November, 1960, to a "Committee of Fifteen," a national panel convened by the U.S. Department of the Interior to help establish future parks, as reported in the Oakland Tribune, November 10, 1960.

Chapter 3: Creating a Regional Greenbelt

Page 72. "The air had..." comment made after a Mott speaking engagement by Rick Sermon in News And Views, The California Department of Parks and Recreation Newsletter, Summer, 1987.

Chapter 4. From Seashore to Mountaintops: A Statewide Crusade.

Page 91. "More than any other state..." quote from an es say, "Movin' Out: A lifelong New Englander pulls up stakes to head for the Left Coast," written by Joyce Maynard for the San Francisco Examiner on August 17, 1997.

Page 97. The Breaking the Glass Ceiling section includes information from a 1997 author interview with Paula Peterson.

Page 97. "Management was another area..." In the September 1993 newsletter marking the 20th Anniversary of the William Penn Mott Jr. Training Center at Asilomar, State Park superintendent Don Lakatos wrote that it was under Mott that the traditional practice of teaching rangers a variety of skills through on-the-job training changed when "the need was recognized for professionally trained park employees, to meet the increasingly complex job of managing California's State Parks."

Page 98. "Mott's decision to add...law enforcement..." Detailed in California State Park Rangers Association Newsletter, June-July, 1991.

Page 118. "The museum, the study said.." refers to a study completed by the Sacramento Trust for Historic Preservation, Inc., entitled Old Sacramento State Historic Park: The California State Railroad Museum. Recommendations for Planning and Development, February, 1972.

Chapter 5. Public-Private Partnerships for Parks

Page 129. "In March, 1976, he threatened..." The Midweek Sun, Lafayette, CA, March 24, 1976.

Chapter 6: Mr. Mott Goes to Washington

Page 167-171. Quotes in the section sub-headed Too Out spoken through the section sub-headed From Watt to Mott, as well as a sense of the general public reaction to Mott's appointment and first several months in office in 1985, are taken from a blizzard of reports in magazines and newspapers, including Newsweek, Parade, The Wall Street Journal, Washington Post, Christian Science Monitor, San Francisco Examiner, San Francisco Chronicle, Oakland Tribune, Contra Costa Times and Contra Costa Sun. Hodel's approval of Mott's 12-Point Plan was reported in Newsweek, September 2, 1985.

Page 170-171. "In my understanding of the Bible..." Mott's discussion with Kitchens was reported in the July/August 1985 issue of Temple Tidings, the newsletter of the First Presbyterian Church of Oakland.

Page 177. "Mott heard young Arkansas governor Bill Clinton..." Mott's 1985 trip to Hot Springs was extensively reported in the Sentinel-Record of Hot Springs National Park, Arkansas.

Page 182-184. Quotes in the Trouble on the Horizon section are taken from and reflected in reports in several newspapers including the New York Times, Christian Science Monitor, Santa Cruz Sentinel and Contra Costa Sun.

Chapter 7: The Year of the Wolf — and the Fire

Page 203. For more on Mott's participation in reintroducing wolves to Yellowstone, see Wolf Wars by Hank Fischer; The Company of Wolves, Peter Steinhart, Knopf, 1966; A Society of Wolves, Rick McIntyre, Voyageur Press, and The Great American Wolf, Bruce Hampton, Henry Holt & Co., 1997.

Page 208-210. Quotes in The Grand Conclave section and the general tenor of the meeting are taken from and reflected in reports by United Press International and the Associated Press as well as from news stories filed by reporters covering the event for the Rocky Mountain News, Deseret News, Sacramento Bee, Daily Sentinel, Denver Post, Minneapolis Star, Arizona Daily Star, San Jose Mercury News, High Country News, and the Los Angeles Times.

Chapter 9. The Vision Persists; The Passion Continues.

Page 253. "Mott wrote not only..." Private correspondence. Family papers.

Epilogue

Page 261. Quotes from Stanley T. Albright and James Ridenour from a National Park Service news release, Sept. 22, 1992, printed along with quotes from Bob Hudson and John DeWitt by the Sacramento Bee, September 23, 1992.

Page 263. "Sunny Californian" reference in Washington Post obituary, September 23, 1992.

Page 263. Melnykovych commentary published in High Country News, October 19, 1992.

Page 263-264. Paul Pritchard comment on Mott as "a true conservationist," from National Parks magazine, January/February 1993.

Sources

Whenever possible, sources have been mentioned in the text. The listings below as well as the Chapter Notes following provide additional information on sources.

Live interviews conducted, taped and prepared
for transcription by Jo Hemphill

William Penn Mott Jr.
Bob Baker
Mary Lou Phillips
Broc Stenman
Dick Trudeau
Mike Findley
Burton Weber

Live interviews conducted by the author
in person or by telephone

Bob Baker
Bob Barbee
Martha Bauman
Ed Bearss
Howard Bell
George Berklacy
Bob Blau
John Blodger

Herbert Brantley
Beverly Clark
John Crompton
Pete Dangermond
John Davis
Loran Fraser
Denis Galvin
Jo Hemphill
Earl Henderson
Donald Hodel
William "Bill" Horn
Hulet Hornbeck
Joanne Lennon
Norman "Ike" Livermore
Putnam "Put" Livermore
Barry Mackintosh
Les McCargo
Josephine "Jo" Mele
Ken Mitchell
Donald Murphy
Joel Parrott
Bill Patterson
Paula Peterson
W.B. Styles
Fred Stickney
Dean Tice
Barry Tindall
John Thune
Richard "Dick" Trudeau
Burton Weber
William Withuhn

Oral Histories

The Bancroft Library, University of California, Berkeley.
  William Penn Mott, Jr., by Ann Lage
  Norman "Ike" Livermore, by Ann Lage and Gabrielle
    Morris
  John Zierold, by Ann Lage
East Bay Regional Park District, all by Mimi Stein
  William Penn Mott, Jr.
  Richard "Dick" Trudeau
  Clyde Woolridge
  Eddie Collins
  Christian Nelson
East Bay Regional Park District by Karana Hattersley-Drayton
  William Penn Mott, Jr., December 27, 1990.
National Park Service
  William Penn Mott, Jr., an Interview, by Barry Mackintosh,
    March 30, 1990, History Division, National Park Service,
    Department of the Interior, Washington, D.C.

Published Documents

*Creating a Park for the 21st Century: from military post to national
  park. Final General Management Plan Amendment; Presidio of
  San Francisco*; Golden Gate National Recreation Area,
  California. 1994.
*Old Sacramento State Historic Park: The California State Railroad
  Museum. Recommendations for Planning and Development*,
  Sacramento Trust for Historic Preservation, Inc., February,
  1972.
*Park Units and Properties Associated with the California State Park
  System*, Park Services Division, July, 1996.

Unpublished Documents and Correspondence

Letters from Pete Hart, Superintendent, Theodore Roosevelt National Park, to WPM, Jr., May-August, 1992. Family papers.

Speeches written, annotated and delivered by William Penn Mott, Jr. Family papers.

Mott resumes and personal letters. Family papers.

Mott Master's Thesis, School of Landscape Architecture, University of California, Berkeley.

Frothinger, Donald, *Children's Fairyland: A Celebration of Children's Literature Design Development 1947 to 1950.* Paper for Landscape Architecture 170 class, (university unknown), Spring 1996.

Scrapbooks, 1962 to 1967, East Bay Regional Park District, Oakland, CA.

Archives, Oakland Office of Parks and Recreation, Oakland, CA.

Jenkins, Michael, *A History of the Hyde Street Pier,* Museum Seminar, Fall, 1977, J. Porter Shaw Library, San Francisco Maritime National Historic Park Historic Documents Department, San Francisco, CA.

Minutes of staff meetings, National Park Service, Department of the Interior, Washington, D.C., courtesy Denis Galvin.

Oral Histories

Bancroft Library, University of California, Berkeley
    William Penn Mott, Jr.
    Norman "Ike" Livermore
    John Zierold
East Bay Regional Park District by Mimi Stein
    William Penn Mott, Jr.
    Richard "Dick" Trudeau
    Clyde Woolridge
    Eddie Collins
    Christian Nelson

East Bay Regional Park District by Karana Hattersley-Drayton
   William Penn Mott, Jr., December 27, 1990.
National Park Service
   William Penn Mott, Jr., an Interview, by Barry Mackintosh,
March 30, 1990, History Division, National Park Service, Department of the Interior, Washington, D.C.

Newspapers

Christian Science Monitor
Contra Costa Sun
Los Angeles Times
New York Times
Oakland Post-Enquirer
Oakland Tribune
Riverside Press-Enterprise
Sacramento Bee
Sacramento Union
San Francisco Chronicle
San Francisco Examiner
San Luis Obispo County Telegram-Tribune
Santa Barbara News-Press
Santa Monica Evening Outlook
Wall Street Journal

Periodicals

California Escapes: American Park Network, San Francisco, 1996
The Courier, monthly publication of the National Park Service.
Legacy, The Journal of the National Association for Interpretation, January/February 1993
Newsweek
Parade
Sierra, the magazine of the Sierra Club, Jan. 2, 1986
Time
U.S. News and World Report

Bibliography

Boyarsky, Bill; *Ronald Reagan: His Life & Rise to the Presidency,* Random House, New York, 1981.

Butler, Mary Ellen, *Oakland Welcomes the World,* Community Communications, Montgomery, AL, 1996

Cannon, Lou; *Ronnie and Jesse: A Political Odyssey;* Doubleday, New York, 1969.

Cannon, Lou; *Reagan,* G.P. Putnam's Sons, New York, 1982

Cannon, Lou; *President Reagan: The Role of a Lifetime,* Simon & Schuster, New York, 1991.

Covel, Paul F.; *Beacons Along a Naturalist's Trail: California Naturalists and Innovators;* Western Interpretive Press in association with Western Heritage Press, 1988.

Crawford, Robert, *Reflections of a Recreation Professional,* National Recreation and Park Association, Arlington, VA, 1993.

Engbeck, Joseph H., Jr., *State Parks of California From 1964 to the Present,* Graphics Arts Center Publishing Co., Charles H. Belding, Publisher, Portland, OR, 1980.

Fischer, Hank; *Wolf Wars,* Falcon Press Publishing Co., Inc., Helena and Billings, Montana, 1995.

Fox, Stephen; *John Muir and His Legacy: The American Conservation Movement.* Little Brown, New York, 1981.

Hughey, Janice & Billy; *A Rainbow of Hope,* Rainbow Studies, Inc., El Reno, OK., 1994.

Mackintosh, Barry; *The National Parks: Shaping the System,* National Park Service, Washington, D.C.,1991.

The National Parks: Index 1995, Office of Public Affairs, National Park Service, Washington, D.C., 1995

Stein, Mimi; *A Vision Achieved: Fifty Years of East Bay Regional Park District;* East Bay Regional Park District, Oakland, CA, 1984.

INDEX